*Planning the development of universities* *
A series of reports based on an IIEP research project

Vol. I.   IIEP seminar on planning the development of universities,
Paris, 7-11 July 1969

(Basic discussion paper/Summary report of the seminar/Case study
on Leningrad State University/Case study on the University of Sussex)

* Other volumes to be published in the series

# Planning the development of universities—I

*An IIEP Seminar, Paris, 7-11 July 1969*

*Edited by* Victor G. Onushkin

Paris    1971
Unesco: International Institute for Educational Planning

The IIEP research project on Planning the Development of Universities is being carried out with financial assistance from the Swedish International Development Authority (SIDA) and the Ford Foundation.

Published in 1971 by the United Nations
Educational, Scientific and Cultural Organisation.
Place de Fontenoy, 75 Paris-7e
Printed by L. Vanmelle, S.A., Ghent

# Preface

During the last decade it has become obvious that there are many problems in the field of higher education which must be solved if higher educational systems are to adapt themselves to the social and economic needs of their respective countries. One of the most important problems is that of improving the management and planning of higher education at different levels (institutional, regional and national), and this is the reason why we have chosen 'Planning the development of universities' as a research topic at the IIEP, under the direction of Mr. Victor Onushkin.

The seminar which took place in July 1969 discussed the aims and methodological problems of this research, as well as the first results and future plan of action. It was very important to have the opportunity to do this at an international forum during the early stage of this research in order to define our aims clearly and to have the benefit of discussion on the methodological problems and methods to be used in this type of research. A document by Mr. Onushkin describing the aims and methodological problems was presented for discussion as well as the results of two exploratory case studies which were carried out at the Universities of Leningrad and Sussex.

These two case studies represented different systems of higher education within countries of different social systems but, apart from this, they proved at the same time that there are many interesting developments occurring in different universities which can be analysed and summarised so that the conclusions can be used by other universities.

One can see, on reading the present volume, that the experience of the Leningrad State University shows how a university functions in a planned socialist economy, and how the university has solved and is solving the problems arising in the process of its development. A very interesting aspect is the administrative structure of the university, where all groups involved in university life, including the students, are represented at all levels of the decision-making mechanisms. Another aspect of value is the organization of the links between the university and secondary schools, and the process of searching for talent among schoolchildren. A particularly interesting part of this case study is that dealing with the planning and management of research work. The indices and criteria worked out and applied at Leningrad State University for measuring the quantity and quality of research work may be utilised by other universities wishing to start or to improve the planning of their research work. The planning of the teaching/learning process and curricula planning are also worth noting.

The University of Sussex is functioning in a different situation, where there is no central higher educational planning at the national level, but it is very interesting to see how the university is attempting to work out adequate mechanisms for planning and management in these specific circumstances. Their experience in creating a flexible planning mechanism, and their organization of periodical reviews of the organizational structure of the university in order to adapt them to the solution of fresh problems, will be of value to other universities. This university also has organized representation by groups of students in university administration and in the different Committees responsible for the most important aspects of the work of the University. The case study also shows how the University of Sussex is trying to solve the vital problem of inter-disciplinary teaching and learning and inter-disciplinary research.

The discussion of materials presented at the seminar was useful in that it proved the necessity for this type of research and confirmed that the methodology suggested was in principle approved by the participants. It also showed that it is important, even when concentrating at the institutional level of planning and management, to take into account higher educational planning at the national level. It was suggested also that in order to get the most useful results from the research, the attention of the research group should be concentrated on planning and managerial problems in specific fields of university activity, such as the creation of a university information system, planning of the teaching/learning process, planning of research work, problems of the training of teaching staff, planning of access to the universities, and employment of graduates, because only by a detailed analysis of the most important aspects of university activity can an over-all picture of the methods and mechanisms of university planning and management be obtained, the necessary conclusions be drawn, and recommendations made.

Many of the participants in the seminar suggested that the results of this research should be presented in the form of a manual for heads of universities and should contain the most interesting and most useful conclusions drawn from existing experience in planning university development in different countries of the world. Without any pretensions to finding the final solutions to a great range of problems connected with university planning, we hope to make our contribution towards their solution and in this way to help the heads of universities in carrying out their complex, important and onerous functions.

We would like to express our thanks to all the participants in the seminar for their contribution to this research, and particularly to Mr. Victor Onushkin, who has had the responsibility of preparing the meeting, introducing the discussion and summarising the conclusions.

RAYMOND POIGNANT
Director, IIEP

# Contents

*Basic discussion paper*

# Some methodological aspects of planning the development of universities

*by* Victor G. Onushkin

# Planning the development of universities

The purpose of this paper is: firstly, to offer a brief description of the existing situation in many universities—a situation which is vastly complicated by rapid changes in the surrounding world; secondly, to suggest possible approaches to the analysis of changes and developments; thirdly, to formulate some theoretical ideas about planning the development of universities; and, lastly, to introduce our plan of work for the next stage of the project.

First of all, what is meant by planning the development of universities? What is a university? What are the important changes which should be taken into consideration when plans are being worked out?

1. What is a university? I am not going to give a new definition of a university. Too many exist already. I would like simply to say that in this project, by university we understand higher educational establishments to which access is available for people with completed secondary education, and which give a term of training of not less than three years—as a rule, from four to six years. I think, for example, that one cannot include so-called junior colleges in this category.

The characteristic features of the modern university are, or should be, as follows:

A teaching process with content and method based on the latest results of scientific research and with a permanent renovation of curricula and methods of training;

an organic combination of instruction and scientific research work, which supplement and enrich each other. This provides for a truly creative atmosphere at the university and inspires students to seek, acquire and apply new knowledge. This is extremely important in the modern world, since it is impossible to provide students with working knowledge for the whole

13

period of their active lives; for this reason, it is important to educate them in such a manner as to enable them to renew their knowledge and to continue their self-education;

a sizeable volume of research work; a combination of many different branches and fields of study facilitates the execution of complex research projects, especially at the meeting-point of different sciences;

training of specialists at the graduate level for research and development, for teaching at higher educational institutions and for managerial and other positions requiring advanced training; a high proportion of graduate students;

a leading role in renewing and improving the qualifications of specialists in different branches of the economy, science and culture, including the whole system of higher education;

a leading role in the preparation of textbooks and other instructional materials for the whole system of higher education and for the general secondary schools;

an increasing volume of activity necessary for the maintenance and running of the teaching process and research work;

an important role in the training of teachers for all levels of the educational system.

These features do not relate to some abstract ideal model of the modern university, but summarize characteristics of the most advanced universities. Not all higher educational establishments have the above-mentioned characteristics. Many of them do not devote sufficient attention to the analysis of their own activities. Indeed, they frequently do not have adequate mechanisms for self-analysis, for flexible planning for the future and for modern management of the complicated processes going on within their own walls.

2. The contemporary situation in many universities is characterized by the following features: old traditions, sometimes mediaeval, play an important role in the life and development of universities—and often in their failure to develop; development is very often understood to be purely quantitative growth, without substantial qualitative changes in the activities of the university; insufficient effort is made consciously to adapt the different functions of the universities to new demands of the changing environment; the university does not pay sufficient attention to internal changes, especially those concerned with the attitude and composition of the student body; in many countries there is no educational planning at either the institutional level or the national level.

In recent years, university management has become an increasingly complex affair for a variety of reasons, such as rapid growth of the size of the university, increasing diversification and complication of the curricula and teaching programmes, growth and complication of research projects and greater involvement of universities in local, national and international affairs. As a result, university expenditures have grown and the economic activities (consequently the economic analysis of these activities and others) have become very important.

Not surprisingly, the old managerial methods have, in many cases, proved inadequate to the new conditions.

3. Recent decades are characterized by marked socio-economic and political changes in the world and by great events in many countries. One of the most substantial contemporary trends is the development of the scientific and technological revolution, which is seriously influencing all sides of social life. It is obvious that there exists a close interdependence and interrelationship between scientific and technological progress, economic and social changes in society, and the development of higher education (the training of highly-qualified specialists).

What are the most important trends and changes which should be considered in the planning of university development? It should perhaps be said here that the principal philosophy which lies behind the changes studied in the project is that of the democratization of higher education. For the sake of clarity, three distinct groups of changes are distinguished:

*External changes,* outside the university, in which are reflected the increasing complexity of the socio-economic environment:

the scientific and technological revolution which is producing changes in the structure, dynamics, and rate of growth of industry and agriculture;

the emergence of new fields of knowledge, a rapid increase in the volume of scientific and technological information, and the rapid obsolescence of previous information;

substantial changes in the manpower structure, an increasing proportion of scientific workers and engineers, and an increasing demand for economists, sociologists and psychologists;

the development of mass communication media: radio, television, etc.;

the increasing demand for higher education which, in many countries, becomes mass education, and at least involves an important proportion of the corresponding age group;

the need for the rapid discovery and development of new talents, because the accelerating tempo of scientific and technological progress demands the training of people who are able not only to use the results of modern science, technology and culture, but also to develop and enlarge upon their knowledge.

*Internal changes,* reflecting the complication of the internal life of the university, which has taken on new tasks to meet new needs, interests and demands:

the development of new teaching disciplines and new fields of training. The importance of reforming structures to ensure inter-disciplinary co-operation and to avoid the situation where each specialist is isolated in his own specialization;

changes in the social composition of the student body, in the student attitude towards education and society, changes in the students' general educational and cultural levels;

the emergence of new fields of research inside universities and the growing complication of all related activities;

the development and use of increasingly complicated materials, new methods, and new technological media in training and research;

an increasing complexity of the university structure and of the management process.

*A complication of the relationship between universities and society,* in which universities show their increased socio-economic role:

the extension of the responsibilities of universities vis-à-vis societies;

diversification of the training of highly qualified specialists;

the growth in the volume and diversity of research, performed both independently and on a contractual basis for outside organizations, which had not previously paid great attention to research;

in order to keep up with rapid scientific and technological change, the university must expand its functions for permanent education and for the retraining of former graduates;

one of the new functions of the university appears to be that of an advisory body; universities play a more and more important role in preparing important decisions in government, in industry, and in other organizations.

4. Of course, all the above-mentioned circumstances manifest themselves differently, with different acuity, and in different combinations with each other in different countries. Nevertheless their existence, to a greater or lesser extent, produces difficulties and contradictions. In the field of university planning and management our attention should be concentrated on these difficulties and contradictions in order to create favourable conditions for university development.

What are the contradictions and difficulties in university development? To summarize some of the points I have already mentioned, they are as follows: a disproportion between limited resources and a rapidly growing demand for higher education; a contradiction between the rapidly increasing volume of scientific information and the limited duration of formal education; a discordance between rapidly accumulating new scientific information and a curriculum slow to change; an imbalance between the existing structures of specialities and demands for new structures and qualifications of graduates; a discordance between the existing professional training of the teaching staff and the necessity to teach new disciplines; a contradiction between the limited material and technical bases of universities and the need to broaden and to improve them in order to increase the quality and effectiveness of teaching and research; limited financial resources, in particular the contradiction between rising unit costs and over-all financial needs, and the rate of growth of national economy and public budget; rapid obsolescence of the organizational structure of the university and the necessity for its systematic improvement. Here, there is frequently a contradiction between structures which isolate disciplines from one another, whereas, in fact, the need is for greater co-operation; and finally, a contradiction between old methods of management and the complication of the university managerial processes. A specific aspect that comes to mind here is the industrialization of research processes within the universities: the use of computers and of all the most up-to-date methods of research demands in turn the most modern management available, if optimum efficiency is to be reached.

The above-mentioned and other existing difficulties and contradictions of university development can be overcome in planning university development only if there are the necessary socio-economic-political conditions in the respective countries. Nevertheless, it should be made clear that we do not believe planning alone is the panacea for all university ills. It is only when planning becomes a specific form of modern university management that it can, in our opinion, be really effective.

5. The necessity of planning the development of universities is determined, consequently, by a number of important factors, some of which have already been mentioned. Above all, I would like to stress here that while there has always been a need for planning universities, that need has lately grown enormously, as a result of vastly accelerated changes in the environments of universities, accelerated increase in the demand for higher education and the many new tasks and pressures being thrust upon universities. The universities must, therefore, now change and adapt more rapidly than ever before and this calls for an essentially new kind of planning which, in turn, is an aspect and function of a new kind of university management.

6. Many authors, in discussing the problems of educational planning, deal only with its economic—or even purely financial—aspects. Certainly, the isolation of the economic side of the problem, with a view to purposeful economic management of higher education, is quite possible. It would be wrong, however,

17

to reduce problems of the planning and management of higher education to this one side of it. The economic approach to higher educational planning is very important but it is, at the same time, only one approach among many.

One should remember that the financing of higher education creates some material prerequisites for its development, but does not create higher education itself. For this reason the analogy between the development of educational systems, or isolated parts of them, with economic processes and industrial enterprises can only be a remote one.

In our opinion the planning of the development both of higher education as a whole and of its various parts can only succeed if, besides the existing socio-economic prerequisites for planning in one or another country, the peculiarity of this field of human activity is taken into account. Its peculiarity is that the system of higher education produces and distributes knowledge and the subject and object of this process is a human being.

When planning the development of higher education or of individual institutions of higher education, one must try to consider, together with the economic aspects, the aims, the responsibilities and the functions of higher education. Higher education has an important social and political role to play in every country, and the organization of the teaching process and what is actually taught will contribute to the fulfilment of this role.

All these elements together, not any individual element, are the subject of higher educational planning. One should also bear in mind that realistic and optimum planning of the universities can take place only when it is not an isolated phenomenon, but is a part of the whole national economic development plan. In a situation where there is no over-all national plan, reflecting the objectives of development, there may be useful planning on different individual levels, but it is less likely to achieve optimum results.

7. In tackling the subject of higher educational planning it is important to distinguish between at least two levels of planning: (a) the statewide or nationwide level, which is the planning of the development of the whole higher educational system, and (b) the individual level, which is the planning of individual higher educational institutions. Both these levels of planning are interdependent and interact very closely and, indeed, it is essential that the plans of the individual universities be co-ordinated at the national level. Just as statewide planning of higher education cannot succeed if it is not itself based on a synthesis of development plans of individual universities, so individual university planning cannot bring the best results if the individual plans are not co-ordinated, on the national level, with the plans of other universities. For example, in view of the unlimited extension of knowledge, universities at the post-graduate level in particular will have to specialize, at least partially. In order to determine

these specializations, a plan at the national level is indispensable. The fact is that the demand for graduates from any one university is so diversified that, even with the best possible internal planning mechanism, the university cannot practically take into account all possible demands, especially those for the future.

In this project we are, nevertheless, concentrating our attention on the level of planning at individual universities. This limitation of the framework of our research, at least in its first stage, has been adopted for obvious reasons and principally in order to have a project of manageable dimensions. We also feel that the activity of individual universities will, in any case, be seen in a national context, because the necessity of an organic combination of statewide and individual plans is clearly understood; that case studies at individual universities in different countries will reveal the common problems which universities are facing in the process of their planning (on the other hand, in statewide or national planning, when it exists, there are greater differences); finally that the investigation of concrete mechanisms for planning the development of universities will create a basis for the future analysis of the broader set of problems.

In order to focus our research as clearly as possible and to make it more purposeful, we shall concentrate our participants' attention only on those aspects of university development planning which are directly connected with *change and development*. In the process of our work on this project we are studying the most interesting experiences in planning accumulated by universities. We are studying those planning and managerial mechanisms which allow university administrators to identify critical problems of university development in time to avoid maladjustments.

On the basis of the case studies, we hope to work out a system of criteria and indices, in order to have a mechanism for choosing priorities in university activity and for maintaining the necessary proportions between different kinds of activity. We are going to use quantitative (figures, relative indices, analytical indices, and synthetic indices) and qualitative indices in order to cover the different aspects of university activities (for example, the social, economic and pedagogical aspects). The quantitative and qualitative aspects are, of course, closely connected and the purpose of this research is to work out mechanisms which will respect the relationship between quantitative and qualitative changes.

It can be seen that *we are focusing our attempt on the adaptation of the university to progress—scientific, technological and social.*

8. The nature of planning the development of universities is that it is a dynamic process. As with all kinds of planning, it includes the following elements: (A) diagnosis and evaluation of recent and existing performances—in relation to resources; (B) formulation of the aims and of the concrete targets; (C) co-

ordination of the resources with the aims and targets; (D) implementation of the plan; (E) feedback mechanism during the implementation of the plan, which is constantly revised and improved.

Adequate information about different aspects of a university's activity plays a very important role.

The necessary instruments of a planning process are the indices of a plan and criteria for the evaluation of performance, trends and emerging problems during the planning process. Let us consider all these elements.

A. *Diagnosis and evaluation of performance and of existing resources* are necessary in order to work out realistic plans which can be implemented. By resources one understands practically all the main internal and external conditions of the university. They cover such facts as: the number of applications to the university; the number of students; the existing teaching and research personnel and sources of its reinforcement; the existing teaching and research space and its growth perspectives; the existing teaching equipment and perspectives for its improvement; the existing research facilities; and the financial resources.

Only by taking into consideration all the important conditions determining present and future university activities can the basis for well-grounded planning be created.

B. *Formulation of the aims and concrete targets for the plan.* A planning process makes sense only if it is purposeful. It is not particularly difficult to formulate partial concrete targets which university administrators are working on or plan to work on. But the very diversity of the problems which arise in the process of university development means that it is essential to see the targets in an over-all perspective and to orientate them towards the more general aims of higher educational development. It would not be hard to find examples showing that the individual university is ill-equipped to define its own objectives in the absence of a national plan. Here again we are facing the need to combine individual university planning with broader statewide aims of higher education.

The question of the aims of different educational systems is not an abstract problem. Many of those who write on the problems of higher education agree that one of the main general problems of higher education is its democratization. But the differences begin here, because a number of different things are understood by the term 'democratization', varying from the necessity to meet the growing demand for higher education to student participation in university administration. In this domain there is, therefore, a really important need to define the national aims of higher educational development, taking into consideration the differing situations in different countries.

The investigation of this question of aims shows that only in a limited number of countries have such aims been clearly stated in government documents. Nevertheless, the question of objectives receives a good deal of attention even when there are no officially proclaimed aims.

There are three groups of systems of higher education with more or less clear attitudes towards the question of their aims: (a) systems of higher education of which the main function is the training of highly-qualified specialists for different branches of scientific, governmental and cultural activity. Under these systems the training of students is clearly oriented—the activities both of the ministries of higher education and of the individual universities are focused on these aims; (b) systems of higher education which do not have clearly stated aims. Here, higher education is considered as the next step inside the system of education. The function of this stage of the system is to provide the possibility of learning to those people who wish it and who have the necessary qualifications and also, perhaps, the economic and social opportunities; (c) systems of higher education which come in between the other two groups as far as the determining of the aims of higher education is concerned.

It is obvious that for the first group the main concern of planning activity is the content of higher education, and all other concerns, including financial, are subordinated to the main one. As for the second and, to a great extent, the third group, the main concern is not the planning of higher education itself, but the providing of some prerequisites for its development. These prerequisites are very important, but they do not unduly influence the main content. Only when one has clearly formulated aims of higher education can one successfully plan the development of universities.

Certain aims, it is true, can be clarified during the process of implementation. In the process of planning university development, concrete targets are formulated. These concern the individual functions of the university and affect interrelationships between all other functions. Examples of such concrete targets might be: an increase in the number of students or the improvement of the composition of the student body (by field of training, by social background, by age, by sex, and so on); a change in the structure of the teaching personnel (by speciality, by level of qualification, by age, by sex, and so on); a change in the student/teacher ratio; the utilization of more efficient means and methods of teaching; closer combination of teaching and research work in order to develop students' research talents; the development of scientific research in definite spheres; the improvement of material bases for research work; an increase in, or a more efficient utilization of, teaching and research space; more efficient utilization of financial resources.

Whichever one of the listed or similar concrete targets we take, we must look at it in relation to the other spheres of university activity, because all of them are interrelated and interdependent. The investigation of mechanisms of intercommunication and interdependence of different aspects of university activity is one of the necessary prerequisites for planning the development of universities.

C. *Co-ordination of the resources with the aims and targets* which are to be achieved in the planned period of university development creates the possibility on the one hand of specifying the targets—to make them more realistic—and on the other hand of looking for new resources, in order to fulfil the plan. At this stage, the most important problem is the methods to be used to achieve the aims.

To this end one could choose the optimum solution among numerous alternatives. From our point of view, the optimum solution is one which offers the possibility of reaching the targets with the minimum resources, while carefully calculating the limiting factors. The limiting factors at the university are not only financial, but also limitations on existing material resources such as personnel, space and equipment, which cannot always be corrected by the use of financial resources, especially in short-term planning.

Planning targets should reflect requirements of planned proportionality. The balance method plays a decisive role; there is also a method of norms, a method of coefficients and some other methods which can be used and which are necessary for almost all planning calculations. In recent years, the experimental and economic-mathematical methods of planning have been used with increasing frequency.

The method of sociological research also plays an important role. At this stage, the model of the planning process can be a very important tool for selecting the best alternative, with the use of a computer. It is clear, therefore, that the planning of university development, in order to avoid crippling mal-adjustments, requires a 'systems approach' to self-diagnosis and planning; that is to say that each university should see itself as a total entity, composed not of independent pieces, each to be examined separately, but of interdependent parts, working together within the university and collectively interacting with the surrounding environment.

The working out of an optimal university plan means optimization from the point of view of achieving the over-all social and economic aims of the country, optimization of plans of each part of the university, as well as optimization of strategy of implementation—of timing, etc.

D. *Implementation of the plan* is the decisive stage of the whole planning process. At this stage one achieves the practical results of planning the development. In the process of the implementation of the current plan, it is very important not to lose perspective. Only the combination of current planning with long-range planning can make planning continuous and efficient. Taking into consideration the peculiarity of the university product (highly-qualified specialists for the future, training of whom takes four or five years within the university alone) one cannot limit the terms of planning to a five-year period. The plan should cover at least a ten to fifteen-year perspective.

As a result of a plan there are new proportions inside the university, such as redistribution of resources among its different parts, its adaptation to new situations, and implementation of the aims and targets. Consequently there is a balanced development of the university towards the planned aim.

E. *The availability of a feedback mechanism* or functioning channels for feedback is an indispensable factor for the implementation of a plan. With such a mechanism one can achieve a permanent comparison of the plan with actual developments. It also ensures flexibility and the possibility of carrying out mid-way adjustments. As a result, resources and efforts can be redistributed better to achieve the aims and targets in the planned period and in the most economic fashion.

A reliable feedback mechanism means the availability not only of timely and sufficient information but also of conditions for operative use of this information by university administrators. These would therefore have the necessary rights and means, and the real possibility of using these rights.

The complexity of the multitude of links between a modern university and its environment makes the creation of a reliable feedback mechanism extremely difficult. Many universities are just beginning to create one. In order to create such a mechanism, one should clearly identify all the links between the university and its environment. As a rule, these links exist between the university and secondary schools, which prepare candidates for the university; between the university and the government; between the university and consumers of its human products—the graduates; between a university and consumers of its intellectual products—the results of research work; between a university and other universities and research organizations in the field of training and utilization of teaching and research personnel; between the university and organizations financing its activities; between the university and suppliers of teaching and research equipment.

There should be a sensitive warning system about present and future changes in all the above-mentioned directions. Very often all these channels are related. For adequate evaluation of these links it is essential to work out a system of criteria and indices for university activity.

9. Obviously, in planning the development of universities one needs adequate and up-to-date information. This information should be sufficient for decision-making at different levels (departmental, faculty, research institute, university) and for controls for implementation of decisions.

At the present time, however, only a few universities have sufficiently complete information about their internal processes. The volume of information about the links connecting the university with its environment is even smaller. Sometimes universities have large volumes of statistical data, but these data are not regularly utilized in the planning and management processes.

In addition, there is no systematization of information in accordance with the level of the detailing and generalization of information, and this creates difficulties for those who use the information at different administrative levels. It is useful to consider the university information system as a complex of information sub-systems and links, with different kinds of information and different levels of generalization and analysis.

The creation of an accurately-functioning information system is a necessary prerequisite for regulating information flows, sorting out necessary information and excluding unnecessary and repetitive information. Only on such a basis can the automatic university information system with the utilization of modern technical means and methods be worked out.

An information system makes sense only when it is based on well-worked-out indices which reflect various sides of university activity. The selection of such indices is one of the purposes of this project, 'Planning the development of universities'.

The main difficulty in working out a system of indices for the university is that it should give not only quantitative but also qualitative characteristics of university activity. *Qualitative* characteristics play an extremely important role at universities. Indices which provide information about: the quality of training (this should be the main concern of university administrators); the fitness of the quality of training to changing demands; the quality and level of research; and the quality of the teaching staff—and similar indices—are absolutely necessary for effective university planning.

It is, however, very difficult to interpret those phenomena in quantitative terms. On the other hand, it is no less complicated to interpret quantitative indices (student/faculty ratios, research costs, library size) in qualitative terms.

Nevertheless, the elaboration of methods for such interpretation is absolutely essential, because without adequate interpretation of existing quantitative indices one cannot observe new tendencies in university development nor discover disproportions and maladjustments. The system of indices characterizing a university can be built up in accordance with the main functions of the university. Different indices reflecting certain specific functions and combined into a system should give a complete characterization of the functions at different managerial levels.

Among the most important complexes of indices from the point of view of planning the development of universities are access to the university; teaching and training; research; the composition of the student body; the composition of the teaching staff; the occupation of graduates; space utilization; finance and economic activities.

Each of the foregoing complexes of indices consists of interrelated indices which should be very carefully selected. There are a number of fundamental absolute indices characterizing the university, such as: the number of students, the number of teachers, the volume of research, available space, and income and expenditure. All these absolute indices are very important but they do not always clearly reflect the dynamics and direction of development.

In planning university development, relative indices, such as the following, are vital:

the ratio of acceptances to applications;

the number of graduates in relation to the demand for them, by field of specialization;

student/professor ratio;

rate of drop-out;

proportion of students doing research work;

proportion of graduate students in the student body;

availability of teaching and research staff and its structure and quality;

distribution of staff time between teaching, research and other activities;

proportion of new courses in the curricula in a definite period of time;

the rate of innovation in research programmes;

proportion of completed research which is of high professional calibre;

ratio of available books per student;

availability of teaching and research equipment;

availability of space;

availability of dormitory space for students;

unit costs per graduate.

Most of the preceding and similar relative indices can be worked out as a result of analysis and combination of the basic absolute indices. Only continuous analysis of indices creates the possibility of planning the development of universities.

10. The necessary elements of planning university development are criteria for evaluation of the existing situation and criteria for planning. It is well-known that some universities have a very solid reputation; in some countries one can see a list of the universities in the country, ranked according to their reputation. In other words, there are attempts to evaluate and compare the results of their activities. In evaluating university activity one cannot use the same criteria as those used by industrial enterprises, the profit motive, for example.

At universities, the guiding principle is quality. Here again, we face the problem of quantitative interpretation of quality. Because of the complexity

25

of the subject, the planning of university development is impossible with the use of only one kind of index. Inevitably, planning must be based on a composite of interrelating indices. Thus, the use of only one criterion for the evaluation and realization of the plan is practically impossible. Certainly the economic evaluation of university activity can be used on a limited scale; one can also use the point system. But the main difficulty again is the quantitative (in points) measurement of qualitative phenomena.

In our opinion, the main criteria for the evaluation of university activity should be the comparative level of the quality of training and the comparative level of the research work. Only in using these qualitative criteria can one carry out this process of planning development—because development is inherently qualitative rather than simply quantitative growth.

11. It is not enough only to give an analysis of the process of university development planning and to draw attention to the existing difficulties. Planning cannot be successful without adequate organizational mechanisms. The organizational structure should correspond to the current problems; it should be flexible and should guarantee planning for development. It is impossible to give any common solution to these problems because of the variety of internal structures in universities.

An adequate solution can be achieved only by taking into consideration the specific conditions, but periodic reconsideration of the existing administrative structure is essential to solving these problems. The experience of many universities has shown that joint consultative organizations can play an important role in planning. These joint organizations include representatives both of the university and of those organizations with which the university is connected. These joint organizations should work regularly and should have the necessary authority to implement decisions.

In the field of university contacts with secondary schools, they may work out recommendations concerning the quality of teaching at the secondary level, professorial guidance of pupils, improving the quality of school teachers, the creation of preparatory courses for university entrance, and so on.

In the field of training specialists, they can work out recommendations concerning the quality of training, curriculum changes, the combination of general scientific and specialized training, content of practical work, improvement of teaching equipment, opening of new fields of training, improving the qualifications of working specialists, and so on.

In the field of research they can work out recommendations concerning research plans, utilization of research results, co-operative research, and so on.

It is extremely difficult to create an organizational mechanism adequate to all the tasks we have described, but it is nevertheless a precondition for really creative planning and management.

12. One very important question, namely the question of the optimum dimensions of a university, has not yet been worked out. Once again, one cannot offer a common solution for different situations, but I think that the principles of optimization of university dimensions merit discussion.

13. The theme, 'Planning the development of universities' is a very broad one which covers many problems. It is possible to take different approaches which nevertheless overlap in many areas. Three examples might be:
A. An analysis of the existing mechanisms for planning development. With this approach one should pay particular attention to working out principles for the creation of flexible planning mechanisms, from the bases which exist. Flexible planning mechanisms here would be a set of instruments used by university managers to allow them to foresee changes and to take them into consideration in the management processes.
B. An analysis principally concerned with the main functions of the university and the changes they undergo in relation to and as a result of economic, scientific and technological changes in the surrounding society. In this approach, the spotlight should be on mechanisms and methods of planning specific aspects of university activity as a preparation for a future analysis of the entire planning mechanism. The following may be indicated as among the most important functions of the modern university: training highly qualified specialists to meet national demand; re-training and improving the qualifications of specialists already in the productive sector; development of graduate courses and training of teaching and research personnel; research work; etc.
C. An analysis of the principal problem areas. Without this analysis one cannot work out flexible mechanisms for planning the development of universities. A list of such problem areas might be rather long; however, we consider the following to be among the most important:
    access to the university;
    planning curricula changes; forms of training specialists; the role of the university in providing permanent education; industrialization of scientific research at the university and new methods of its management; development of graduate courses and the training of teaching and research personnel; information flows between the university and the environment; cost analysis; etc.

14. To analyse the mechanisms of planning the development of universities we use both direct investigation of the individual universities by IIEP staff and

questionnaires sent to selected universities. On the basis of the answers, we will choose universities for further case studies, for investigation of the methods they use for planning their development.

We think we can get useful information by asking universities the following three groups of questions:

a. What are the major changes your university will face in the next decade?
b. What information, which can be used as a basis for planning development, does the university have about itself and its present situation and about its prospects relating to the changes discussed above?
c. What mechanisms and procedures does the university have or require in order to plan for and implement major changes?

Our project is being carried out on the basis of case studies in both developing and developed countries. At the next stage of research, which will begin after this seminar, we plan to carry out a number of case studies at universities of different types, situated in different regions. In this way we will be able to discover, to generalize, and to disseminate the most interesting experiences in planning the development of universities.

The purpose of this research and the subsequent synthesis report, which will be based on it, is to find various ways and means of managing and planning the development of universities which will be useful to educational planners and university administrators. The results of this research will be published in a form which will make the useful, practical experience of a number of universities available to educators.

These results will be very useful to universities in developing countries because they will include the most advanced and diversified experiences of different countries in the world, and might well be helpful in working out university planning mechanisms in applying new management techniques, which take into consideration local conditions. They will also be of great interest to universities in developed countries, since many of those universities are also looking for flexible managerial and planning mechanisms.

Work on this project is being carried out by the staff of the IIEP, with the help of experts in the field, on a contractual basis. We seek and welcome the co-operation of individual universities in the execution of our project and we are very grateful to those universities which have already taken part in our project or have agreed to participate in it in the future.

# Summary report of the seminar

*by* Gaynor Bartagnon

# 1. Introduction

The seminar on 'Planning the development of universities' took place at the International Institute for Educational Planning from 7-12 July 1969. Representatives from more than a dozen countries and from many international organizations took part. In his opening speech Mr. Poignant, Director of the Institute, stressed the urgency of the many problems of higher education in countries all over the world. He expressed the hope that the project undertaken at the IIEP would contribute substantially to a clear identification of the problems and show the way to some possible solutions. The opinions and advice of those present were of great value, since they would throw new light on the subject and help to orientate the future direction of the project.

The summary of the seminar which follows is based on a number of necessarily arbitrary decisions. The seminar opened with the presentation of the basic discussion paper by Prof. V.G. Onushkin on methodological aspects of planning the development of universities. The actual presentation of this document and of the case studies has not been included since the discussion paper and two of the studies are published in this volume. The discussion which followed upon the presentations has, of course, been incorporated into the body of argument given here.

During the five days of the seminar, the two principle aims were, to a large extent, achieved. Firstly, it was hoped that those present would give their opinions on the project 'Planning the development of universities' and secondly, that there would be an open debate on the problems of higher education. The reaction to the project was that it was indeed relevant to the needs created by existing circumstances and the broad outline of the work involved met with the approval of the majority of the participants. Some doubts as to the usefulness of a questionnaire in the early stages were expressed. Certain participants felt that a questionnaire rarely evokes information on anything other than purely formal structures. Another point of view which was put forward was that the questionnaire—even if not fully answered—would provide a useful basis for future research, which might well go beyond the limits of the project under discussion. Another argument in favour of the questionnaire was that it made possible an extremely wide sampling in the initial stages.

There was general approval for the method of problem-oriented case studies. It was emphasised, however, that here, as throughout the project, it is essential to take account of planning at the national level, where it exists. Another participant urged that the case studies should go as deeply as possible into the selected problems in order to get at the reality behind the facts. If this were done, they would indeed provide invaluable material. In addition, this was probably the only reliable way of identifying the real managerial problems and of finding the levers for change within the administration.

Several participants felt that the project was breaking new ground, since there exists no established theoretical framework for the research to be under-taken. This, however, was in no way discouraging. The project would create this framework as it went along, using all the experience gained along the way. It was pointed out that those working on the project could not afford to ignore research being done on higher education in different countries, notably in the Soviet Union, where important research on higher education is being carried out by official bodies.

The idea of producing a manual for university planners and administrators met with general approval. Two recommendations for the manual were made. Firstly, that if it is to indicate alternatives and options in management and planning, different national structures must be taken into account. Secondly, the manual should, if possible, deal with factors to be considered in planning at every level. Every effort will be made to meet these two specifications.

The general attitude towards the project may be considered as encouraging. The consensus of opinion was that there are certainly great difficulties, both of matter and methodology, to be overcome but that the investigation of the problems of planning in higher education is extremely valuable and answers an urgent need.

As for the second aim of the seminar—a debate on the problems of higher education—this was more than satisfactorily achieved. The general discussion allowed the participants to raise the aspects which appeared to be the most important to them and to give a wider airing to some of their preoccupations. During the five days, the participants ranged far and wide over a multitude of problems connected with higher education. For the summary, it was therefore necessary to adopt a firm framework in order to present the numerous topics. This may appear to impose an order which is somewhat arbitrary, but it never-theless serves the interests of clarity and discipline and it is to be hoped that none of the ideas and theories expressed have suffered from the structural implications.

# 2. Higher education and economic and social development

There was a lively debate on the specific relationship between the development of higher education and rapid economic growth. The first idea which was called into question was the assumption that there exists a clear link between economic expansion and the development of higher education. Some participants felt strongly that the contribution of higher education to economic development was of great importance. Others were less convinced of this. 'As members of universities, as officials of universities, it serves us well to believe that universities are important contributors to economic development, but, in fact, the evidence is very confusing on this issue.' This remark was followed up by the example of the Industrial Revolution in England which led to vast and rapid economic growth and to which the universities contributed nothing but opposition, being categorically opposed to industrial development. The argument was reinforced by mention of the economic growth of Italy during the 1950s; growth which was not accompanied or indeed preceded by an expansion in higher education. Even more categorical was the reference to a study carried out by the OECD which shows that, as far as the developed countries of Europe are concerned, there is no direct measurable relationship between the expansion or non-expansion of higher education and economic growth, whether expressed in GNP *per capita* or in growth of GNP *per capita*. Here, it was added, however, that the relationship is far more complicated than a simple one-to-one relationship and that, in considering this problem, the stages of economic development of the country in question must be taken into account, along with many other factors.

This sounded the opening note for a middle of the way opinion in between the two opposed positions on this problem and the need for a wider study of its complexities. If the relationship between economic growth and the expansion of higher education is considered in isolation, the result may be disastrous, from whatever angle the problem is approached. A concrete example of this was offered from India where the relationship was seen, in a sense, in reverse. Counting on a high rate of economic growth, the government had approved a policy of rapid expansion in higher education. The expected growth rate was not achieved and there was therefore a surplus of graduates, resulting in serious unemployment. This would seem to indicate that there is room for more specific studies to explain at what level of development large economic investment in higher education is absolutely necessary for economic growth. It may well be that in many situations, reasons other than economic ones call for investment in higher education and that, in these cases, needs other than economic ones are served.

Without denying the contribution—to a greater or lesser degree—of higher education to the economy, we can accept that we must be concerned with other equally important factors and with other goals of the social system at the same time. From this discussion one can also conclude that in many instances universities are not sufficiently oriented towards the complex socio-economic needs of their countries.

It is important to consider not only the contribution of higher education to the economy, but also the demands which it makes, in competition with other services, on the public purse. If higher education is to expand, it will need greater resource allocation and, at the same time, demands from other services of the social system are growing. It is therefore essential to be clear about what higher education is offering society. Along this line of thought, one participant in the seminar said: 'I do not think that the statement that a modern technological or a modern industrial society requires the expenditures of these vast sums of money in order to create these vast professional elites is a demand that is going to withstand scrutiny very easily'. It is, in fact, fairly simple to demonstrate the insufficiency of this reason and so another rationale must be found. The university must fit the needs of the economy, and of the social system as a whole, if it is to justify the large sums of money being spent on it and to be spent on it in the future.

One element in the fitting of the university to the needs of a nation is the way in which it does, or does not, respond to the demands of society. The modern university has a responsibility to the society and the policy of the university towards satisfying social demands may be, in part, illustrative of its commitment to society and to the state. A tool which controls this response, to some extent, is the admissions policy. The problem of social demand and, with it, admission policies, evoked a great deal of comment and a good deal of information. It is interesting to note that a participant from India made the point that in a developing country the admissions policy cannot be based solely on economic demand: 'If a university is not only to serve society, but also to influence and lead, its thinking and its policies must reflect more than the

34

economic concerns'. The central problem is that finance and resources for higher education are limited, whereas the demand may be well beyond these limits. The question for a rapidly developing country—and indeed for the developed countries—is how to solve this conflict in a democratic and acceptable way. In some cases, it was pointed out, the fact that economic and social demands are not necessarily compatible is swept under the carpet and it is therefore essential to make this a central issue for discussion. One way of doing this would be to analyse the reasons for which the demand exists. It is no longer possible to subsume it under the heading of preparing people for individual tasks. A closer analysis of the reasons for growing demand for higher education might well bring about an understanding, which would make the demand easier to harness and control.

A concrete example of the difficulties which arise when the capacity of the university cannot meet the demand for places was given. In the United Arab Republic it is impossible to put the brakes on enrolment. The secondary schools graduate each year between fifty and sixty thousand students, all of whom apply for university places. The capacity of the university is between twenty and twenty-two thousand. The gap here and the pressures and tensions, which are created by the situation, are obvious. There is, however, a further complication in that about 50 per cent of those who do not succeed in gaining a place, try again the following year. The effects of this on the educational plan are, needless to say, extremely serious.

The same problem was raised from another angle, namely that of the recruitment of the student body, as opposed to simple demand. Clearly, there are different methods of planning student recruitment and these methods may do much to influence the situation of the university. A sharp distinction was made between the system of the Soviet Union for example, where student recruitment is carefully planned, and systems where recruitment is almost totally conditioned by individual demand and, yet again, systems where the universities organize their own recruitment of students.

Another response to the needs of society can be studied through the output of the university, in other words its graduates, and where this exists, research. The graduates produced must be of a nature to be useful both to the economy and to themselves. The problem of overproduction of graduates and the production of the wrong sort of graduates in developing countries was raised for discussion. The attitudes of graduates towards their work and towards the demand which society makes upon them was considered as an important factor, but difficult to measure. Those who refuse to work in rural or disagreeable areas can become a drain upon the economy. Where student recruitment and deployment of graduates is carefully planned, it is easier to avoid this unfortunate situation.

35

Output of graduates was also discussed in more general terms, taking into account as far as possible the future demands of a changing world. Many participants seemed to feel that the aims of university training have shifted from that of simply giving a professional training for life towards that of training professionals who are at the same time well-rounded, intelligent people, who will understand the future, be able to live in it and to participate in forming and changing it. It is unlikely that, in a world where knowledge itself is growing at an almost alarming rate, a person may be given a training over a period of three or four years which will last him for life. It is no longer possible to produce an 'educated' man, we must try to produce an educable man whose desire for knowledge in whatever field he may be will remain lively and unsatisfied.

# 3. Some aspects of teaching staff formation and the student body

Certain aspects of what may be considered as the 'inputs' into higher education were discussed during the week and teachers in higher education appeared to be one of the main concerns. The expansion of higher education, which brings a large increase in the number of teachers, will, apart from all its other effects, change the composition of the teaching staff and also have an effect upon the role of teachers in higher education. A concrete example of this came from India. In 1951, there were between twenty and thirty thousand university teachers. Today there are a hundred and ten thousand. Not only does the recruitment of teachers on this scale become a problem, but, clearly, not all the teachers can be first class and our ideas of what we expect of them must change. A possible area for adjustment here is that of the rather haphazard selection or self-selection of future university teachers from among the brighter university students. It should be possible to present university teaching as a career among others in a much more standardized and much less mystical way.

The question of whether university teachers should have some pedagogical training was raised. This is again perhaps a part of the demystification of the profession. If teaching methods are to evolve as quickly as technological progress would theoretically permit, university teachers will certainly need a pedagogical training, besides their intellectual one, in order to be able to exercise their profession at all. More information about the size of class which teachers may reasonably be expected to teach, given their subject-matter, is urgently needed. This is so not only because it may affect the kind of training needed and the number of students recruited, but also because it may have consequences for unit costs.

Another point which was raised was that of the qualifications of university teachers. This too can affect unit cost and also, as was clearly shown in one case, the recruitment system. At Cairo University all teachers must have a Ph.D. This makes recruitment difficult, by making demands which are possibly too high, and affects the career pattern of the teachers. If they already have a Ph.D. when they enter the profession, the motivation of adding to their qualifications and thereby speeding up their promotion is removed. Career patterns for university teachers everywhere, it was pointed out, could be more clearly mapped out than they are. If the university is to compete on a level with other organisations in society, they must offer comparable career structures.

Two concrete examples of the problems of staff recruitment in developing countries were given. In Ethiopia the main difficulty is the replacement of expatriates by nationals. This is a lengthy and expensive business, which is tending more and more to have the aspects of a vicious circle. The vast expansion of higher education has meant that although the proportion of nationals on the staff is increasing gradually, the absolute number of expatriate staff is also increasing.

In Cairo, the problem has rather different aspects. There are no full-time expatriates on the university staff so that recruitment does not have replacement to contend with. Indeed until 1954 there was a plan which was close to fulfilling the needs. Five hundred students were sent abroad for post-graduate studies each year and the majority of these returned to take up teaching posts. Since then, however, there has been a rapid university expansion and there has been difficulty in recruitment for different reasons. One of these is the brain drain to the developed countries. Out of an average of twelve hundred graduates a year studying in the United States of America, between fifty and sixty a year return to the United Arab Republic. To counter this, there has been an effort made in developing post-graduate studies in the national universities. At Cairo University there are now ten thousand post-graduate students and on an average one hundred Ph.D.s are awarded each year and one hundred and fifty masters degrees. In spite of this, however, the problem is not solved, since there are other aggravations. Since 1961 there has been an intensive programme of industrialisation, which has created a brain drain away from the universities and into industry, within the United Arab Republic. This is a problem which is well-known in the developed countries as well, but which obviously needs to be solved more urgently in a country where highly qualified manpower is not over-abundant.

The student input, in terms of social demand, was raised elsewhere, but other aspects of the student body were discussed here. Although there were a few dissenting voices, it was decided that student unrest did not come within the brief of the seminar, as it would merit much more profound attention than could be given to it, during the short meeting.

One of the aspects of the student population discussed was that of the socio-economic mix of the student body. Data on this is sadly lacking in many countries, and, in the developing countries, unless a definite policy to counteract the present trend is adopted, it is inevitable that students will continue to come from urban areas, where the possibilities of continued schooling are much greater. There is here not only the question of the aims and duties of the university, but of the formal definition of those aims. If it is part of the university's ideal of service to recruit students from every possible socio-economic group, or indeed to make particular efforts as far as disadvantaged groups are concerned, a policy which makes this possible has to be worked out in clearly defined terms.

In a more general context concerning these 'inputs', the staff/student ratio came under discussion. Several rather scathing remarks about its usefulness as a measurement of quality or indeed of anything else, were made. One participant quoted Charles Johnson of Fisk University as saying, 'If you try to improve the student/faculty ratio, you may have to make some compromises of quality in the faculty; in which case all you will have accomplished will be to enable the faculty to communicate their mediocrity in a more intimate environment'. Yet another participant remarked that 'the question of the staff/student ratio is, in fact, a fundamental question in all discussions of university planning and, in the absence of many other indicators, it is one to which we commonly resort as a quick rule of thumb...'. He went on, 'If you have no faculty, you have no teaching. If you have one faculty member per student, you probably have pretty good teaching. Everything else falls somewhere in between those two extreme statements'. There is no ideal staff/student ratio, nor even a norm which tells us anything about the effect that these numbers have on teaching. Indeed, if the ratio is considered in isolation from other factors, it becomes worse than meaningless. It may frequently be a figure which has more significance in budgetary terms than in academic ones. Many universities believe that it would be a 'good' thing to reduce the number of students per members of staff, but there is no proof that this would change a great deal. This concern may even be a screen, which covers a multitude of other issues and problems.

# 4. Teaching and research programmes

The programmes of universities came under discussion, which varied from curriculum development to the financing of research projects. It is probably fair to say that there was a consensus of opinion as far as dealing with the curriculum and with teaching methods as such were concerned. This was that the aim of the programme and of the methods used is to teach people so that they themselves can continue to improve their knowledge. The difficulties involved in this cannot be minimised and one major problem was summed up in this way: '... one should not think that, at any given moment, education is rationally co-ordinated with the system of human knowledge. The influence of the system of knowledge upon education takes place slowly and always with some delay ... it is nevertheless essential to have a system of education which corresponds harmoniously to the requirements of modern life, modern industrial methods and the development of knowledge itself'.

Beyond this basic concept, opinions and experience were varied. Closely linked, however, to the idea of turning out students who will adapt and continue to learn in a changing world is the emphasis, which must be put on how the teaching of the subject is done. It was stressed that, if only for reasons of self-reliance afterwards, students need to learn to study alone. A participant from the Soviet Union, where there is a considerable development in independent study, said that experiments were going on at the present time to establish the optimum ratio between obligatory lecture courses or tutorials and periods of independent study. 'The main task of the teachers is not to give prepared knowledge to the students, but to organise the activity of the students and, in particular, their independent activity.' This point emphasised the difficulty of isolating teaching methods from the staff/student ratio, which may be radically affected by new methods. At one point, the problem was clearly stated as a need to define what we want to accomplish and subsequently to invent a teaching system which will help to achieve the defined objectives. Up to now, only too often in teaching methods and even in subject-matter, the new is super-imposed on the old and does not, as it should, replace it. It is, in fact, time to admit that patching up will not serve for ever. The essential aspects were seen by one participant to resolve themselves into two problems: the intensification of the teaching process and its 'economisation'. This implies rapid teaching and reasonable and economic usage of the students' potentialities, the most expedient selection of material for training and a rationalisation of methods of teaching and learning.

An example of an experimental way of combining new methods and new subject-matter came from the University of Louvain. A group of students, who are to study for a given qualification, meet together with the teachers who will teach the course. Where numbers make the participation of all students impossible, there are elected representatives. At a series of meetings the group defines first of all the objectives to be realized through the learning process. Next they decide what subjects they need to learn and what teaching methods would be the best to enable them to achieve their objectives. A priority rating is given to each objective, to each subject and to each of the teaching methods envisaged. The information is then programmed and run on a computer. The students and teachers can then, having seen the full implication, draw up a programme, which best answers their defined needs and objectives. The next move is to fill out a form showing the number of hours needed per subject, the number of teachers needed, the amount of equipment and all other relevant demands. This information is then run on a computer in order to see whether the financial resources available are sufficient to implement the programme. When it has been seen what adjustments have to be made for financial or other reasons, there is an attempt made to maximise the objectives on a computer, using all the information available from all groups. This process could allow for student participation in working out teaching programmes and might offer interesting possibilities for varying structure, content and teaching method of courses.

Following on from this came an example of curriculum study from Humboldt University. Here the interest was centred on the kind of learning situations which different programmes, with different subject-content, need. What subjects for instance are suitable for full-time study or—to define the term more precisely—what subjects really necessitate full-time study? There is a real possibility that some courses, which at the moment are offered as full-time three-year courses, involving concentrated study over the period, might usefully be taught as part-time courses, spread over a longer period. In this way, they would combine more effectively the practical and theoretical aspects of the work concerned. The use of part-time education may also be a way of avoiding the dangers of over-specialization. These dangers are inherent in a concentrated

41

programme of study, which has a fixed beginning, a set amount of content and a fixed end.

The problem of over-specialization and the risk of overloading courses, as knowledge expands and new ideas or techniques have to be added, brought out another crucial element of curriculum design. Since the attempt to add Greek and Latin culture to the basic theology programme in the mediaeval universities, men have been successfully adding on and grafting new curricula to old. This is the easy way out of a complex and difficult situation. What we will have to learn to do—and this is not easy for many reasons—is to drop subjects or parts of subject-matter from the curriculum. It is probably simpler to do this if one has a completely new approach to curriculum building. One of the factors which stands in the way of ruthless programme revision is the vested interest of members of teaching and research staff. In addition to this, their position is frequently reinforced by their security of tenure. It was pointed out here that a system such as that of the Soviet Union, where teachers come up for re-election to their posts every five years, obviates some of these difficulties. Further contribution to this discussion from the Soviet Union provided an interesting description of this problem. If we accept that of the knowledge gained by a university student during his studies about 10 or 15 per cent remains useful and directly applicable and that the rest is gained afterwards during his working life, what is the best attitude towards curriculum planning? Two solutions suggest themselves. Either one may attempt to include in the course as much concrete knowledge as possible, thereby slightly increasing the percentage of useful knowledge, or one may devise a curriculum which offers a wide general background. These two contradictory points of view are always represented when programmes are worked out, but the second attitude would seem more likely to produce students who are both useful to society and themselves satisfied with their own education. This opinion seemed to be shared by the majority of the participants.

The implications which the adoption of new teaching programmes may have for research were raised and this led to a general discussion on research programmes. One aspect of the problem which was raised was that of research choices and the planning of research options. It was questioned whether the means by which research projects are selected are really effective. Examples of research projects chosen by individual professors, who have succeeded in finding funds for them from outside the university are frequent. Cases of research being undertaken hastily and under pressure because a problem has manifested itself in the social system, where with a little forethought the research might have preceded the problem, are numerous. Examples of grants being given to universities which then find themselves committed to increased current expenditure which they can ill afford are not uncommon. All this would seem to indicate a need for more rational planning of research within the universities in many instances. One way of tackling the problems of research, which for one reason or another is not in tune with economic or social needs, would be to improve the communication of research results. This needs to be done not only on the national scale but on the international one also. All universities should have means of access to world knowledge and, at the moment, it was stated frequently this is not so. There is a need then to facilitate communications among the producers of research themselves—the universities and their institutes—and also between the producers and the consumers of research—the universities and the communities in which they exist.

An example of the setting-up of research units within universities came from New York State University at Buffalo. In setting up the research units at Buffalo, an attempt was made in the first place to cut across hard and fast departmental and disciplinary divisions. The University has seven large faculties and a series of small colleges. All students and all faculty members are attached both to a faculty and to a college. An example of the interdisciplinary nature of studies is the School of Social Sciences and Administration. Besides the traditional disciplines, this school includes a professional welfare school, management school and other related studies so that there is a good admixture of theoretical and applied disciplines.

As far as research itself is concerned, each faculty research institute is run by a Council of teaching members of the faculty. There are two basic principles which underlie research programmes. The first is that a research programme should involve students, and secondly that it should also involve other faculties, where this is possible. Another criterion, which is applied, is the contribution of the research programmes to teaching. There is also a determined attempt to build impermanence into the system, since no project is financed for more than five years. At the end of that time, the programme is reviewed in the light of the above criteria, and also in the light of any other criteria which the faculty may have seen fit to invoke. This system does not unduly limit the freedom of the individual professor, but means that if he wants extensive funds from the university, he must accept the checks and controls established by the university. The question of criteria for the research itself, rather than for how it is carried out, is somewhat flexible in that each faculty plans its own research. Clearly, there are some constraints, such as the availability of facilities and resources, imposed from without. One principle in the area of free choice, however, is that of putting energy only into projects where the university can be strong. A definite attempt to avoid slavish imitation of other universities and to avoid entering into useless competition with them is a notion lying behind all choices of research areas. Going one step further than this, it is considered important to maintain and develop links with other universities in the research field and,

where possible, to share facilities. This can obviously have important consequences for the economising of scarce resources, and represents on the part
of the individual university an interesting move towards stemming the dangers
of spreading the talent too thinly. The participation of students in university
research projects was emphasised by one of the participants from the Soviet
Union. Not only is the student's contribution to research valuable in itself but
the training such co-operation offers him is being increasingly considered part
of his education.

The wider problem of whether the university is autonomous in its research
choices or to what extent it is influenced by outside pressures was summed up
in this way. 'There is a necessary tension here between the notion that universities are completely autonomous and the notion that the social system has
a set of requirements of its own. I think it is fruitful to let that tension exist.'
The conclusion here was that in this state of affairs, some research choices
will be made independently of the social system and others will be dictated
by it. A corollary to this was added in the form of a warning about the constraints placed on research choices, when the money for financing the research
comes from outside the university.

The value of an information system for research was mentioned and an
example was given of the setting-up of an information system to make a complete inventory of research going on at the university. There will be three
stages in the procedure. First of all the identification of research, secondly
the decisions taken for each activity and thirdly an inventory of achievements.
The most striking problem revealed initially by the inventory—though perhaps
one should not be too surprised—was that the definitions for what is and
what is not research appear to be large and loose. In one instance, an important
research centre listed three topics of research being carried out, whereas in
fact there were many more which were worthy of the title. Other centres had
a tendency to count as research topics which were not. Since this is an area
where a university needs to know a great deal about itself, one might also add
that it needs to know what it is knowing. One stage further than the inventory
of research, the problem of evaluating the research work carried out at universities is found. Measures of evaluation employed in the Soviet Union were
described. At the moment an attempt is being made to formulate indices for
this purpose. The effectiveness of fundamental research is determined to a
certain extent by comparison with the work of other countries in the same field.
The evaluation is carried out by the State Committee for Science and Technology
and the Academy of Sciences. Conferences, symposia and seminars are also
used as useful meeting-grounds for evaluating all research activity. There are,
in addition, certain quantitative criteria. Among these are the volume of
research work and the possibility of its application to industry, the number of

successful candidates for higher degrees, the number of patents granted, the volume of contractual research and, in the case of applied research, the effectiveness of its application to industry. In this way, both quantitative and qualitative criteria are used in evaluation.

# 5. Innovation

Another area into which the discussion fell was that of innovation and change, and of resistance to both. In the realm of more general problems, one of the participants from the United Kingdom made the point that the concept of systematic innovation is a relatively new one. This means that for the moment there is no theoretical framework in existence, to which ideas may be fitted. A useful and even essential move therefore is to create this framework, rather than to continue to use models derived from other sectors of the economy, which are totally inadequate for the job. First of all, change and innovation must be differentiated the one from the other. Change may be considered in the form of unintentional alteration, which occurs as a result of undirected stimuli, or unforeseen events. An example of this would be a rapid expansion of the system of higher education to include a population bulge in an unplanned way. Innovation, on the other hand, is a planned operation, where one or more variables are deliberately altered in order to achieve the prescribed goals more effectively. A third area within this framework is that of development which results from a situation in which one is forced by innovation to reconsider and possibly to modify goals. Within the framework then it is important to distinguish between indices which relate to the three different areas.

Although the participants in the seminar were urged to respect this definition in the discussion, it must be said that the boundaries between change and innovation frequently seemed to overlap and the distinction was not always respected.

A controversial point with regard to innovation was made early on in the discussion. The idea was put forward that in old-established institutions, it is extremely difficult to do more than innovate at the margins. Although this initial statement was hotly contested at once, other ideas of a very similar nature came to join it. It was suggested that growth in one direction or another could perhaps be considered as a prerequisite for fundamental changes. Two other preconditions which were suggested were pressure from either inside or outside the university. Most people would probably prefer to consider these pressures as possible causes rather than prerequisites. A quotation of Sir Herbert Butterfield, Vice-Chancellor of the University of Warwick, summed up the attitude of some participants towards the necessary conditions for change. 'If there are to be radical changes or even interesting experiments, it would seem that these can emerge only in the newest universities of all. One of the most exciting features of present-day educational movement is the special creative opportunity that is open to the new universities, just where originality is urgently needed and older universities are too committed to existing systems.'

Two additional points of view, which somewhat modified this position, were given. It was pointed out that although new universities may be in a strong position to innovate initially, there is the subsequent counterweight of pressure for stability within them. Indeed, at the other extreme, some new universities may consciously imitate the old-established ones in the hopes of recruiting a certain kind of student. Another possibility is that, though they may have difficulty in introducing innovation, older universities are more likely to be under pressure from outside and inside sources and may therefore find themselves in a situation where pressure becomes the cause of innovation.

A more detailed discussion followed of why and how innovations were introduced and of the means by which they might be introduced in a planned way. Two participants spoke very strongly on the importance of knowing where the centre of power for change lies whether it be within the university structure or outside it. This implies an identification of different possible levels of change and such a process might well go beyond the limits of the university and find centres of motive power within the national government or elsewhere. This identification would make it easier to define the kinds of change or innovation, both quantitative and qualitative, within the compass of the groups involved. It was urged that a study of this kind should not remain abstract and impersonal but should deliberately concern itself with the 'human element' and the persons concerned at the different levels. The more complex aspect of this problem is the difficulty involved in seizing hold of and differentiating between formal and informal structures—whether they are within the university or a part of some other official body. It will, however, be difficult to pin-point and define them as responses to questions on this rather delicate subject tend to fall back on the formal structures.

There followed several concrete examples of change and innovation, with explanations of where the impulse for change came from and how it was implemented. The introduction of Black Studies into a number of American universities was clearly the result of pressure of student demand. A participant from the United States of America told the seminar how this discipline was introduced in at least one university and the method is interesting mainly for its lack of originality. That is to say that the introduction went through the normal channels for introducing a new course of any kind; the only difference being that the usual processes were greatly speeded up. It is interesting to speculate as to whether one should conclude from this that university procedures can move faster than they do and therefore be more efficient, or whether it is simply an example of an innovation being squeezed into and passed through the traditional forms. The relentless grind of conventional machinery may frequently blunt the cutting edge of innovation.

Another example came from Latin America. In the University of Chile, there was a generally accepted belief that change of many kinds was needed. A commission to study university reform was set up by the rector. The report of the commission was presented and received with enthusiasm by all concerned. It turned out, however, that an enthusiastic reception had nothing whatsoever to do with action or implementation. One year later, since nothing had been done, the students overthrew the university authorities and took over the university. This gives an illustration of the gap between understanding the need for change and the translation of this understanding into meaningful action. The reasons for such a gap are many and various and it is essential to understand and define them in order to be able to combat them.

Many of the participants were interested in the splash-over effects of innovation. The question was raised as to whether innovations remained innovatory, in the true sense of the word, long enough to become contagious or whether they became only too quickly standardised, as they were swallowed by traditional structures. The danger of this is evidently less in a new university, which is starting everything from scratch. However, the influence of the new universities in the United Kingdom over the older establishments was not seen to be particularly encouraging. At first sight, the impact does not seem to have been very great, though, as yet, no precise research has been done on the subject. The difficulty here is that no experience is directly transferable and in this case the very specific conditions which obtain in the new universities may mean that transference is even more unlikely. It was added here, however, that even if we are obliged to accept certain limitations it might be reasonable to hope that a new university would blaze the trail for other *new* universities.

A plea was made for a somewhat more limited approach to the subject. We should be clear that we were not talking about theories of change and innovation in depth, but were concerned with the change or innovation implied by certain defined problems. Three basic questions needed to be asked. First of all what kind of information does a university need to have about itself in order to plan for the right innovation? What kinds of information flows are necessary

48

to ensure that problems and the need for change are quickly identified? Lastly what are the mechanisms which will guarantee a rapid transition between analysis and action? These questions are relevant to all universities and of particular significance in those developing and developed countries where the emphasis has been on quantitative expansion. In many cases the irresistible pressure to expand has meant that systems of higher education have simply gone on adding more of the same. There has been no time to study what was going on, as all energies were devoted to responding to the pressure of student numbers. The result is that the need to adjust, to adapt and to change in order to avoid maladjustments was largely ignored and is now making itself felt with correspondingly greater strength.

There are certain areas where one can be certain that change will come if only because of technological progress outside the universities and because a university with ten thousand students is not the same thing as a university with twenty thousand students. The changes implied must, however, be foreseen and planned by the universities themselves, for if they happen in an unplanned way they may simply be seen as a threat to present standards.

A word of warning was given here on the dangers of innovation; more particularly in curriculum development. There are often practical difficulties, such as the obtaining of new material for new courses. Assessment may prove very difficult indeed. This warning was elaborated on and some ways of avoiding the dangers of innovation were suggested by other participants. All innovations should be carefully tested and experimented with on a small scale before being generally disseminated through the system, and before any innovation is even tried out one should ask what the final aim in mind is and to what extent the new methods or innovation will contribute to achieving it.

A description of the methods used for introducing innovation in the Soviet Union was given. There exists a group of methodological departments and councils within the Ministries of higher and specialised secondary education. On the instigation of these departments and councils, innovations are tested at one university. The results of the experiments are discussed at meetings in which all parties concerned participate. If the new course or new teaching method is found to have been successful, it can then be introduced into other universities. This work goes on continuously. Meetings are held annually or bi-annually and in this way innovations can be introduced smoothly, without disrupting the day-to-day work of the university. In recent years the process of introducing new courses has been moving more rapidly as the march of technological progress gathers speed, and this method is allowing the system of higher education to respond well to new demands in a changing world.

There were several brief comments on the problems encountered in the form of resistance to innovation. Undoubtedly there are as many forms of resistance as there are individuals who resist, but understanding of their motivations may help to devise mechanisms for overcoming resistance.

A forceful and optimistic note on the problem of resistance to innovation brought the discussion to a close. In order to convince people of the need to innovate, one must be able to confront them with the real problems which are their concern, with possible alternative solutions to these problems and with the data relevant to all the stages of analysis and diagnosis.

# 6. Some problems of university planning and management

The planning of universities, for obvious reasons, occupied a place of primary importance in the discussions. All the participants were in agreement on the need to differentiate between planning at the institutional level and planning at the national level, where it exists. This led straight away to the heart of the problems of different political and social situations and of differing stages of economic development. It was pointed out that perhaps the most interesting studies on planning and management at universities would come from those universities which were responsible for their own planning decisions. However, this clear statement on the value of university autonomy was counterbalanced by a sharp element of doubt on the ability of universities to govern themselves in a period of rapid change. If universities allow themselves to get stuck in deep ruts or to fall behind in the march of progress, is this not an indication that they are unable to plan for themselves and that the planning will have to come from the outside? This could perhaps be formulated as a word of warning. If institutions of higher education do not set to and plan for themselves, then either they will find they are subject to and victims of contradictory pressures from the world around them, or some outside agency will step in and plan their development. A humanising word of warning was put in here: 'We should remember that the modern and efficient organisation of the planning and the economics of education is not only an economic but also a social problem.'

What appeared, at first sight, to be a compromise view between a study at the institutional level and studies at the level of national planning came from Chile. Here the emphasis was put upon the fact that what goes on in the individual institutions can only be properly understood within the framework of the national scene. At all events, in Latin America, university development is linked by an umbilical cord to the national situation.

This view was firmly shared by one of the participants from France: 'In

51

my opinion there is no such thing as "the university phenomenon". There is a fundamental shared existence between the university and the nation. The university must live within the nation and within all the traditions, which a long history implies, within certain structures and a given constitution. The proof of this which I can bring is the experience of a group of enthusiastic academics who said to themselves last July, 'We are going to reconstruct the universities', and who realised when they came to discuss with the constituent bodies of the nation and with the Parliament that the nation had a profound and real existence and that the constraints imposed by this existence were considerable. This, I think, is the problem we must formulate. Does the university exist independently of the nation in which it lives?' The problems of planning may then imply, at the very least, an analysis of the system as a whole.

A method of categorising universities in broad groups, which might take account both of differences between individual universities and their national situations, was suggested. The first group would include universities which are planned neither from the inside nor the outside. Many Western European universities and many Latin American ones would come into this category and any university where there is a complete absence of planning mechanisms and where the central or regional government takes no hand in planning higher education would be included. The second series would consist of those universities whose internal planning mechanisms are weak or undeveloped, but supplemented by a strong external planning system, at the government level. Universities which have inadequate structures for planning and which tend therefore to be planned by an external authority either because of their inability to plan themselves or for other reasons would be in this category. Thirdly, there would be a group for those universities which have deeply-rooted planning structures of their own, and which plan their own affairs independently of any external authority. The last group would be made up of those universities which have strong internal planning mechanisms, but which are also the object of firmly structured external planning mechanisms. Here one would suppose that there was some division of labour between the two kinds of planning. It is not intended to imply that any of these categories are static and unchanging. There is movement in different directions at all times within them. Highly centralised countries are and will be dispersing some of the responsibilities for planning and countries with widely diffused responsibilities are and will continue to concentrate some of them at the centre.

Nevertheless, these broad categories might provide a working basis, which makes, in itself, an attempt at definition. Use of this basis would mean that studies could indicate different alternatives and options available in different situations to both developing and developed countries.

A final point which introduced a strong note of pragmatism was made here.

The essential, in planning terms, is to be clear whether we are talking of national aims or whether we are talking of mechanisms at the level of the individual institution. In discussion, it is possible to separate these elements, although in practice it is not.

Another area where there are problems of definition and, therefore, a distinct need to know what is being talked about, is that which covers planning, management and administration. Several participants felt that one should be able to delimit clearly the domain of each three. It was pointed out that planning has become a branch of modern management and the links between these two fall into an understandable perspective. The third area may be introduced here in the form of a question. Given this definition and the consequent implications, how are the concepts of management and planning to be inculcated into the administrators? How are the managers of university planning to be trained and who are they to be? Although it was generally agreed that this was an important question, few answers to it were forthcoming. It would perhaps be fair to say that there was a general feeling that an academic training was not a bad background for an administrator but that aptitude and some further training is also necessary.

An example of brief administrative training sessions made available to the rectors of universities came from the Institute of Higher Education at Humboldt University. Courses are held at the Institute for those rectors and heads of departments who wish to attend and they have been very warmly received. The rectors have the chance to hear theoretical discussions of administrative problems and also—perhaps most valuable of all—to exchange views, air their particular problems and hear of solutions devised by others for similar problems. The courses are organised by the participants themselves and constitute a firm effort to rationalise the management of education which is —as it was said—one of the biggest of our industries.

Distinct changes in the role of the administrator, in part a result of changes elsewhere in the system and in part a result of planning demands, were foreseen for the future. One of the obstacles to efficient management in universities up to now has been the 'closed shop' perceptions of those involved. There has always been a tendency to see the administration, the faculty, the students and the outside world as separate groups, cohabiting—occasionally rather uneasily—for the purpose of pursuing, collecting and disseminating learning. A form of management which is concerned with all these groups without being committed to any particular one would break down these barriers and produce a more objective and, therefore, more efficient approach to the different interest groups concerned. They would in effect no longer be considered as mutually exclusive groups with possibly conflicting interests. This new management would imply a break away from the notion of *the* administrator and an acceptance of the idea of management teams, working full-time on planning, administration, management and evaluation. This also implies the complete integration of the management team into university life.

In order to achieve this, we must be able to see how management processes function in the face of problems and how they resolve the various difficulties. This is in order to ensure that the improvement of management processes evolves towards some required end.

One particular problem to which management and planning should be directing their efforts is that of managing rapid growth. Many institutions have been the victims of runaway expansion, which management techniques would have been able to organise in a more rational and productive way, had they been applied.

The participation of different groups in the university in the planning process came under serious scrutiny. The discussion ranged from the very practical aspects of the problem: how does one set about implanting a planning office in the university, where should it be located both physically and in the hierarchy? to more speculative and theoretical difficulties: how is it possible to move the focus away from academic prestige towards planning prestige? An essential ingredient of the successful implantation of planning mechanisms is a wide participation of all those who are involved by the planning process. The participation, in some cases, may take the form quite simply of distributing adequate information, at the right time. This can lead to more willing co-operation through understanding and lies at the basis of any reasonable feed-back mechanism. The size of the university can create problems here. The University of Calcutta with two hundred thousand students was given as an example of the difficulties of communication, which may become fundamental.

Before it is even possible to envisage participation in the planning of institutions, there is a need to decide who or what are the constituent bodies or elements who should have a say in the planning process. A voice must be given to those who have a right to express themselves and who will use the right of expression to contribute constructively. This implies that the university will know who can and will influence the development of the university on all fronts. It was the opinion of some participants that this knowledge is confined to the micro-level of planning and is not available at the macro-level. On the other hand, one may ask whether a professor is likely to have a sense of his institution *in toto*. Some kind of balance between the two approaches to participation is obviously desirable.

On the question of student participation in planning and administrative processes, it was pointed out that such participation should be focused on areas where students can play a dynamic role in the teaching and learning processes. To this point was added another aspect of student participation.

In some countries and particularly in the Soviet Union participation in the running of the university is considered as an integral part of the students' education. Their involvement and that of members of staff in university planning activities was explained. The faculty academic council, which has the dean as chairman and all heads of departments as members and representatives from among the academic staff and from student organisations, prepares draft plans for changes in instructional methods, curricula, scientific activities and also for the assessment of these activities. The draft plans are sent to the university council and from there to the Ministries of higher and specialized secondary education. In this way the faculty academic council acts as a platform which allows the entire staff and the student body to take part in the decision-making structure of the university.

The students' role in these activities is also reflected through the student academic council in each faculty. In addition, a great majority of the students are members of the *Komsomol* and trade-union organisations which have members on the faculty and university councils. The student academic councils make recommendations on teaching methods and on curricula.

It was pointed out that human relations and how they work are probably just as important as the planning mechanisms which surround them. It is essential to know how the university works as a human concern, in order to be able to define the various roles in the establishment clearly. An example of the insufficient definition of the human situation was that professors and other academics frequently appear to be bad administrators simply because their role in this field is not clear.

# 7. University information systems for planning

On the practical side of techniques for planning, there was a contribution on 'information systems'. As the nature of university planning changes and becomes —necessarily perhaps—more and more complicated, the importance of efficient and wide-ranging information systems becomes evident. One problem, which may seem elementary, but is, in fact, crucial, is that there is a very loose use of terminology. Words are frequently ill-defined and come to mean anything the speaker wants them to mean. The result is that two people talking of 'information systems' rarely mean the same thing. A good approach to this difficulty is to start with a very simple question: 'What sorts of information do universities need to have about themselves?' The following three areas of information where universities are in general rather ignorant were mentioned here as examples.

Few universities have sufficient data on student wastage. Both the rate of loss and the causes behind it deserve more detailed study.

Another area where there is frequently a lack of sufficient information is that of the costs of different programmes and activities. There is some difficulty in getting at these costs, because of the problems involved in breaking them down in the necessary detail. An adequate analysis implies separating the research and teaching load in order to distribute costs accurately. However, it is only if this is done that another aspect of development can be studied. This is the future impact on an institution of new programmes and activities. Too often the effects of new activities on the commitment of personnel and of resources are not calculated in advance, because the information is lacking.

The university library was another topic which came under fire. There are very rarely reliable figures on the number of titles in the library; and the number of volumes, which can usually be found, is not a very revealing figure. Again, there are no measurements of the services of the library. A great deal of use may be made of materials which never leave the premises and lack of measurement, knowledge and information about these facts may lead to inefficient use of resources.

All these areas selected for attention reveal the fact that the development of an information system is not just a question of re-shuffling information already available, but of finding new information. This, of course, implies the creation of new sub-systems to produce the information desired and may lead the universities to consider problems which, up to now, they have been hastily brushing under the carpet.

The information system is indeed a key element in planning, if for no other reason than that it influences and reflects the levels at which planning takes place. The information system must be organised to provide for those who have the power vested in them to make decisions. It can help to improve the quality of decision-making by improving the quality or increasing the quantity of data on which a decision is based. What is also necessary, however, is a means of collecting data which corresponds to the needs of the system. Unfortunately, university planning is usually linear and additive and one of the reasons for this is the way in which data is collected. University personnel and in particular the academics find it difficult to think in the three dimensional terms of systems, and yet, if decision-makers are to see the consequences of their decisions clearly, there must be a systems analysis approach to the collection of data.

A striking example of the evaluation of university activity, leading to a more rational planning of the system came from the Soviet Union. A series of indices, summarising in the main what the university needs to know about itself, have been worked out. They have been in use since 1966 and are therefore well-tried. There are four principal groups of data comprising the characteristics of research and teaching personnel, the characteristics of teaching and methodology, the characteristics of research work and, lastly, characteristics of the non-academic activities of students. Each group is made up of between five and seven indices. A system of weighting for the indices has been worked out and this means that the activity of any institution of higher education, however much they may vary in strength and size, can be evaluated objectively. Each year on the basis of these indices, the results of work are summarised. They are then discussed at meetings of all the university rectors. The experience of the last three years shows that this system of evaluation has stimulated development in every institution of higher education.

Some months ago the same system was introduced at the level of chairs and faculties within the universities. This allows for a comparison of activities of the different faculties and of the chairs within the faculties, and the system of indices is used in a way which reflects the main concerns of the moment. This system does not include economic indices, since the system of national accounting furnishes this information for planning purposes. It should be said that the use of the system of indices does not mean that no other method of evaluation is used. Expert opinion is frequently consulted but the system of indices is a way of narrowing down the field of problems and of allowing for a selection of the most urgent problems for consultation.

# 8. Conclusion

It can be seen from the range and depth of the ideas reported here, that the IIEP seminar provided a forum for many different opinions and attitudes to the problems of higher education. The discussions were most valuable to the members of the IIEP engaged on the research project 'Planning the development of universities' and they would like to thank all the participants for their contributions to this project and for their encouragement.

# Leningrad State University: planning and management of teaching and research work

*by* K.Ya. Kondrat'ev, V.A. Zubkov, V.M. Petrov *and* L.A. Shilov

# Introduction[1]

The Soviet Union is a country with a widely developed system of higher education. Higher education is free of charge—on the principle of the equal right to education of all USSR citizens, irrespective of race, nationality, sex, financial or social standing, and religion—with a view to the wide development of the culture, national in form and socialist in content, of the nations of the Union. Higher education is given by universities, academies, institutes, technical colleges and other similar establishments. The main tasks of higher educational establishments are:

the training of highly qualified specialists with profound theoretical knowledge and the necessary practical skill, versed in Marxist-Leninist theory, and in the latest achievements in science and technology, both at home and abroad, brought up in a spirit of Communism, Soviet patriotism, the friendship of peoples and proletarian internationalism, with skill in the organization of mass-political and educational work;

constant improvement of the quality of the training of specialists, taking into account the requirements of present-day production, science, technology, culture and their prospective development;

scientific research work to further the building-up of Communism;

the production of high-quality textbooks and teaching aids;

the training of sufficient numbers of research and teaching staff;

raising the standard of qualification of the teaching staffs of higher and secondary specialized educational establishments, and that of experts with higher education employed in corresponding branches of the national economy;

fostering in students a sense of duty and a readiness to protect the socialist motherland;

1. This study of the Zhdanov State University of Leningrad is based on the personal assessment of the four co-authors.

dissemination of scientific and political knowledge among the people;
physical training and measures to fortify the health of students.

Higher education in the Soviet Union has undergone a development unprecedented in history. Up to the Great October Socialist Revolution, there were in Russia (within the present-day boundaries) only 105 higher educational institutions (VUZ).[1] In 1914-15 these had rather more than 127,000 students, who were the children of noblemen, officials, clergy, bourgeoisie and in part the Kulak heads of villages. With few exceptions, higher education was out of the reach of the workers. Non-Russian peoples inhabiting our country were completely cut off from higher education.

The Great October Socialist Revolution brought a radical transformation of the higher schools. Higher education in our country became accessible to all who wished to learn. A wide network of higher-educational institutions was created.

While in Tsarist Russia for every 10,000 of the population there were eight students at VUZy and three at secondary special schools, the figures at the present time in the USSR are 181 and 176 respectively. In 1970 there were 4.6 million students at 800 higher educational institutes spread over all the republics.

One of the brightest pages in the history of our cultural revolution is the flowering of education in the national republics. National minorities in the remote regions of Tsarist Russia have made such headway in social and cultural development as, under the old conditions, would have taken a century to achieve.

Before the Revolution, literacy among the populations of Central Asia and Kazakhstan did not exceed 0.5-0.7 per cent, and there was not a single establishment of higher education. These are now regions of full literacy. In the Turkmen SSR there are five VUZy, in the Tadzhik SSR seven, in the Kirgiz SSR nine, in the Uzbek SSR 38 and in the Kazakh SSR 43. In the numbers of students per 10,000 of the population, all these republics have by far outstripped the developed capitalist countries.

Under the Soviet system, freedom and equal rights as members of Communist society were given to women. They received equal rights with men to education. In 1967, of engineers with higher education, women formed 30 per cent; of agronomists, zoo-technicians, veterinary doctors, foresters, 39 per cent; of doctors, 73 per cent; of teachers and other workers in education, 67 per cent; of economists, 60 per cent.

The network of higher educational institutions in the USSR is a well organized system, equal to the tasks of developing the national economy and

---

1. VUZ: *vyssie učebnye zavedenya* (higher educational establishments).

culture and taking into account the economic and cultural interests of the republics of the Union. There are VUZy in all the republics, which in the main supply all the specialists they need.

The higher educational system includes universities, embracing natural and social sciences and humanistic specializations; multi-faculty polytechnics, training engineers with a wide knowledge of various branches of industry. In addition, there are a large number of specialized VUZy including technical, agricultural, economic, law, pedagogical and medical institutes; and higher educational institutions of art, teaching music, theatre, painting, etc.

There has been a wide development of higher education by correspondence courses and in evening institutes, which offer the vast majority of the specialized subjects taught in our VUZy. With the object of improving the management of correspondence and evening education, ordinary, correspondence, and evening courses have been combined into a single 'faculty' system, by which all teaching and academic work is directed by the same departmental management, thus ensuring uniformity of educational treatment to the students of full-time, evening and correspondence schools. The quality of the training of the specialists so produced is, without doubt, thereby improved.

Higher education in the Soviet Union owes its outstanding development to the constant attention which the subject has received from the Communist party and the Soviet government, and the uninterrupted development of industry has made it possible to provide establishments of higher education with a sound and up-to-date infrastructure of material facilities and laboratories.

Higher education, being free of charge, is accessible to all who desire it, and the system of state grants makes it materially possible to follow a complete course of study in any higher educational establishment. More than 70 per cent of all students receive such grants.

Outstanding students receive higher grants, the best among them being awarded the V.I. Lenin scholarship. Students in the social sciences and humanities receive the Karl Marx scholarship; other awards have been established in the name of famous men who have contributed to party, government or society, science, technology or culture.

Students enrolled in evening classes or correspondence-courses are accorded substantial privileges by their employers, enjoying a shorter working day or week and receiving extra leave of absence with pay.

Students following courses away from home are provided with lodgings at very low cost.

The Communist party and the Soviet government, translating Lenin's theories on industrialization into reality, are devoting much attention to the expansion of higher technical education, and outstanding results have already been achieved in this connexion.

Before the first world war, the industry of Russia was served by only about 8,000 specialists with higher technical education. The Russian Empire, with its 160 million inhabitants, had only eighteen technical institutes, with an enrolment of 24,900 students specializing in twenty subjects.

Immediately after coming to power, the Communist party and the government set about creating a new technical intelligentsia from members of the working class. By 1928 there were already three times as many higher technical educational establishments in the USSR as before the Revolution; and in 1937, twenty years after the establishment of Soviet power, the number of graduating engineers was four and a half times greater than the total number of engineers in Tsarist Russia.

During the recent post-war period, the training of engineers has increased enormously. In seven years alone (1958-65), more than a million engineers have been trained. In the years since the Revolution, their number has increased to more than 250 times the pre-revolutionary figure, reaching more than two million at the present time with 230 establishments of higher education providing training in 260 subjects.

Whereas in Tsarist Russia there were fourteen higher educational schools of agriculture with 4,600 students, there are now ninety-eight such establishments in the Soviet Union with a total enrolment of 443,000 students.

Teacher-training institutes (VUZy) are particularly numerous in the USSR (206 in all, with an enrolment of approximately 900,000 students). Pre-revolutionary Russia had only two such institutes.

In 1914, Russia had only six higher educational schools of medicine. Today there are eighty-one, with a total enrolment of 274,000 students.

In 1914, Russia had five conservatoires. Today there are sixty-one higher educational establishments of art and culture.

In 1969, in accordance with a decision of the Central committee of the CPSU and the Council of ministers, departments designed specially for the training of young workers for entering VUZy were created in a number of higher educational establishments. In the academic year 1969-70, such departments were functioning in 191 VUZy.

The intensive development of science and technology, and the major role of scientific research in solving the problems of the national economy and the defence of the country, bring the institutes of higher education face-to-face with new problems. At the moment it is not enough to increase the output of specialists with higher education considerably: the more pressing problem is to improve the quality of their training. In addition, more scientific workers and science teachers must be trained, and their qualifications improved.

Under the conditions of the scientific and technical revolution now in progress, with the continuously developing synthesis and differentiation of the sciences, an important role belongs to the universities, as institutions embracing representatives of both the natural and the humanistic sciences and having the most favourable conditions for complex theoretical investigations and the training of specialists.

Among the higher educational institutions of the Soviet Union, a leading place is occupied by the universities, as the true centres of science and culture, playing a major role in the training of specialists with wide qualifications in scientific and humanistic learning.

In pre-revolutionary Russia, the universities were important centres of culture and enlightenment, contributing to the development of progressive scientific thought and serving as the cradle of the revolutionary movement.

After the October Revolution, the universities received the active support of V.I. Lenin, who valued them highly as a means of uniting science with education, and considered it essential to work for their over-all development and improvement. As early as January 1919, in the midst of disorder and famine, the Council of people's commissars, under Lenin's leadership, decreed the establishment of six new universities. In 1920, the Urals and Central Asia were provided with foundation-stones for higher education with the creation of the universities of Ural and Turkestan (now Tashkent).

The Soviet period has seen a notable extension of university education. Tsarist Russia had twelve universities, catering for only 41,000 students; today, the Soviet Union has fifty universities, with a total enrolment of approximately 500,000.

Universities have been established in all the union republics, and in a number of autonomous republics.

A deep and wide general theoretical training of specialists—the organic bond between scientific work and the educational process—is the basic principle of university education in USSR. In the universities are gathered together learned men who develop the sciences forming the theoretical basis of technical progress—physics, mathematics, chemistry, biology, geology. In university laboratories many very important discoveries have been made, which have laid the foundations for the development of new branches of science and technology. The universities have also played a large part in the development of higher education and in the training of teachers in the VUZy and the raising of their qualifications.

Scientific and technical progress emphasizes the urgency for improving university education and the training of specialists in natural, social and humanistic sciences. Many present-day technical problems, bound up with the development of the national economy, cannot be solved without specialists with a profound knowledge of mathematics, theoretical mechanics, chemistry, biology, economics, psychology, i.e. specialists who can be trained to sufficiently high level only in the universities.

In addition, the universities, embracing in themselves all fundamental lines of thought in the fields of the natural and humanistic sciences, provide the best conditions for solving the big theoretical and practical problems which arise at the 'junctures' of the sciences. This in its turn creates great possibilities for the training in them, on a considerable scale, of scientific workers and teachers, the need for whom in research institutes and VUZy continues to grow.

Finally, alongside the fulfilment of these basic functions, many universities train highly educated teachers for ordinary schools, and produce textbooks and teaching aids for many educational institutions. All these great and crucial problems confronting the universities determine the very nature of these higher educational institutions and their place in the system of higher education.

The system of education in our universities has certain characteristics which distinguish these higher education institutions from others. The training includes obligatory participation in research work together with members of the faculty and under their guidance. Preparation for this participation is given in the courses, where the students master the methods of research, and acquire skill in the use of scientific information. The obligatory diploma work of the graduating student often takes the form of a serious scientific investigation, or his thesis will require independent solution of a small research problem selected by the author.

Another characteristic of university education is the fact that first- and second-year students usually follow a curriculum which is uniform for the particular faculty in question, afterwards passing according to their choice, to specialized departments, i.e. those having a curriculum of their own. A large number of special courses are available, obligatory and optional, which include all the latest developments in any given branch of knowledge.

The system of scientific seminars, with wide-ranging discussion of published and experimental material, is another speciality of university education.

Soviet universities are expected to ensure the training of specialists in natural and humanistic sciences who will be in a position to take part in scientific research, teach in VUZy, work in government institutions, etc. The necessity for constant improvement in knowledge is inculcated, together with the ability to use scientific information and to find one's way about in its vast volume. The very structure of the university and the system of instruction make possible the training of specialists of the required type.

The kind of training given to a specialist must be determined not only by the character of his work and the depth of his knowledge of his special subject, but also by the breadth of his thought, the level of his general culture, his understanding of the social problems of our society, his ability to carry out educational work, and his enthusiasm in the battle for the Communist cause.

At the present time, the educational side of the activity of the VUZ acquires special importance as a part of the general problem of education of the new human being.

The role and responsibility of the higher educational institute are particularly great, since it prepares the future intelligentsia: teachers, scholars, managers of industry—in a word, people who by their very position have to set an example for creative work and for Communist principles and morality.

The activity of the VUZ is oriented towards the future, and this is particularly true of the university, the graduates of which will be working in science, culture, and education.

The Soviet Union is generously sharing its experience in the development of higher education. International contacts at the level of higher education constitute a significant element, both in scale and significance, of Soviet foreign relations. These contacts are constantly expanding and growing in strength and variety, with the aim of sharing success in science and culture and promoting international understanding and friendship, on the basis of full equality of rights, mutual understanding and strict regard for the principles of national sovereignty.

In 1946, 250 nationals of socialist countries were studying in the USSR. Today, more than 13,000 are attending VUZy and technical institutes. In 1956, fifty-six students from the developing countries came to the USSR; today, more than 12,500 citizens of African, Asian and Latin-American countries are working as students or teachers in Soviet establishments of higher education. Ten years ago, forty Soviet teachers were working in the developing countries: in the academic year 1969/70, this figure has risen to approximately 800.

In 1960, 1,266 Soviet citizens travelled abroad under the auspices of the Ministry of higher and secondary specialized education. This figure rose to more than 10,500 in 1969. Since the second world war, more than 48,000 professors, teachers, graduate students and students have travelled abroad for scientific or other academic purposes, 38,000 of them to socialist countries.

## Basic information about the university

The 20th of February, 1969, marked the passing of 150 years since the founding of Leningrad State University of the Order of Lenin and the Order of the Labour Red Flag, named after Zhdanov.

The university was founded on 20 February 1819, with three faculties: philosphy and law (later the Faculty of Law); history and philology; and physics and mathematics. It was formed by reorganization of the Chief Pedagogical Institute. In 1854 a fourth faculty was added—that of oriental languages. The university continued thus for almost 100 years, right up to the Great October Socialist Revolution.

Before the Revolution, Petersburg University was one of the largest centres in Russia of science and culture for the training of the intelligentsia. Professors of the university wrote many brilliant pages in the history of Russian and world science. And during its long and glorious history, the Petersburg-Petrograd-Leningrad University has been the repository and transmitter of the most progressive and revolutionary ideas conceived by Russian society and has been truly served by its advanced intelligentsia.

The history of the university reflects all the main stages in the development of the revolutionary movement in Russia. A special place in the history of Petersburg University is occupied by V.I. Lenin who in the spring and autumn of 1891 took the external examination in the faculty of law and was awarded a diploma in the first class. The Great October Socialist Revolution opened a new chapter in the history of the university, which marked the beginning of its intense growth and flowering. For the half-century following that October, its activity widened and deepened immeasurably.

In the near 100 years of its pre-revolutionary existence, the university produced 25,000 specialists; in the fifty-two years of Soviet power, 80,000. Its organization has also improved. At the time of the Revolution, four faculties were in existence; they now number fourteen. In 1917, for example, the teaching of mathematics, mechanics, and physics, having passed through a period of intensive growth, was nevertheless represented by only three departments; now there are about thirty mathematics and physics departments.

In 1917 there were in the university about 200 professors and lecturers. Now the teaching and scientific body of the Leningrad State University numbers about 2,700 people. Among them are twenty-nine members and corresponding members of the USSR Academy of Sciences and its branches.

The conditions of study and the life of the students have changed radically, for they now have up-to-date scientific and teaching laboratories, bases and stations in the Caucasus, the Crimea, on Lake Ladoga, the reservation Forest on the Vorskla in the Belgorod oblast, and others. One of the largest scientific libraries in the country, the Gorki library, is at their disposal with a valuable stock of four million volumes. The university has ten students' hostels, accommodating 5,500 students from other towns. The sports club provides facilities of various kinds for about 8,000 students.

After the Revolution, the scientists at the university, continuing and developing the best traditions and achievements of their predecessors, greatly widened the scope of investigations and enriched Soviet science with many outstanding discoveries. For outstanding scientific discoveries ten scientists of the university have been honoured with the title of Laureate of the Lenin prize, and fifty-one with that of Laureate of the state prize.

Leningrad University trains about 1,000 students and graduates from foreign countries each year. Very substantial help is given to other socialist and developing countries in the training of their specialists. In the years 1951-68, the university trained over 700 young specialists and 300 graduate students for socialist countries. A number have come from the developing countries of Asia and Africa, and the year 1966 saw the graduation of the first batch of specialists from these countries.

Leningrad University is now one of the most important higher educational institutions in the country, and an important centre of Soviet science. It has fourteen faculties: mathematics and mechanics, physics, chemistry, soil-biology, geology, geography, economics, philosophy, law, psychology, history, philology, oriental studies, and journalism, divided into 153 departments. There is a large staff of highly qualified professors and lecturers, which on 1 January 1969 numbered 1,829 and included 281 doctors of science and 811 'candidates' (of science). To these must be added members of the staffs of scientific research institutes who assist to some extent, e.g. by giving special courses, supervising work for diplomas, etc., among them forty-five doctors and 369 masters of science.

On 1 January 1969 there were 19,064 students, comprising 10,029 full-time, 5,046 evening, and 3,989 correspondence students. The faculties having the largest numbers were the mathematics, mechanics, physics, and philology faculties. The periods of study are: for full-time, five years, and for evening and correspondence, six years.

Evening courses are given in all faculties except oriental studies, and there are correspondence courses in nine faculties: mathematics and mechanics, geography, history, philology, economics, law, philosophy, journalism and psychology. Having regard to the conditions of teaching in the evening and correspondence divisions, the university tries primarily to attract people whose work matches the nature of the subject selected.

The training of the students follows individual study plans. The university, with its special traditions of scientific activity and specialist training, and its great scientific resources and up-to-date equipment, has the right to prepare its own curricula for the training of students. Keeping in view the provision of broadly-based specialist training, the faculties at the same time envisage a deeper specialization by students in subjects selected by them. In some cases, specialized work in one department of the university may overlap into another department. A given department may have to provide numerous special courses, seminars and laboratory practice, which reflect the latest developments in science. Specialization and consequent distribution of students among departments, begins in the third and fourth year courses, and is completed by the student writing a diploma thesis on a subject selected by him and approved by the department.

Recently an ever greater part in the teaching work is being played by very gifted students after special individual plans of study have been given by the department. This method is of particular importance in the training of students who have a complex plan of work, it ensures that they have the possibility to widen their knowledge and experience of subjects not taught in the particular faculty in question, but which are yet essential to the training the student is undergoing.

At the present time the faculties of the university offer the opportunity to specialise in forty-five different fields of study.

The staff of the university is successfully carrying out its task of training specialists for various branches of the national economy, science, education and culture, and for the solution of basic scientific problems in order to ensure the further scientific and technical progress of the country.

# Teaching activity of the university and tendencies in its development

## 1. University and school—the discovery of talent

To ensure the successful accomplishment of the many tasks for development of education and science proposed in the programme of the USSR Communist party, special importance is attached to strengthening the bonds between the higher educational establishment and the secondary schools and establishing greater continuity between them. Leningrad University has had for many years continuous and close ties with the schools in its city.

These ties take many different forms: some of these have now become traditional, such as, help given by members of the university in the work of the Leningrad branch of the Pioneers; the organizing and conducting of mathematical, physical, and chemical 'olympiads'; the organization of societies in schools; a series of lectures given to school children at the university; the establishment of a junior school on social principles at the university: organization of industrial practice for scholars in the laboratories and research institutes of the university; measures for raising the qualifications of the teachers; and so on.

Preparation for admission to university entails a long and painstaking effort to discover the most able pupils, but these have come to the fore in clubs of young mathematicians, physicists, chemists, biologists, historians, geologists, and also in the traditional olympiads in physics, mathematics, chemistry, etc., held in all towns. These olympiads are large-scale events in which thousands of school children take part. University teachers have long taken an active part in the conducting of olympiads, in setting the tasks for the second and third (the most difficult) rounds, and in ascertaining and verifying the results.

Extensive work with school children has long been a tradition of the mathematical and mechanical faculty of the university. This work is of great importance to the faculty: it not only helps to attract the most capable pupils, but also engages a considerable number of students of the faculty in social work of a particularly suitable nature.

A Junior Mathematical School (JMS) has been organized. Formerly in the faculty there were mathematical circles for school children, in which, under the guidance of students, they solved difficult problems, and learned facts beyond the range of the school curriculum. These circles were, however, unconnected with one another and small in number. In 1960 the JMS was created in their place. It differs from the circles firstly in its size, and secondly in the fact that it has one uniform programme. It has about 400 pupils from classes 7 to 10 of the Leningrad schools. Instruction is given in the evening twice a week, by about forty students and graduates of Leningrad University.

The ranks of the students are supplemented by 'graduates' of the school. Almost all the victors in the Leningrad mathematical olympiads are pupils of the JMS. So were members of the Leningrad contingents which were successful in the All-Russia mathematical olympiads of 1964 and 1965. Five pupils of the JMS were victors in past years in the international olympiads of the socialist countries. In 1967 the USSR contingent included four candidates from Leningrad, three of whom obtained first prizes.

Since 1934, when, on the initiative of a group of teachers of the mathematical and mechanics faculty at Leningrad the first mathematical olympiad in the country was held, such olympiads have become traditional. Last year there were thirty mathematical olympiads. In different years the olympiad jury has included many leading Leningrad mathematicians. The Leningrad olympiad is not only the oldest, but also the largest, in the country. Even in the second round, about 6,000 people take part, of whom 600 reach the final round.

The experience of many years has shown that the winners in the olympiad become the best students in the mathematical and mechanics faculty, and go on to fill the ranks of the scientific staff. It can be said without exaggeration that the majority of actively working middle-aged and young mathematicians in Leningrad have been olympiad winners. Each year fifty to seventy teachers and students of the faculty take part in conducting the olympiad. Since 1964 the faculty has been the organizing centre of the mathematical olympiad not only in the city, but also in the regions and autonomous republics of the north-western RSFSR. The faculty prepares the curriculum for the olympiad; in each region of the north west and during the regional round a teacher of the faculty is present; he helps in compiling the questions and in the actual conduct of the olympiad and gives lectures to the teachers and pupils.

For the third year the olympiad organized by the newspaper *Komsomol' skaya Pravda* is taking place. The checking of work for the north-west area is being done by students of the faculty. Members of the staff are taking an active part in the organization of the All-Russia 'olympiad', as in 1967 in that of the first All-Union 'olympiad'.

The mathematical and mechanics faculty initiated the organization of the first specialized mathematics school in the town. Besides general guidance in the organization of mathematics teaching in the school, teachers of the faculty gave instruction in programming of the computer Ural-2 set up in the school.

Since 1965 the mathematical and mechanics faculty has housed the north-western mathematical correspondence school, which has room for 1,000 students per year; about 700 are enrolled at the moment. The faculty compiles the papers for this school (which is closely linked with the similar one at the Moscow State University) and the students and graduates work in it. The school is probably the main support of the faculty in its relations with the secondary schools in the north-western RSFSR.

Members of the mathematical faculty have played an active part in the elaboration and discussion of new programmes of mathematics for secondary schools. Close ties exist between the faculty and the physico-mathematical school No. 239, the work of which is conducted by members of the physics faculty staff.

More than 180 pupils are taught in the circles of the physics faculty. In view of the introduction of a new school physics programme, the physics faculty, with the teacher-training institute, organizes two-year courses for re-training of physics teachers in Leningrad secondary schools.

The chemistry faculty has been working systematically with school children for more than twenty years, with olympiads for the pupils, lectures, reports, excursions, etc. The faculty is the centre of organization of the All-Union chemistry olympiad for the north-western regions of the RSFSR. For the organization of the olympiad each year twenty to thirty staff members go to Murmansk, Tallinn, Riga, Pskov, Petrazavodsk, Vologda and other towns.

Since 1966 a group of young chemists has been working at secondary school No. 208. The young chemist's club has been founded for pupils of the schools in the Vasilii Ostrovskii district.

In the soil-biology faculty, school societies are regularly at work on human and animal physiology, zoology of invertebrates, hydrobiology, ichthyology, zoology of vertebrates, etc. In 1966 in the Vasilii Ostrovskii district a school for biologists was opened, to take pupils interested in biology, from classes 8 and upwards, in all schools of the district. For the course, a group of staff members of the university and the USSR Academy of Sciences drew up a programme, wrote a textbook called *General biology,* and completed the preparation of a series of instructional tables for this department. Numerous lectures were given by faculty members in the Teacher-Training Institute. Biological olympiads were organized and conducted in the towns.

For more than fifteen years at the Leningrad branch of the Pioneers a club for young geologists has been in existence, comprising fifteen different sections. Geologists of the university, besides working at the club, have organized expeditions and excursions to geologically interesting areas of the Leningrad region, to Transcarpathia, and to the Urals.

In the historical faculty a young historians' club has been running successfully since 1965, with a membership of over 200. It has several sections: history of the USSR; history of international relations and diplomacy; history of the Middle Ages; history of the theatre; history of art; archaeology. Students of the faculty take an active part in the assistance given by the university to Leningrad secondary schools.

Work of considerable diversity among school children is also done by other faculties of the university. Systematic help is given to teachers and pupils by the pedagogical department. In conjunction with the teaching body it has published a collection of articles on 'Interrelations of school and life'. Members of the department take part in practical-scientific conferences of the schools of the Vasilii Ostrovskii district, and give lectures to teachers and parents on the problems of Communist education.

There is probably not a single faculty of the university which does not take an active part in helping teachers and pupils.

A very large part is played by the university in the work of the specialized boarding school No. 45 at Leningrad State University, created in 1963. This school provides completion of general secondary education and at the same time gives more thorough training in mathematics, physics, chemistry and biology, and professional training in accordance with the special subject studied. Organization of the school is one of the forms of methodological help given by the university to secondary schools with a view to raising the general level of teaching of mathematics, physics, chemistry and biology, by the following means: the olympiads, the production of books of exercises and teaching aids, the giving of lectures and the conducting of competitive selection in the school. These activities are carried out by the school under the guidance of the university in conjunction with the regional education authorities, pedagogical institutes and other interested organizations in the north-western regions according to the list ratified by the Ministry of education of the RSFSR.

The boarding school accepts children from the seventh to eighth grades from the regions and republics of the north west: Pskov, Novgorod, Vologda, Archangel, Murmansk, Leningrad, Komi ASSR, Baltic Republics, etc.; principally children of Kolkhoz workers, workmen, officials, needing state help for the completion of their education.

Much painstaking work over admission to the school is done by the acceptance committee, representatives of which go to the regions and republics of the north west for this purpose. They speak on radio and television, give information in the local press, and supervise examinations held by the local authorities. The results of the work of the schools, and in particular the success of pupils in examinations for admission to the VUZ, speak in favour of the basic course, and especially of the method of selection. In the scholastic year 1967/68 of 153 finishing at the boarding school, 123 were accepted by the day department of the university; of these forty-three by the physics faculty, thirty-three by the mathematics and mechanics faculty, nineteen by the chemistry and soil-biology faculties. The evening department of the university, and other VUZ, took twenty. In the scholastic year 1966/67, of 133 school leavers, 120 entered the university. No less important is the fact that the students from the school make very good progress at the university.

The programmes for qualifying subjects are drawn up by the relevant faculty of the university, and then considered by the methodological committee of the school, which is headed by Professor D.K. Faddeev, of the mathematical and mechanics faculty, corresponding member of the USSR Academy of science, and one of the most eminent scholars of the university. Intensified physico-mathematical training takes place principally during time allotted in the plan to subjects of the student's choice. The experience of the boarding school, as of other specialized schools, is of interest in connexion with the proposed change to new programmes in all secondary schools.

Thus, for instance, the programme for biology at boarding schools, which had proved its value in practice, was taken as a basis for a model programme for all schools in the country and was accordingly approved by the Ministry of education of the USSR.

Considerable extramural work goes on at the school, special attention being paid to the aesthetic training of the students. Meetings are arranged with writers, artists, scientists and veterans of the revolutionary movement and labour organizations. The school runs interesting aesthetic activities, with a compulsory course of work at the Hermitage and at the Museum of Russia. Great attention is paid to physical education and sport, there being at present twelve different sports sections in the school. The number of sportsmen with an official rating increases every year.

Alongside this extensive and varied work with secondary-school students, the university strives to facilitate university entrance to anyone whose studies have been long interrupted, i.e., those who since they left school have worked in industry or agriculture, served in the army or those who feel they are not properly equipped to take the university entrance examinations.

For all such persons a set of preparatory courses is available where at a modest charge they can prepare themselves for university entry. These consist mostly of evening courses for young people of secondary education working in Leningrad. The courses last nine months, the curriculum being such that entry to any faculty of the university is possible. In this connexion, the courses include study groups in physico-mathematics and the humanities. The annual intake to these courses is 900-1,000, the students being drawn from industry and various other occupations in Leningrad. The studies are based on semesters with two sets of intermediate examinations, and are run by the university staff. Completion of the courses does not entitle the students to any privileges; they are simply better prepared for the faculty examinations.

Whereas the evening preparatory courses are designed exclusively for young persons living in Leningrad, young persons from other town and country areas wishing to prepare themselves for university entrance can take correspondence preparatory courses. These are for people with secondary education, and last ten months, with suitable curricula. The students of these courses regularly receive material and textbooks on their chosen subject, and exercises which they have to complete and return to the school. At the end of the course, those who wish can go to Leningrad where for one month they can attend tutorials on their chosen subjects, run by the university staff. The advantage of the correspondence courses is that they cater for a wider circle of young people wishing to enter university from different towns, regions and areas of the country.

The above-mentioned courses are supplemented each year by short-term courses of one to three months, run by the university branch of the Association '*znanie*' ('knowledge'). These courses consist of survey lectures on mathematics, physics, biology, history, literature and other subjects, with tutorials, and are designed to familiarize the young with the university's requirements.

In addition to fee-paying courses, the university operates preparatory courses for young persons leaving public rural schools. As is known, despite the enormous success of the public-education system in the USSR there are still some differences in the level of preparation at rural and urban schools. This is due to the obvious differences between town and country and the facilities they offer. Short non-fee-paying preparatory courses for young agricultural workers wishing to enter university are designed to remedy this situation. Local education authorities each year select students from rural schools. These students are interviewed to determine their knowledge and ability, and those suitable go to Leningrad for one month for daily study and tutorials. All the students' requirements during the courses and preparation for examinations are catered for by hostels. As a rule, 70 to 80 per cent of those attending these courses pass the university entrance examinations.

For some years now, a preparatory faculty for workers from industry and for young agricultural workers, has been in operation at the university, running nine-month courses for 100-200 persons. This faculty originally fulfilled the functions now provided by the short courses for those leaving rural schools. Today the faculty serves, among others, young workers engaged in the construction of a complex of new buildings for Leningrad University in the Peterhof area. Attendance at the faculty is free.

In accordance with the decree of the central committee of the Soviet Communist party and of the council of ministers, of 20 August, 1969, to raise the general educational level of workers and rural youth and to improve the necessary conditions of admittance to higher educational institutes such as Leningrad University, special preparatory departments are to be organized from the 1969/70 academic year onwards.

Students admitted to preparatory departments include successful workers, collective-farm workers and men demobilized from the Soviet armed forces who have completed their secondary education. Those admitted are required to follow a practical course for one year at least. The selection of students is made directly by leaders of industrial enterprises, transport and communication bodies, state and collective farms, and by commanders of military units acting on the recommendation of party, *Komsomol* (young communist league) and trade-union organizations. Nominations for preparatory departments are discussed at consultative meetings of workers in industrial enterprises, at sessions of collective-farm boards and of collective farm-workers, and of social organizations generally.

Admittance is decided by committees comprising the head (chairman) of the section concerned, representatives of the party and the *Komsomol* in the higher educational institute, teachers of various disciplines and representatives of various establishments and organizations. The committee makes its choice, in accordance with the approved plan of admission, following interviews with every candidate in order to ascertain his aptitude for training in a given section.

Registration at preparatory departments is made in accordance with the results of the above interviews by order of the rector, and the line of study in the preparatory department depends on the subjects presented at the entrance examination to the higher educational institute concerned.

At the end of their studies, students sit for their final examinations which are supervised by a Commission appointed by the rector. This state examination commission includes professors, qualified instructors and the head of the preparatory department. The chairman is either the rector or his deputy.

Students in preparatory departments, who have passed the final examinations, may register at the corresponding faculties for special study without taking the usual entrance examination.

In certain specific cases, students, who have finished their course in a preparatory department, may then enter a higher educational institute with a different specialization; this depends on the approval of their establishment or organization. On entering another higher educational institute these students sit for all the compulsory examinations for admittance to the special study concerned and compete on the same footing as students who have followed a practical course for at least two years.

Those who pass out with the mention 'excellent' are examined in only one of the major disciplines as decided by the higher educational institution.

Those who pass examinations (written and oral) in this subject with the mention 'excellent', are exempted from further entrance examinations. The mentions 'good' or 'satisfactory', however, entitle students to exemption from examination in none of the subjects laid down by the rules of admission to the higher educational institute concerned.

Students in preparatory departments receive study grants on the same basis as first-year students from the university scholarship fund. Scholarship grants may also be paid directly by industrial enterprises, or by state and collective farms, who send students for training, the allowance being 15 per cent higher in this case than for first-year students.

Tuition in preparatory departments may consist of the normal daily, the evening or the correspondence courses; the length of each is eight months full-time study. A period of ten months is prescribed for evening or correspondence courses, which do not entail absence from regular work, and in this case students are entitled to an extra fortnight's leave.

## 2. Entry to the university

The plan of entry to the university (based on the university's proposals) is ratified each year by the Ministry of higher and secondary special education of the RSFSR.

Entry to the university is handled by a central entry committee and fourteen faculty entry (selection) committees set up each year.

The rector is the chairman of the committee, which is made up of the faculty deans, representatives of public organizations, teachers and students.

The central entry committee discharges control and procedural functions, arranges organization and issue of documentation, checks the examination procedures, ensures observance of entry procedures, and ratifies the resolutions of the faculty committees and the entry of the students. The faculty entry committee, consisting of the dean, his deputy, representatives of the professorial and teaching staff, and students, is responsible for the acceptance of candidates for examinations (documents etc.).

Examination committees are set up for examinations in Russian language and literature, mathematics, physics, chemistry, biology, history, geography and foreign languages. These committees are appointed by the rector and those for 1966-68 included prominent scientists of the university, and professors.

Admission to the university is the responsibility of the entry committee. The meetings of this committee are attended by representatives of the city committee for checking entry to Leningrad higher education establishments, and of the Ministry of higher and secondary specialist education of the RSFSR.

Entry is strictly in accordance with procedures, and is based on the ratings of the candidates in their entrance examinations, and other specified factors. The ratings in subjects other than that selected for study are also taken into account in assessing the pass mark.

Applications for entry are checked daily at the times specified in the entry procedures, with alternation of the day and evening entry application times.

The entire work of the entry committees is based on the principles of open discussion. Major problems are resolved conjointly at meetings of the central entry committee.

Anyone who has taken the examination and who wishes to see his written papers can do this on application to the entry committee of the faculty, which forwards the application to the examination committee concerned and informs the candidate of the date and time of his appointment with the instructor and the deputy chairman of the entry committee. Groups made up of the chairman of the examination committee or his deputy, and highly experienced senior instructors, decide doubtful cases relative to ratings made by the examination committees.

To illustrate entry to the university, the criteria involved and the admissions procedure, we will now consider the system and data concerning entry to the university over a period of three years (1966-68).

Entry work includes a number of preparatory measures designed to acquaint young people with the university, to select the most suitable among them, to prepare them for examinations, etc. This work goes on throughout the year, especially in the case of school leavers and young working people, and consists of a system of preparatory courses, societies and other forms mentioned in the preceding section. Mention can also be made of some of the measures taken in organizing entry for 1968. In that year the university held several 'open days'. The rector's department circularized various organizations in the north west of the USSR, asking them to carry out the necessary preparatory work to make up a short list of experienced and able young people capable of studying at Leningrad University. The professors and university instructors went several times to the north west of the USSR to assist directly in this work of attracting young people to the university. The instructors of the economics faculty visited industrial works in the city, where they explained the work of the faculty. Much was done in this connexion, also, by previous students, closely associated with works and factories in Leningrad. The press, radio and television are other important means of attracting young people to the university. Thus many of those attending the philosophy faculty (up to 20 per cent of those admitted) were found to be acquainted with works and articles of leading faculty members published in the press, and broadcast on radio and television, and confirmed that their selection of subjects had been directly influenced by these works. Articles on the university, designed for the workers, have been published in large circulation works newspapers of the main firms in the city, and also in some regional newspapers.

The students' sociological group, operating under the direction of the Institute of complex sociological research, and carrying out a sociological survey of up to 95 per cent of the candidates for day courses and about 10-15 per cent of the evening and correspondence students of one of the faculties, has played a useful part in the correct selection of candidates.

About 500 instructors and staff of the university took part directly in work for the examination and entry committees in 1968. The basic principle in organizing the work of the entry committees was to avoid excessive centralization of entry formalities and to obtain a high degree of independence and initiative by faculty entry committees. Much of the routine entry work was handled by the faculty entry committees, who were able to organize the entry process individually. The central entry committee acted in a control and co-ordinating capacity. In addition, this minimized the inevitably doubtful and boundary cases raised, with or without justification, by the candidates for examinations with the faculty entry committees and the examination committees. The daily meetings of the central entry committee dealt mainly with general questions concerning all the faculties, but also considered doubtful cases—admission to examinations, the entrance examination procedure or various complaints by the students. Each individual case of admission of candidates for examination with half the pass mark was considered fully and very carefully. All the candidates who wish to see their own written work may do so. The candidates are then informed of their mistakes by the examination committee chairman personally, and their work is discussed. Altogether, seventy examination scripts on mathematics and about 400 on Russian language and literature were discussed in this way.

Entry to the university over the years 1966-68 can be characterized as follows in Table 1.

TABLE 1. Entry to the university, 1966-68

| Years | Section | Planned capacity (number of places) | Number of students admitted to examinations | Students on competitive examinations list | Number of newly enrolled students | |
|---|---|---|---|---|---|---|
| | | | | | % Men | % Women |
| 1966 | Full-time | 2 000 | 9 001 | 2 000 | 55 | 45 |
| | Evening | 1 140 | 4 191 | 1 140 | 42 | 58 |
| | Correspondence | 726 | 2 747 | 726 | 57 | 43 |
| 1967 | Full-time | 2 008 | 8 390 | 2 008 | 51 | 49 |
| | Evening | 1 075 | 4 023 | 1 076 | 34 | 66 |
| | Correspondence | 725 | 2 884 | 725 | 53 | 47 |
| 1968 | Full-time | 2 005 | 7 949 | 2 015 | 52 | 48 |
| | Evening | 1 000 | — | 1 000 | 41 | 49 |
| | Correspondence | 700 | — | 700 | 54 | 46 |

# 3. Classification of student entries

The annual number of students at Leningrad University exceeds 19,000, averaging 10,000 on day courses, 5,000 on evening courses and 4,000 on correspondence courses. (Table 2.)

The greatest individual increases over this period were in the chemistry, mathematics-mechanics, physics, and biology-soil faculties, due to the ever-increasing demand for specialists in these fields at the scientific research establishments, in industry, and in agriculture.

There was also an increased tendency to enter faculties teaching philosophy, scientific communism, journalism and psychology. (Table 5.)

TABLE 2. Numbers of students at the university on 1 January 1968

| Type of course | Total number of students | Number of women |
|---|---|---|
| Full-time courses (Soviet students) | 9 720 | 4 881 |
| Evening courses | 5 246 | 3 171 |
| Full-time courses (foreign students) | 524 | 82 |
| Correspondence courses | 4 255 | 1 739 |
| Total | 19 745 | 9 873 |

TABLE 3. Distribution of students over faculties on 1 January 1968

| Faculties | Full-time students | | | Evening students | | | Correspondence students | | | Total | | |
|---|---|---|---|---|---|---|---|---|---|---|---|---|
| | Total | Number of women | | Total | Number of women | | Total | Number of women | | Total | Number of women | |
| | | total | per cent | | total | per cent | | total | per cent | | total | per cent |
| Mathematics-mechanics | 1 474 | 568 | 38.5 | 327 | 153 | 46.7 | 339 | 108 | 31.8 | 2 140 | 829 | 38.7 |
| Physics | 1 805 | 405 | 22.4 | 356 | 79 | 22.1 | — | — | — | 2 161 | 484 | 22.4 |
| Chemistry | 905 | 577 | 63.7 | 401 | 355 | 88.5 | — | — | — | 1 306 | 912 | 69.8 |
| Biology-soil | 788 | 511 | 64.8 | 490 | 366 | 74.7 | — | — | — | 1 278 | 877 | 68.6 |
| Geology | 679 | 333 | 49.0 | 145 | 57 | 39.3 | — | — | — | 824 | 390 | 47.3 |
| Geography | 479 | 296 | 61.8 | 229 | 127 | 55.4 | 185 | 85 | 45.9 | 893 | 508 | 56.8 |
| Economics | 379 | 177 | 46.7 | 566 | 345 | 60.9 | 270 | 102 | 37.7 | 1 215 | 624 | 51.3 |
| History | 411 | 236 | 57.4 | 431 | 285 | 66.1 | 711 | 344 | 48.4 | 1 553 | 865 | 55.7 |
| Philosophy | 413 | 231 | 55.9 | 204 | 69 | 33.8 | 403 | 91 | 22.5 | 1 020 | 391 | 38.3 |
| Psychology | 185 | 102 | 55.1 | 144 | 95 | 65.9 | 211 | 97 | 45.9 | 540 | 294 | 54.4 |
| Law | 322 | 235 | 73.8 | 806 | 324 | 40.1 | 1 178 | 324 | 27.5 | 2 306 | 883 | 38.2 |
| Philology | 1 368 | 1 005 | 73.5 | 1 040 | 890 | 85.1 | 471 | 344 | 73.0 | 2 879 | 2 239 | 77.7 |
| Journalism | 229 | 106 | 46.3 | 107 | 46 | 12.9 | 487 | 189 | 38.8 | 823 | 341 | 41.4 |
| Orient | 283 | 99 | 34.9 | — | — | — | — | — | — | 283 | 99 | 34.9 |

TABLE 4. Breakdown of undergraduates, post-graduates and students of faculties and courses for higher qualifications (excluding foreigners) as on 1 October 1968

|  | 1940 | 1950 | 1955 | 1960 | 1965 | 1968 |
|---|---|---|---|---|---|---|
| Total number of undergraduates | 8 087 | 11 134 | 13 209 | 14 183 | 19 130 | 19 609 |
| full-time | 6 060 | 9 834 | 9 251 | 7 936 | 9 102 | 10 135 |
| evening | — | — | 193 | 3 125 | 5 243 | 5 228 |
| correspondence | 2 027 | 1 300 | 3 765 | 3 122 | 4 785 | 4 246 |
| Total number of post-graduates | 423 | 507 | 645 | 523 | 1 026 | 1 244 |
| full-time | 423 | 504 | 579 | 387 | 913 | 921 |
| evening | — | 3 | 66 | 136 | 113 | 323 |
| Number of teachers | — | 284 | 319 | 268 | 511 | 520 |
| Students of courses and faculties to improve qualifications | — | — | — | — | 390 | 700 |

TABLE 5. Entry of students according to faculties and subjects (full-time courses)

| Faculty<br>Subject | 1940 | 1950 | 1955 | 1960 | 1965 | 1968 | 1970 scheduled |
|---|---|---|---|---|---|---|---|
| *Mathematics-mechanics* | *146* | *129* | *224* | *237* | *302* | *309* | *350* |
| Mathematics | — | 46 | 123 | 125 | 145 | 153 | 150 |
| Astronomy | — | 22 | 15 | 34 | 31 | 27 | 25 |
| Mechanics | — | 61 | 36 | 78 | 126 | 129 | 125 |
| Applied mathematics | — | — | — | — | — | — | 50 |
| *Physics* | *170* | *280* | *311* | *276* | *326* | *324* | *305* |
| Physics | — | 252 | 311 | 276 | 229 | 230 | 230 |
| Geophysics | — | 28 | — | — | 25 | 24 | 25 |
| Radiophysics | — | — | — | — | 75 | 70 | 50 |
| *Chemistry* | | | | | | | |
| Inorganic chemistry | 121 | 169 | 206 | 132 | 175 | 175 | 175 |
| *Biology-soil* | *92* | *134* | *132* | *110* | *145* | *176* | *175* |
| Botany and biology | — | 109 | 107 | 54 | 95 | 53 | 55 |
| Physiology | — | — | — | — | — | 48 | 45 |
| Biophysics | — | — | — | 23 | 12 | 12 | 12 |
| Biochemistry | — | — | — | 11 | 13 | 15 | 15 |
| Soil science | — | 25 | 25 | 22 | 25 | 48 | 48 |
| *Geology* | *94* | *135* | *155* | *100* | *125* | *150* | *125* |
| Exploration: minerals | — | 109 | 86 | 75 | 125 | 120 | 100 |
| Geophysical methods and surveying for minerals | — | 26 | 28 | 25 | — | 30 | 25 |
| Geochemistry | — | — | 41 | — | — | — | — |
| *Geography* | *181* | *128* | *78* | *70* | *100* | *100* | *85* |
| Geography | 181 | 128 | 78 | 70 | 75 | 75 | 85 |
| Meteorology | — | — | — | — | 25 | 25 | — |

[*continued*]

TABLE 5. *(continued)*

| Faculty<br>Subject | 1940 | 1950 | 1955 | 1960 | 1965 | 1968 | 1970<br>scheduled |
|---|---|---|---|---|---|---|---|
| *Economics* | *33* | *50* | *25* | *56* | *72* | *77* | *75* |
| Political economics | — | 50 | 25 | 56 | 20 | 26 | 25 |
| Economic cybernetics | — | — | — | — | 52 | 51 | 50 |
| *History* | *256* | *88* | *85* | *53* | *52* | *84* | *75* |
| History | — | 88 | 85 | 53 | 46 | 75 | 66 |
| History of art | — | — | — | — | 6 | 9 | 9 |
| *Law* | | | | | | | |
| Jurisprudence | — | 188 | 144 | 126 | 75 | 102 | 125 |
| *Oriental studies* | — | *194* | *38* | *64* | *50* | *70* | *70* |
| Oriental philology | — | 166 | 22 | 51 | 26 | 51 | 50 |
| Oriental history | — | 28 | 16 | 13 | 14 | 19 | 20 |
| *Philology* | *362* | *205* | *177* | *229* | *278* | *250* | *250* |
| Russian language and literature | — | 74 | 100 | 75 | 61 | 58 | 58 |
| Latin/Germanic languages and literature | — | 99 | 61 | 120 | 181 | 150 | 150 |
| Slav languages and literature | — | 25 | 11 | 19 | 21 | 24 | 25 |
| Classical philology | — | 7 | 5 | 5 | 5 | 6 | 5 |
| Mathematical linguistics | — | — | — | 10 | 10 | 12 | 12 |
| *Philosophy* | *62* | *66* | *25* | *25* | *90* | *95* | *100* |
| Philosophy | — | 66 | 25 | 25 | 90 | 51 | 55 |
| Scientific communism | — | — | — | — | — | 44 | 45 |
| *Journalism* | | | | | | | |
| Journalism | — | 52 | 25 | 35 | 50 | 52 | 75 |
| *Psychology* | | | | | | | |
| Psychology | 2 | 12 | 5 | 5 | 15 | 60 | 75 |
| *North faculty* | — | 35 | — | — | — | — | — |
| Over-all total : | 1 519 | 1 865 | 1 630 | 1 518 | 1 855 | 2 024 | 2 060 |

TABLE 6. Entry of students according to faculties and subjects (evening courses)

| Faculty<br>Subject | 1955 | 1960 | 1965 | 1968 | 1970 |
|---|---|---|---|---|---|
| *History* | *26* | *76* | *100* | *84* | *75* |
| History | 26 | 59 | 85 | 72 | 60 |
| History of art | — | 17 | 15 | 12 | 15 |
| *Philosophy* | | | | | |
| Philosophy | — | 30 | 48 | 52 | 50 |
| *Psychology* | | | | | |
| Psychology | — | 23 | 26 | 33 | 25 |

[*continued*]

TABLE 6. (*continued*)

| Faculty<br>Subject | 1955 | 1960 | 1965 | 1968 | 1970 |
|---|---|---|---|---|---|
| *Philology* | *57* | *189* | *202* | *204* | *150* |
| Russian language and literature | 57 | 80 | 75 | 108 | 50 |
| Latin/Germanic languages and literature | — | 109 | 127 | 96 | 100 |
| *Journalism* | | | | | |
| Journalism | — | 25 | 25 | 29 | — |
| *Law* | | | | | |
| Jurisprudence | — | 156 | 150 | 153 | 150 |
| *Mathematics-mechanics* | | | | | |
| Mathematics | — | 43 | 85 | 78 | 75 |
| *Geography* | *53* | *26* | *53* | *54* | *50* |
| Geography | 53 | 26 | 53 | 27 | 50 |
| Cartography | — | — | — | 27 | — |
| *Geology* | | | | | |
| Aerial photography | — | 24 | 28 | — | — |
| *Economics* | — | *74* | *125* | *120* | *125* |
| Political economy | — | 22 | 50 | 50 | 50 |
| Economic cybernetics | — | — | — | 25 | 25 |
| National economic planning | — | 52 | 50 | 25 | 25 |
| Statistics | — | — | 25 | 20 | 25 |
| *Physics* | | | | | |
| Physics | — | 35 | 95 | 60 | 50 |
| *Chemistry* | | | | | |
| Chemistry | — | 64 | 79 | 51 | 50 |
| *Biology* | | | | | |
| Biology | 57 | 103 | 83 | 82 | 75 |
| *Over-all total* | 193 | 868 | 1 099 | 1 000 | 875 |

TABLE 7. Entry to correspondence course 1 according to subjects

| Faculty | 1950 | 1955 | 1960 | 1965 | 1968 | 1970<br>schedule |
|---|---|---|---|---|---|---|
| Mathematics-mechanics | 48 | 100 | 40+22 | 78 | 50 | 50 |
| Geography | 45 | 50 | 21 | 27 | 25 | 25 |
| Biology-soil | 37 | 50 | — | — | — | — |
| History | 40 | 100 | 126 | 149 | 125 | 125 |
| Philology | 84 | 200 | 95 | 50 | 50 | 50 |
| Journalism | — | 150 | 61 | 83 | 100 | 100 |
| Economics | 28 | 25 | 26 | 60 | 50 | 50 |
| Philosophy | 20 | 30 | 59 | 103 | 50 | 50 |
| Psychology | — | — | 24 | — | 25 | 25 |
| Law | 58 | 245 | 192 | 200 | 225 | 225 |
| Total | 360 | 950 | 666 | 750 | 700 | 700 |

TABLE 8. Entry of undergraduates, post-graduates and students to faculties and courses to improve qualifications

|  | 1940 | 1950 | 1955 | 1960 | 1965 | 1968 | 1970 schedule |
|---|---|---|---|---|---|---|---|
| Total entry of undergraduates to course | 1 483 | 2 265 | 2 778 | 3 140 | 3 795 | 3 821 | 3 785 |
| full-time | 1 483 | 1 865 | 1 630 | 1 518 | 1 855 | 2 029 | 2 060 |
| evening | — | — | 198 | 868 | 1 100 | 1 000 | 875 |
| correspondence | — | 360 | 850 | 666 | 750 | 700 | 750 |
| foreign students | — | 40 | 100 | 88 | 90 | 92 | 100 |
| Total entry of post-graduates | 140 | 150 | 138 | 296 | 406 | 307 | 427 |
| full-time | 140 | 150 | 103 | 238 | 296 | 228 | 314 |
| Total entry of students | — | — | — | — | 220 | 700 | 700 |
| full-time | — | — | — | — | 70 | 590 | 590 |

TABLE 9. Data concerning changes in number of undergraduates over the years 1966, 1967 and 1968 (full-time courses)

|  | 1966 | 1967 | 1968 |
|---|---|---|---|
| Intake | 2 005 | 2 012 | 2 034 |
| Transferred from other higher educational establishments | 57 | 79 | 79 |
| Transferred from evening and correspondence courses of the university | 192 | 279 | 231 |
| Returned to university | 118 | 180 | 89 |
| Completed period at university | 1 366 | 1 135 | 1 488 |
| Transferred to other higher educational establishments | 60 | 28 | 64 |
| Transferred to evening or correspondence courses | 139 | 104 | 57 |
| Left before completing period at university | 386 | 495 | 515 |

TABLE 10. Data concerning drop-outs in 1966

|  | 1st year | 2nd year | 3rd year | 4th year | 5th year | 6th year |
|---|---|---|---|---|---|---|
| Pupils who left university before completing course | 98 | 128 | 79 | 44 | 28 | 9 |

As will be seen from these data, about 60 per cent of all drop-outs occurred in the lower courses (1st and 2nd years). The main reasons were: 50 per cent family circumstances and personal wishes (move to another town, desire to stop studying and start full employment, etc.), 30 per cent difficulties in assimilating the university course and the resulting failure to keep up with the curriculum; these factors are most predominant at the start of study.

## 4. New subjects and specializations

Over the last ten years a number of new subjects and specializations have grown up at the university.

These developments were brought about by the scientific and technical revolution, a process of synthesis and differentiation of science and rise of new scientific trends, and the development of economic, scientific and cultural relationships with socialist and other countries, especially the developing countries of Africa, Asia and Latin America.

Thus for example the use of mathematical methods in economics led to the formation in 1958 of the subject 'economic cybernetics' in the economics faculty and later to the introduction of 'econometrics' in the mathematics-mechanics faculty.

The use of physics methods of investigation in biology on the molecular level gave rise to 'biophysics' in the biological-soil faculty and the parallel subject 'molecular biophysics' in the physics faculty.

The mathematical methods which have developed in linguistics over the last ten to fifteen years and the use of machine translation gave rise to 'structural and applied linguistics' with the specialization 'mathematical linguistics'.

The strengthening of the economic links with foreign countries, and aid to the developing countries of Africa and Asia, resulted in the rise of the subject 'economics of contemporary capitalism' in the economics faculty.

The need to deepen and expand knowledge of man in society gave rise to such subjects and specializations as sociology, scientific Communism, ethnography and anthropology and social psychology, etc.

The rise and development of new subjects and specializations at the university and the preparation of specialists on the subjects who have a scientific leaning, will subsequently facilitate the creation of similar subjects and specializations of an applied nature in higher education establishments.

New subjects arise and develop from a study of the domestic and foreign scientific literature concerning the appearance of new trends in science, or as a result of some scientific discovery made by a scientist or his school at the university.

At the same time, the obvious need for specialists in this field of knowledge in the future is studied and predicted. In order to open up a new subject and specialization, the university prepares future instructors from among the post-graduates. Their preparation is usually the work of one of the leading scientists in this field, selected from the professors and scientific staff of the department. If no specialists are available at the university, then staff are drawn from the scientific research establishments of the USSR Academy of sciences and the trade associations to instruct the candidates and organize the new subject. After a few years, once qualified instructors are available, the work of instructing undergraduates in the new subject and its specialization begins. This requires the consent of the academic council of the faculty and the university and the approval of the Ministry of higher and secondary specialized education.

At first, the number of undergraduates reading the new subject is small. The curriculum for the new subject has to be formulated, and the immediate needs of the scientific research and higher education establishments and the national economy for specialists in the new field have to be determined. Then the new subject is listed among the subjects and specialization approved by the Ministry, and it is allocated an individual number. Usually the scientific research establishments are the first to require specialists in the new field, and some of the graduates stay on at the university to work for higher examinations.

After several years the specialists trained at the university join the staff of other higher education establishments, as well as scientific research establishments and—depending on the subject concerned—industry and agriculture.

Thus, for example, when the specialization 'economic cybernetics' began, it was studied by ten undergraduates. Most of these found employment in planning organizations and at scientific research establishments. Now the entry is fifty persons. Some of these, on completing their studies in this specialization, go to higher education establishments as instructors, either directly or indirectly, after post-graduate study, and present a thesis for a candidate's degree (Ph.D). The number of requests from the planning organizations for graduates in this specialization has increased.

The pattern is also similar in the case of the subjects 'structural and applied linguistics', 'biophysics' and the specializations 'social psychology', 'sociology', etc.

At present much fruitful work is being carried out at the university in the field of improving the learning process, teaching methods, and the transition to independent study by the undergraduate.

One of the ways in which such conditions can be attained, and one which is an excellent means of training undergraduates for research work is to allow some of them to select their own individual study plan on the higher courses. Today—when the differentiation and synthesis of scientific knowledge is rapidly developing—this form of study is particularly promising, especially at universities, where conditions are most favourable for exchange of scientific information between representatives of natural and humanitarian sciences, for the development of new scientific trends on the boundaries between various branches of knowledge, where many specialized courses exist, and where there are research institutes and experimental laboratories. It is at the universities that specialists can be trained in the differentation and synthesis of science, through extensive general theoretical and specialized training, in particular that of specialists in new research methods.

All this is confirmed by experience at Leningrad University, where in most of the faculties undergraduates have been studying in accordance with individual plans over the last three years; occasional experiments along these lines were carried out even earlier. Three main aims are evident here.

The first is to give a more differentiated training to the future specialist in his selected field. Thus, those following individual study plans in the law faculty also attend special courses and study foreign languages; the undergraduates in the history faculty improve their knowledge of the language of the country in whose history they are specializing, while those studying in the ancient history and archaeology department take Greek and Latin. For example, three undergraduates specializing in the history of Latin America are studying the Spanish and Portuguese languages, while a future archaeologist is studying ancient Greek; those studying in the oriental faculty also learn one oriental or European language and attend a course on the geography of the corresponding country; three future journalists are acquiring extensive training in the sphere of radio and television reporting, while another is learning the German language, the history of German literature, and journalism.

The second is to provide training in two or three allied specializations of the basic subject. Thus, some undergraduates studying in the physics faculty select special courses in not one but two departments. In particular, those studying physics of the atmosphere also take various spectroscopy courses under the direction of the optics department, while twelve evening-course students—training to be radio-physicists—attend parallel specialized courses in several departments.

The third aim is to train—initially only a few—specialists in the synthesis (integration) of science in such directions as mathematical methods of research in economics, biology, linguistics, chemical methods of research in biology, geology, physics, sociological methods of research in philosophy, economics, jurisprudence, with parallel study in several faculties. Thus, two undergraduates in the physics faculty—future specialists in molecular biophysics—are attending a course on general biology in the biology faculty, and at the same time students in the department of molecular spectroscopy are attending specialized courses for two years in the astronomy department of the mathematics-mechanics faculty.

For some years now, the chemistry faculty has been encouraging undergraduates to adopt individual study plans in order to turn out specialists with biological or physico-mathematical leanings.

The philosophy faculty has been organizing individual study plans for five years now. Much experience has been accumulated here, indicating the advances made in this method of study. While ensuring satisfactory general training of the undergraduate, the individual plan enables him to start specializing earlier in particular problems, to maintain and extend his scientific interest, and to strengthen his contact with the instructor. About thirty-five undergraduates have worked on this basis in the faculty. They have acquired considerable additional knowledge in wide fields—in law, ethnography, economics, biochemistry, genetics, etc.

To whom is the privilege of individual study accorded, and by whom?

As was stated earlier, this privilege is granted to promising undergraduates of higher courses who display good scientific ability. Exceptionally, individual students in the second year are also granted this privilege, if they have displayed a special ability for scientific work. Such exceptions have been made in the physics and journalism faculties.

The question of the study plan of the individual undergraduates is handled by the department concerned, with the co-operation of the instructor and the social organizations; upon the agreement of the dean the plan is authorized by the rector.

The main way of checking the work of these undergraduates, apart from examinations and tests, is through a report made on them once each semester to the departmental conference, and in some cases through an essay on a selected topic.

As will be seen from the above, individual plans differ from the general faculty plans, in that they include not only the compulsory subjects, but other general or specialist courses and special 'seminars' involving taking a test or examination. Sometimes students are allowed to omit certain specialist courses in their faculty by the department and dean's office concerned. For example, two students in the chemistry faculty specializing in biology and allowed to omit the study of chemical technology, high-molecular compounds, chemical processes and engineering, took courses on genetics and selection, genetics of micro-organisms and cytology. They also did applied practical work and carried out diploma work at the Institute of natural compounds. Another student specializing in organic chemistry took a course in quantum mechanics and did applied practical work in the department of theoretical physics.

In the philosophy faculty, individual plans are approved in the subject field. General subjects are compulsory. This system allows examinations to be taken early or to be postponed to a later date. The over-all dates for academic courses are not as a rule altered in these cases.

In general the teaching of students on individual curricula provides interesting material for a study of the question of maximum periods and methods of teaching and of the differentiation of programmes to suit the capacity of students, etc. This aspect poses many problems of method and organization.

A complex question, for example, is that of the acquisition of a qualification by students, studying on individual curricula—in the case where the student specializes in a neighbouring field in a different faculty or obtains in parallel an additional qualification, for example, a chemist in the field of genetics, a philosopher in mathematics or law, an arts student or an oriental specialist in some language outside the curriculum of the faculty.

In general an individual curriculum is worked out by the head of department and confirmed by the dean of the faculty. If this curriculum deviates significantly from the general or department curriculum, it must be confirmed by the faculty council with the participation, if necessary, of a representative of the other faculty.

Other points of practical importance are obligatory attendance at lectures by the particular students, their attachment to other higher educational establishments to gain practical experience, their attendance of specialist courses and the supervision of their studies. In Leningrad University, students, studying individual curricula, are normally exempted from obligatory attendance at some lectures and sometimes from practical work also. Exemption is granted by the agreement of the head of department.

Where necessary, students on individual curricula may be sent to another higher educational establishment to attend specialist courses or sit examinations. They may also be sent on an individual basis to another higher-educational establishment or scientific institute to obtain practical experience.

One undoubted advantage of individual study is of course the serious participation of students in scientific work. Such students—active participants in the work of the department and the students' scientific society—normally complete their course and diploma studies more rapidly and obtain better qualifications than other students.

# 5. Planning and organization of the teaching process at Leningrad State University

A plan for organizing education exists at Leningrad University as in every other higher education establishment. The main principles involved in drawing up the curriculum are based on tuition of an ideological and scientific character to train all-round specialists and to equip them with indispensable scientific knowledge, in their special field of study.

A wide range of subjects is selected in accordance with these principles for each speciality, the study of which, along with educational and industrial practice, enables the students to apply the latest research methods in their practical work. All this determines the content and structure of the university curriculum in which general theoretical training is somewhat broader than in other higher educational institutions and more subjects on a compulsory or optional basis are taught, and in which the programme of work in courses and for preparing a final degree as well as for the practical work in laboratories, etc., is far wider.

Educational planning at Leningrad University is conducted in accordance with the decree of the central committee of the Communist party and of the council of ministers of the USSR on the development of higher education and science, and in accordance also with orders, instructions and recommendations issued by the Ministry of higher and secondary specialized education and its branches in the union republics.

At the same time, the professorial and teaching staff plays an essential part in drawing up the curriculum and in organizing practical teaching as is shown by the activities of university departments, methodological committees and academic faculty councils.

The fact that Leningrad University to a large extent trains research and teaching personnel for higher educational institutions proves the individual character of the organization of education at the university.

The drawing up of curricula and the planning of education is based in general on the specific character of Leningrad University, its schools of learning and research trends, and on the opinions of its teaching staff. Students also have a part to play in educational planning and their representatives sit in academic councils and take part in the work of methodological committees and research councils.

The curricula are systematically revised and brought into line with the requirements of science and technology as well as with those of the national economy.

In the first place, the methodological committee of the faculty, which comprises such highly qualified officials as professors and lecturers, changes the curriculum when new special subjects have to be included or traditional special subjects improved. Furthermore, any proposed curriculum is reviewed by the academic council of the faculty, who make modifications and additions with due regard to the views of leading members of the faculty.

Thereupon the proposed curriculum is submitted to the rector for approval and finally confirmed by the Ministry of higher and secondary specialized education in the USSR.

Once, however, the proposed curriculum has been confirmed by the Ministry, the rights of the academic council of the faculty remain as great as before.

The faculty council is entitled to modify the number and succession of lessons allotted for any subject in the curriculum (except for disciplines the volume of which is scheduled by the Ministry) on the strict understanding that students obtain the minimum of scientific knowledge prescribed by educational programmes and without exceeding the maximum weekly load.

The academic council also determines every year the subject and volume of specialized and faculty courses and approves their programmes.

Thus, a decisive part in setting up the curriculum is played by councils (kollegia) of scientists, including members of methodological committees and of the academic councils of the faculties.

The following are basic elements in the curriculum:

— subjects connected with general education;
— subjects regarding a certain speciality or specialization;
— educational, industrial or pedagogical training;
— diploma thesis *(diplomnaja robota)* and state examination.

The general and specialized educational training is organized in the form of seminars, lectures and laboratory research and practical work. The combination of different specialized training courses depends also on the specific structure of the faculty.

Thus in the 'history' curriculum, for instance, 55 per cent of the study time is devoted to lectures and 45 per cent to seminars and practical work. In the speciality 'history of the arts', lectures account for 63 per cent and seminars and practical work for 37 per cent.

Educational and industrial practice, according to the specific nature of the specialized subject, is carried out in the laboratories of academic institutes, universities, specialized research institutes, industrial undertakings, natural reserves, experimental stations, state and collective farms, government foundations, planning boards, higher educational institutions, schools, museums and scientific expeditions.

Experimental diploma projects and theses are carried out in accordance with industrial requirements.

Educational training ends with the defence of a diploma thesis and by passing the state examination before the state examination commission which is headed by a leading specialist or scientist selected, as a rule, from some co-operating research institution. This ensures that the standard of knowledge is appraised and that the corresponding qualifications are awarded objectively. At the same time, leading experts of science of the faculty or department concerned, are introduced before the same commission. The staff of the state commission is selected by heads of faculties and submitted to the Ministry for approval. A major part of the diploma theses represents original research work, and often contains valuable suggestions and conclusions for the development of specific branches of the national economy. The basic content of many of these diploma theses is issued in the scientific publications of Leningrad University and other scientific-research establishments. The best diploma theses are to be seen at the Exhibition of Soviet economic achievements, and their authors receive medals, testimonials or money awards.

The curriculum is drawn up, above all, with due regard to the requirements of national economy, science, technology, culture and education to obtain highly-qualified specialists.

In the present stage, it is the synthesis and differentiation of science and the scientific and technical revolution (i.e. the enormous social changes of yesterday and today in our country), which influence the content of the curriculum considerably.

A specially strong influence on the development of the humanities curriculum is exerted by the extremely high number of research projects on mankind and society. This also results in a strikingly high intake for the faculties of humanities or for those faculties of science which are directly concerned with the study of mankind and the characteristics of organic matter.

Not only objective factors influence the content of the curriculum but also subjective ones. There is, for example, the tendency observed among professors or prominent scientists in certain faculties to strengthen student training in that speciality which they consider to be most important at that moment. These factors, however, are less determining than the others.

At the present time, almost every faculty of the university is an important educational institution in itself, with its own independent and specific character and its own tradition of research and tuition acquired over many decades. Hence also the curricula of various faculties, though following the same general principles, may differ considerably in structure.

Existing curricula may be divided into three types:

1. The first refers to third-year students, or to the students in the first half of their fourth year, dealing with general studies, after which they start specializing. Figuratively speaking, a curriculum on these lines resembles a pine tree (see Figure 1), with a ramified top (faculties of mathematics and mechanics and physics and chemistry, on the one hand, faculties of journalism, psycholgy and law on the other).

2. The second refers to first-year or second-year students dealing either with one single subject of study, or courses in two or three studies, prior to splitting up for specialization. This plan is like a tree with a narrow top (fundamental biology, history, economics)—see Figure 2.

3. The third refers to the specialization of students which starts immediately with the initial course; students read only specific subjects, mainly of a general educational character, in one single subject of study (faculties of geology and philology and the school of oriental studies). This plan, in graphic form, resembles a widely branching shrub.

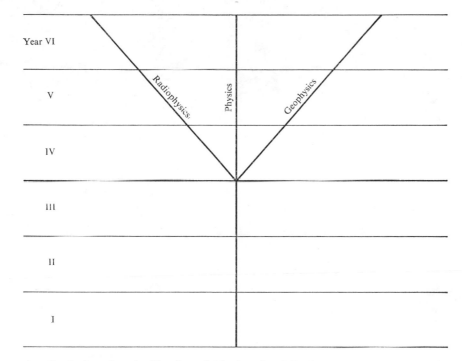

Figure 1. Curriculum for the Faculty of Physics. Specialisation starts at Year IV; the study period is five years and five months.

The specific importance of the various disciplines varies in the curriculum.

Above all, every discipline in the curriculum has to be divided into two groups: a compulsory one which every student has to follow and an optional one which students follow if they so desire. The specific importance of optional subjects in the curriculum (10 per cent) is generally limited.

Compulsory subjects may also be split up into general educational, sectional and specialized subjects.

General educational subjects are those read by students of all faculties, the number of hours being fixed by the Ministry. They refer to social and economic subjects (the history of the Communist party of the USSR, political economy, Marxist-Leninist philosophy, the scientific bases of communism and atheism), a foreign language (optional) and physical training.

Sectional studies refer to general educational disciplines for a given faculty or group of faculties. Thus, mathematics and physics, for instance, for the mathematico-mechanical and physical faculties, and for those of fundamental biology, geography, geology and chemistry; Soviet history and general history

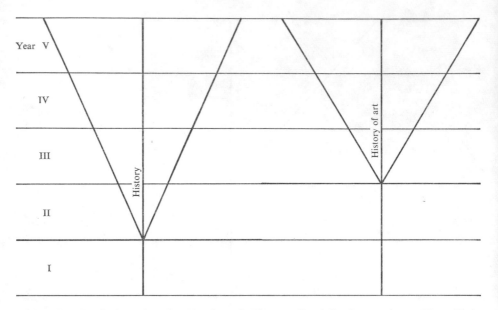

Figure 2. Curriculum for the Faculty of History. Specialisation starts at Year II in special history and from year III in history of art; the study period is five years.

for the faculty of history, political economy for the school of economics and so forth.

Special subjects are those in a given speciality (special courses and seminars). They are also split up into compulsory and optional courses.

The specific importance of each of these subjects in the curriculum is unequal as stated above.

General educational subjects usually take up from 20 to 23 per cent of the total number of hours in the curriculum, sectional subjects from 40 to 50 per cent on an average. Special subjects take up from 30 to 45 per cent according to the nature of the faculty.

Furthermore, it should be pointed out that nearly all the study categories listed may be studied in addition on an optional basis.

The curriculum is thus one of the leading factors (but not the only factor) for educational planning.

Another factor is the student quota which determines the number of lecture courses and training groups. As the number of lecture courses increases, and the training groups grow fewer, the volume of study work in hours is accordingly higher.

The next factor to condition educational planning is the calculation of the teaching load in hours imposed by the Ministry. In lectures and practical work, for instance, one hour is assigned to teachers for every hour of study. A quota of fifteen hours a year for every student is allotted for the guidance of students in accordance with nature of course followed and character of faculty. In the humanities this figure usually ranges from three to six or eight hours a year and from six to thirteen or fifteen hours in natural sciences. A total of thirty-five hours per student is assigned for the guidance of diploma theses and their defence before and review by the state examination commission. A total of fifty hours a year is assigned for post-graduate guidance.

Furthermore, the material and technical equipment of the university influence educational planning: the number and capacity of lecture halls, the capacity of laboratories and study rooms, the availability and complexity of educational facilities, the extent of technical research for teaching purposes. The basic unit for teaching and scientific work is the department *(kafedra)* which plans the work for the academic year in accordance with the curriculum of the student and the post-graduate quota of its faculty and with the demands of other faculties and departments on the basis of current standards for the calculation of hours. The volume of work in a faculty, which is submitted to the administration office, is based on the structure of these departments.

The administrative office also determines the amount of work to be carried out in faculties and departments within the university as well as the proposed student and post-graduate quota for the coming year, and plans the composition of the professorial and teaching staff on that basis.

The volume of teaching work in a faculty, having thus been determined, is divided into the average teaching load of every instructor, which determines the number of permanent and non-permanent instructors needed for the faculty. In order to work out more precisely the correlations between professors, lecturers and research assistants, the total volume of work is also split up among the professorial and reading staffs (lecture courses, guidance for diploma theses and post-graduate work), and likewise among the research assistants (seminars, practical courses, laboratory tuition and guidance). Thus the various categories of work are shared out on an average as follows: professors 500-600 hours, lecturers 600-700 hours, assistants 700-840 hours.

We are dealing here with the breakdown of the professorial and teaching staff in the various faculties. The staff as a whole is, however, established in accordance with the student and post-graduate quota, which depends on factors of admission, drop-out and graduation.

Thus, the principal criteria for educational planning rest with the curriculum and the student and post-graduate quota.

Having fixed the student and post-graduate quota at the beginning of the academic year, with regard to the admission, drop-out and graduation of students, the administrative office and the financial planning section proceed to fix the time-table of the professorial and teaching staff within the university according to approved standards of calculation, and submit it to the rector for approval. Thereupon, the Ministry of higher and secondary specialized education in the RSFSR approves the salary fund and professorial and teaching strength on the basis of data submitted by the university. On receiving the approved staff schedule, the rector's office divides it up among the faculties and general studies departments in accordance with the student quota and the volume of teaching work. For this purpose, the total volume of teaching load within the university does not include general university subjects such as social sciences, foreign languages, physical training; or subjects taught commonly at a faculty for several different departments, such as general mathematics, general physics, analytical chemistry (inter-faculty departments).

The volume of teaching work in departments for general university studies is divided into the average teaching load per teacher and the number of teachers needed for these departments is thus determined. If the student and post-graduate quota has increased, the additional staff is divided up among the general university studies and inter-faculty departments and afterwards among those faculties in which the number of students has gone up or new specialities or departments have been created. When the student quota remains unchanged, the professorial and teaching staff is maintained at its previous level and only certain departments, in which the volume of teaching work has increased considerably, receive additional staff.

On the basis of the volume of teaching work and the composition of teaching staff, the rector's office, acting on reports from the various faculties and departments, determines the number of additional part-time staff-members and likewise the expenditure per hour on teachers who, without being on the regular staff, are nonetheless indispensable for the organization of specialized courses, for the guidance of undergraduate and post-graduate students, and for the tuition and pedagogical training of students.

Thus, the volume of teaching work planned for the academic year comprises, on the one hand, the work of the regular professorial and teaching staff, including teachers working on a part-time basis, and on the other, the work of non-permanent teachers paid on an hourly basis. The second category seldom accounts for more than 10 per cent of the total figure.

According to the scheduled amount of work, approved by the rector with due regard to the curriculum and the student and post-graduate quota, the deans of the faculties and heads of departments distribute the burden of work among the teachers and submit it to the rector for approval.

Thus the university teaching strength, as a whole, is fixed in accordance with the student and post-graduate quota, and the distribution of the staff among the faculties and departments is based on the volume of teaching work.

The practical supervision of tuition is ensured by heads of departments, deans of faculties and by the office of the rector. At the end of the academic year, every instructor submits to the office of the dean a report on the teaching and scientific work performed by him.

The head of the department plans, at the same time, the teaching load for the next academic year in accordance with the curriculum and with the probable student and post-graduate quota.

Such, in brief, is the system of planning, distributing and assessing the work of the professorial and teaching staff.

The total strength of the professorial and teaching staff on 1 January 1969 was 1,829, including 281 doctors of science and 811 candidates of science (equivalent to Ph.D).

TABLE 11.   Characteristics of the professorial and teaching staff in terms of academic qualifications

| Year | Total teaching staff | Including | |
|---|---|---|---|
| | | Doctors of science | Candidates of science |
| 1940 | 992 | 161 | 376 |
| 1950 | 998 | 172 | 381 |
| 1955 | 1 265 | 184 | 619 |
| 1960 | 1 409 | 201 | 653 |
| 1965 | 1 517 | 221 | 676 |
| 1968 | 1 769 | 281 | 811 |
| 1970 (schedule) | 1 774 | 290 | 850 |

TABLE 12.   Distribution of the professorial and teaching staffs by academic qualifications and appointments

| Academic degree | | | | | | Academic appointment | | | |
|---|---|---|---|---|---|---|---|---|---|
| Doctors | | Candidates | | Academicians and corresponding members | | Professors | | Lecturers | |
| full-time | part-time | full-time | part-time | full-time | part-time | full-time | part-time | full-time | part-time |
| 210 | 35 | 141 | 15 | 13 | 10 | 172 | 23 | 493 | 9 |

The total volume of teaching activity in the university exceeds a mean 1,200 thousand hours annually. More than 90 per cent of this teaching is given by established professorial and teaching staffs, and the remainder by non-established teaching staffs, who are paid by the hour, and by scientific workers of lower grades.

The average teaching load for the professorial and teaching staff is 600-700 hours annually and in the oriental studies faculty 500 hours annually.

The extent of the teaching load depends on the qualifications of the particular teacher and the nature of the task (lecture, practical work, supervision of theses). In general the teaching load for department heads and professors is less in terms of quantitative indices than that of lecturers and assistants and the load for lecturers slightly less than that of junior teachers and assistants.

The reason for this distribution is the nature of the load on each category of teacher. The more laborious forms of teaching load, requiring higher scientific qualifications and experience (general and specialized courses of lectures, specialist seminars, directing the studies of aspirants) fall on the professors and lecturers.

The greater part of the teaching load, falling on assistants, consists of practical work, supervision and laboratory work.

In individual cases the teaching load may be reduced by 50 per cent or the teacher may be temporarily relieved of teaching duties for a few months, such duties being redistributed among the remaining members of the staff or undertaken by non-established teachers. This procedure is followed where the teacher is completing work on a dissertation, preparing an officially planned textbook or is sent on an assignment outside Russia, etc.

The criteria for tenure on the professorial and teaching staff are primarily the scientific and pedagogic qualifications of the teacher and his previous scientific-pedagogic experience.

The weekly load for students in terms of obligatory periods is thirty hours per week for students on junior courses and twenty to twenty-four hours for students on senior courses. The number of obligatory periods is at a minimum for fifth-year students and at a maximum for first- and second-year students. The ratio of the load on students as between lectures, practicals and independent work is approximately 1 : 2 : 3, although the ratio will of course depend on specific conditions (speciality, specialization, particular course).

Attendance at classes is obligatory for all students except in the case of certain optional and specialist courses, for which preliminary registration is possible. The numbers, registered for specialist courses should not, as a rule, be less than five.

At the present time the following staff/student ratio applies at Leningrad University: one teacher for 9.1 students on full-time courses; one teacher for 20 students on evening courses; one teacher for 53 students on correspondence courses. There are deviations in either direction, depending on the specific situation of each faculty or department, but the over-all deviation is in general small.

The number of hours allocated to consultations is 10 to 12 per cent of the number of lecture hours.

The organization of the teaching process on a scientific basis makes provision for specific experiments. It is unlikely that the optimal ratio between lectures/seminars and individual work by students will be arrived at in any other way.

Experiments of this type are being carried out in three of the university faculties simultaneously. From 1965/66 onwards an 'experimental stream' has been established in the physics faculty. Four groups of first-year students were separated into a special stream, and the number of lecture and seminar periods was reduced for them by half, while the same programme and examination requirements were retained. This experiment was subsequently extended and at the present time several groups of first-, second- and third-year students are studying on this basis.

Prior to this experiment considerable preparatory work was undertaken with the participation of very well-known scientists (academician V.I. Smirnov, corresponding member Ac. Sci. USSR S.F. Frish) on the structure and content of lecture courses, methods of practical instruction, etc.

It has been found, after several academic years with the experimental stream, that the level of success is slightly higher than with the normal system. But the main point is not so much this, but that the students of the experimental stream have a more conscientious and creative attitude to their study and show far greater independence in their work. Third-year students in the arts and oriental studies faculties work on a doubled academic period (eighty minutes without a break). The level of success has remained the same in this case, while the conditions for individual and social work have been improved, since the new system eliminated the overloading of students, previously typical of that faculty.

The experiment in the physics faculty has been given positive assessment. The essence of this interesting experiment has been on the one hand the adoption of a different approach to students with different standards of previous knowledge and, on the other hand, the inculcation of habits of independent work right from the start of the first course. This is a result of an increased requirement for scientific and theoretical preparation in young research workers.

As regards the experiment in the arts and oriental languages faculties, which has now been extended to include the faculty of philosophy, the main aim here is to find a correct ratio between obligatory studies and lectures in the educational process and at the same time to provide free time for independent work by students in accordance with the specific character of these faculties and to allow for increased departmental control. This experiment has proved most successful with a group of students in the department of Far-Eastern history, where the introduction of various forms of supervision of students' independent work has increased the proportion of time, devoted to the latter, and the quality of the students' preparatory work.

The experience of these faculties is of course still insufficient for broad conclusions to be drawn, but the value of the experiment seems quite clear in that it provides a scientific method of determining the optimum ratio between obligatory periods and time for independent work.

The improvement of specialist training depends to a large extent on the way the teaching process is organized.

These problems were considered to be of high priority in the long-term plans of university development which were elaborated by the rector's office with the support of professors and students. In 1970-80 the curricula and programmes of all the faculties in the university will be continuously improved and perfected, in accordance with the development of science and the national economy.

Hence further improvements in the curriculum and programmes will cut out premature specialisation, and additional emphasis will be put on general theoretical training in the selected field of study and on the two stages in the curriculum, namely: 1. not less than two-three years' general theoretical training in a given field of knowledge; 2. a thorough specialization, based on knowledge acquired in a more restricted field, with emphasis on methods of research and reduction in the number of compulsory subjects, greater scope for individual work and possibilities of individual study for the most promising students.

High priority in education will be given to improvement of pedagogic proficiency and teaching qualifications, the creation of closer links between general and specialized training, the rationalization of the teaching process, extensive use of social-sciences, television, films and other modern technical teaching appliances.

At the same time, more favourable conditions will be promoted for a thorough and creative study by students of the Marxist-Leninist theory and of the theoretical and practical activity of the party.

Work will continue, for this purpose, with a view to publishing textbooks and manuals on the history of the Soviet Communist party, the Marxist-Leninist school of thought, political economy, scientific communism, the improvement of the material and technical resources of general libraries and departmental reading rooms.

One possible means of improving the curricula and programmes lies in reducing the students' weekly time-table, leaving time for individual study and making educational training by the university teaching staff more effective. Hence it would be advisable to reduce the average length of lectures once students have methodological aids. Between 1970 and 1975 the curricula for a series of specialities and specializations will be reviewed, with the aim of increasing the future professional possibilities of students. Complex cross-education will be imparted by transferring students, after two or three years of tuition, from certain specialities to others, which will make for more flexible and rational use of potentialities. A certain number of students studying mathematics, physics and chemistry are expected to follow advanced courses in biology, geography and economics up to the corresponding qualification, e.g. 'biologists using mathematical methods in their speciality', etc.

It is advisable for students in philology or oriental studies to follow advanced courses in the economic, historical, legal and philosophic activities of the country in whose language they are specializing.

One of the most important problems in university education is the perfecting of teaching methods with regard to changes in the number of students and teachers, the increasing amount of scientific information, sources of information and output of literature on teaching methods, etc.

The perfecting of demonstration techniques and the widespread use of films, television and tape-recording as well as the use of methods of computer-aided instruction will play an essential part in the improvement of specialist training.

# 6. Special courses and seminars

A feature of university education, as stated before, is the large number of special courses and seminars which enable students to specialize more thoroughly in selected branches of knowledge. The fundamental aim of special courses and seminars is to acquaint students with the latest data in the branch of knowledge in which they are specializing, to acquaint them with basic scientific problems and prospects of development, to promote the habit of individual scientific work and make them familiar with methods of research. Hence special courses and seminars occupy an intermediate position between the educational and scientific work of students and come closer to the latter; the part they play in promoting the habit of research work is highly significant.

The number of special courses also depends on the specific nature of the faculty and as a rule is fairly high. In the faculty of physics, for instance, in the academic year 1968/69, there were 179 special courses, including sixty in oriental studies and 107 in philology.

Special courses and seminars are held by the highest qualified specialists —members and correspondents of the Soviet academy of science, professors and doctors of science, senior staff members of academic institutes and other specialized research institutes and museums.

Furthermore, qualified specialists with practical experience in a variety of branches of the national economy, public administration, cultural and general educational establishments—engineers, agronomists, planning-establishment personnel, members of local soviet committees, lawyers and public-prosecution officials, etc., are also invited to hold special courses.

Hence, besides members and correspondents of the academy and staff professors and doctors of science, who give courses and direct seminars, highly-qualified specialists from other establishments are invited either as permanent part-time teachers (0.5 of salary), or as non-permanent collaborators paid on an hourly basis.

At the faculty of physics, for instance, in addition to permanent members and correspondents of the Soviet academy of science and professors there are highly qualified specialists from academic and other specialized institutes working on a part-time basis as staff members on subjects such as semi-conductors, physico-technical and optical research, etc.

Special courses and seminars, at the faculties of history and oriental studies, are conducted by a large number of highly qualified specialists from the National Hermitage Russian Museum, from the institutes of ethnography, anthropology and archaeology of the peoples of Africa and Asia, and from the department of oriental studies at the academy of the USSR.

The faculty of economics invites engineers and economists from large industrial plants, planning bodies and state and collective farms to organize special courses.

Officials from the executive committees of local soviets, the law courts, public-prosecution and investigation departments, boards of arbitration, customs offices and members of the legal profession are invited by the faculty of law for the same purpose.

The faculty of journalism invites members of newspaper, periodical, publishing, radio and television staffs to hold special courses and seminars.

This wide range of highly qualified specialists in charge of special courses and seminars facilitates the development of existing, and the opening up of new, specialities and forms of specialization, for the thorough study by students of any chosen speciality, for the organization of study at individual level, and for specialist training of a related or synthetic (integral) type, together with extensive training in a narrow field.

Any talented student may choose to follow additional special courses in related specialities.

As a rule, the length of every special course is limited, as compared with the total number of lessons (thirty-two to forty-eight hours).

Teachers giving special courses renew and perfect the programmes every year in accordance with the latest scientific achievements and make additions to the list of works recommended for individual study.

Thus, specialized courses contribute not only to the training of highly qualified specialists but also to suitable methods for dissemination and practical application of scientific knowledge.

A well developed teaching-practice in the university is an essential requirement if students are to become familiar with their special subject-matter and acquire practical skills in that field of study.

The purpose of teaching-practice in the faculties of fundamental biology, geography and geology, for instance, is to make the students familiar with the basic methods of field research and to consolidate, under natural conditions, the knowledge acquired at lectures and in laboratory and practical courses, to prepare them for their future practical work.

Teaching-practice is acquired under experienced instructors in educational workshops, botanical gardens, natural reserves, educational and experimental farms, computer centres, and scientific expeditions. Leningrad University has a whole series of centres for this purpose at its disposal, locally and in the Belogorsk, Crimean and Caucasus regions. During the practical-training period, students gather plants for herbaria, make systematic studies of plants and collect minerals, observe animal and plant life and micro-organisma, and conduct meteorological studies in the atmosphere, etc.

# 7. Students' practical work

One of the indices of a future widening of the bounds of teaching-work in the university is perhaps the present state of educational, productive and pedagogic practical work, undertaken by students in the university. In all its aspects (economic effectiveness, scientific value of investigations of junior grades, variety and range of basic institutions, undertakings and organizations), student practical work in recent years has been marked by further successes. As before, students from the LSU (Leningrad State University) have undertaken practical work in different areas of the country: in Moscow, where undergraduates from the economic, oriental languages, law, history and other faculties are sent regularly, in leading scientific research and teaching centres of the RSFSR and other republics, and over wide areas, including Siberia (geology, geography), the Pacific coast and the Kuriles (biology, oriental studies), Central Asia (archaeology, astronomy) and the Far North (geography).

International student exchange has recently assumed considerable proportions. In 1968 the number of countries participating in the free exchange of students, and also the number of student groups sent overseas and the number accepted by Leningrad University, stood at a very high level. At the instigation of the LSU the circle of countries and co-operating higher education establishments, participating in student exchange, has been widened. In addition to the German Democratic Republic, and Hungary and Czechoslovakia, who have previously accepted our students, Poland and Mongolia were included in these exchanges in 1968. The list of specialized departments sending people abroad for practical study has also been greatly extended: the ranks of philologists, physicists, geologists, geographers and chemists, who have traditionally participated in exchanges, have now been joined by groups of historians, economists, philosophers, journalists and students of oriental languages. The results of the practice of international exchanges have fully confirmed the educational and ideological importance of this promising development and have already yielded good results.

Foreign assignments of students from language departments have extended to countries located at great distances from the USSR: Afghanistan, Iraq, Syria, United Arab Republic, Singapore, the Korean People's Democratic Republic, Italy, Algeria, Somalia and Cuba.

A recently compiled list of university assignments demonstrates clearly the wide range of places where our students gain practical experience. It includes more than 300 progressive undertakings, foundations and organizations in different branches of the national economy, science, culture, education and state administration. The effectiveness of practical instruction does not of course depend primarily on the number of people, but also on where it is carried out, and most of all on the nature of the work, which our students are called on to perform. Over a period of years the university has maintained close relations with a number of large scientific centres, where graduate workers have gone as research students, such as for example the A.F. Ioffe physico-technical Institute, the Combined Institute for nuclear studies, the Institute for semiconductors, the Pulkovsk Observatory, the Institute for the economics of peace and international relations, the All-Union Institute for scientific and technical information and other organizations, where students can always expect to undertake interesting research projects under the direction of experienced specialists.

The university with its constituent, creative scientific departments and schools provides a sound basis for carrying out investigations and experiments (a widely-based system of scientific research institutes, problem-solving laboratories, etc.) and in a large number of cases, organizes very successful practical training in its departments, employing research students for the execution of contract projects. The scientific research activity of the whole department, to which the students are attached in the process of such work, widens the horizons of knowledge and removes the deadening influence of previously acquired theoretical knowledge, connecting knowledge to life and to practical requirements. In the execution of research projects, entrusted to the VUZ by individual undertakings and organizations, students are frequently able to see concrete results emerge from their investigations and applied under practical conditions. This form of organization of practical work has the further advantage that it brings students into personal contact with the staff of the department. Direct contacts and relationships between students on senior courses and scientists, acquire a very close and intimate character during productive practical work and diploma investigations, and are one of the most effective methods of ensuring the real education of students. This explains why during the past year a large body of students (over 800 in number) have undertaken contract projects in the course of their practical training and in some of the natural science faculties the great majority of students have taken part in such projects (125 out of 162 of the fourth year chemistry students).

During the execution of contract projects many research students have undertaken interesting and promising lines of research. For example, students in the section of economic cybernetics studied the determination of the optimal structure of a laboratory of economico-mathematical methods. Their fellow-students took part in the devising and development of methods for solving problems in relation to the best possible use of reserves for the *giprospetsgas* institute. Particularly noteworthy was the practical work of students from the department of specialized economics, who carried out some extremely creative work in the Institute of economics of the Latvian SSR on drawing up the projected plan for the Daugavpilss region in 1980, and obtained agreement for this plan from the production directorate. Students from this department carried out calculations for a metal products factory, based on the Tekhpromfinplan. Chemical students effected numerous complex syntheses of organic compounds, required in the specifications of contract projects, displaying in the course of their investigations considerable initiative and introducing a number of improvements to the previous method of synthesis. Student soil-scientists worked as collectors on the staff of the LSU agrochemical expedition, undertaking on a contract basis the investigation and mapping of soils of arable land on virgin *sovkhozes* (state farms) in the Barabinsk Steppe. All applied scientific materials, agricultural maps and cadastres of the investigated soils were handed over to the originators of the contract, thus enabling them to undertake agricultural production on a scientific basis.

Representatives of the humanities have also participated actively in important sociological investigations. Russian language students, for example, passing through the Karelsk ASSR and the Pskov, Archangel and Murmansk provinces in the course of practical work on Russian dialects, collected material for a

'Dictionary of dialects in Karelia and the White Sea', for a 'Pskov province dictionary' and a 'Panslav dialect atlas'.

Many students have written papers, based on material collected during their practical work, which have been of sufficient scientific value and have been of sufficient importance to be published.

In 1968 some of the work, begun in the previous year, was continued and extended. Philologists in the third and fourth years, specializing in the study of old Russian literature, again carried out practical work in palaeography. The student expeditionary detachment visited numerous villages and hamlets in the Pinezh region of the Archangel province in their search for evidence of the old northern written culture of Russia. The students collected valuable material—seventy-six manuscripts from the fifteenth to the nineteenth centuries and some twenty very early printed books, which have been added to the collection at the Institute of Russian literature (Pushkinskii Dom) and in the A.M. Gorki library of fundamental science. Among the recovered texts were many new inscriptions from literary tombstones and some compositions, hitherto unknown to science. All the manuscripts were described and dated by the students themselves.

A new form of practical work for political science students deserves attention among the innovations of 1968. The economic faculty sent a group of fourth-year students to businesses and organizations in the Vasileostrovsk region. They organized a series of lectures for manual and salaried workers. The students delivered and conducted more than 100 lectures and seminars in several factories. This form of practical work promotes habits of independent and systematic work, brings the student in contact with people outside the university and enables the student to master aspects of pedagogic and preparatory work.

For the oragnization of practical work a typical future development will be an extension of the number of specialized secondary educational establishments and schools, to which students can be sent from the philology, history, soil-biology, geography, philosophy and psychology faculties.

Teaching-practice for students is one of the most important elements in the system of education at the university. It develops the teaching and organizational capabilities of the students and establishes their interest in the teaching profession. Its important and close relationship to the practice of teaching is shown by the following figures: out of 780 students, following this form of practical course in 1968, 500 passed with 'excellent' gradings.

The 'Regulations on productive practical work by students at higher educational establishments (VUZ) in the USSR', which appeared in 1968 and were compiled in the light of the results and in accordance with the economic reform recently introduced in the Soviet Union, were an important step towards the general improvement of this aspect of education. It enabled VUZy to standardize

110

the payment of specialists taken on to supervise the practical work of students and provided for educational visits by students engaged in practical work. The economic advantage of this as a means of exchanging information and experience among large educational and scientific centres in the country has been frequently stressed by our university.

Finally a decision taken by the Soviet council of ministers on 8 August 1968 represented an important step in the plan to improve the material circumstances of students during their training periods, and shows the attention paid to their needs. It provided a significant increase in the funds of the individual student, and enabled university authorities to select as centres for practical work not only economically successful undertakings, but also centres of creative interest.

The passing of these important measures opened promising new perspectives for improving the practical work of students and raising the standard of education of highly qualified specialists in the different fields of knowledge.

# 8. Distribution of university student output to employment

The most important characteristic of the Soviet system of higher education and its greatest triumph is the fact that the state guarantees all those completing courses at a VUZ employment in his own specialized field. This guarantee is met on a planned basis by means of the state plan for the distribution of young specialists, drawn up by the planning bodies on the basis of demands by the relevant ministries and staff requirements.

As a result of this system, without which a planned distribution of the whole output from higher schools would be impossible, day students are bound to accept work related to the specialized qualification obtained on conclusion of a specified period (three years) at a VUZ.

The university receives a state student distribution plan from the Ministry of higher and secondary specialized education and within the framework of this plan, when allotting jobs to the student output, takes into account their wishes, capabilities, inclinations and other factors also.

In general, university graduates are posted to scientific research institutes, higher educational establishments, industrial undertakings, cultural foundations, planning and other state organizations. Some of the students, finishing the course, are sent to secondary schools as teachers.

Students displaying an inclination for research during their university career, stay on to continue their studies as research students (aspirants).

Students posted to employment from the university, prior to taking up their duties, are sent on paid leave, with travel expenses paid and living accommodation provided.

In recent years there has been an increase in the proportion of graduates posted to research institutes in union republics, and to higher and secondary educational establishments, and in those continuing as research students.

To illustrate the distribution of young specialists who have completed university courses, we give some figures for the past three years. In 1966, for example, Leningrad University placed the student output to 107 ministries and directorates, to twenty-four higher educational establishments and to a number of industrial enterprises. In 1967 graduates of Leningrad University were employed by ninety-six ministries and directorates. Some were employed as teachers in thirty-four higher educational establishments throughout the country. In 1968 out of 1,400 graduates 1,225 were distributed among ninety-four ministries and directorates: 138 became teachers at higher education establishments, and 124 continued as research students.

# 9. Educational work: and student organizations

Formal instruction of students is only one aspect of university education. No less important is coping with problems related to the Communist education of young specialists and the formation of their ideological and civic qualities. It is important that the young specialist should be trained not only in his chosen discipline, but that he should also obtain a wide political background, cultural erudition, and a sense of the responsibilities of citizenship, and in fact become an intelligent member of society in the full Communist meaning of the word.

Participation of the professorial and teaching staffs in the ideological education of the students follows two main lines: (a) during teaching periods and (b) in extramural activities.

The inculcation of a scientific attitude to life is an extraordinarily complex and wide-ranging process, depending on the interaction of a whole number of factors. It is effected both during the teaching curriculum and outside it, by the exercise of a deliberate ideological influence on the student body within the walls of the VUZ, and by the effect of different situations outside it, all of which play a part in forming the ideological background of the student.

The formation of a Marxist-Leninist attitude to life is organically linked with other forms of Communist training—ideological, political, work-oriented, aesthetic, physical and moral. The various disciplines and the various forms of instruction give the teacher the opportunity of influencing the student in different ways, depending on the nature and content of the subject, the degree of contact with the audience, the personality of the teacher, etc. The social sciences play a leading part in this field.

In their application of the Resolution of the central committee of the Communist party and the Council of ministers of the USSR 'Measures for improvement of the training of specialists and perfecting the management of secondary and higher specialist training in the country', the teaching staff of Leningrad State University set themselves the task of evolving methodical principles for the long-term planning of instructional-educational work over the whole period covered by the university course. On the basis of proposals by workers and social organizations in the LSU, the laboratory for the socio-logical investigation of problems of student education of the NIIKSI drew up a draft plan, which was approved by the social and political organizations and the scientific council of the university and recommended for implementation in the academic year 1968/69.

Long-term teaching and educational planning at Leningrad State University follows certain imperatives, namely: to guarantee a consistent and systematical educational training of the student; to bear in mind the specific character of teaching and educational work in every course; to subordinate problems of the whole teaching and educational work to the objective of fostering in students those qualities which are indispensable for building up the Communist society; to combine the acquisition of knowledge, standards and rules of conduct with their practical realization; to combine individual forms of teaching and education with tuition in groups; to find methods of checking the effectiveness of teaching and educational activities.

The basic objectives of the plan are as follows:
1. introducing scientific planning methods which, like the effective organization and supervision of teaching and educational work, rely on the use of the latest pedagogic data, social psychology and the study of the mentality of students, theories of Communist education, the scientific organization of work and management of university life and of specific sociological research;
2. achieving complete unity of tuition, scientific research and educational work within and outside the teaching process, taking into account the influence of all educational factors (urban surroundings, environment of students who do not live in hostels, influence of the press, radio and television, etc.), independent of the university environment;
3. achieving more effective interaction and co-ordination in the activities of the professorial and teaching staff, departments, party, young communist league (*Komsomol*), trade-union and other public bodies and of student associations; the differentiation of functions and the removal of overlapping;
4. development of the social self-government of students in solving educational problems; the uniform distribution of teaching, educational and social tasks among all members of the university and their participation in active social work;

5. organizing of all teaching and educational activity, on the basis of a thorough all-round study of the personality of school leavers and students, and of characteristic social-demographic and socio-psychological peculiarities of student bodies, on the basis of the latest scientific data and comparative studies of changes and application of specific methods of sociological research.

In framing the plan, the office of the rector and the party committee follow decisions made by the Soviet Communist party and government, instructions from the ministries concerned in the USSR and the RSFSR, material from the first All-Union student conference, the results of opinion polls in the university, certain data resulting from concrete sociological research carried out at Leningrad University and other higher educational institutions in the country, the experience of long-term research in planning educational work in the state universities of Kiev and Lvov, Leningrad and Kiev polytechnical institutes, and also proposals made by faculties, departments and other sub-divisions of Leningrad University.

The great majority of students studying at the university are members of *Komsomol* and trade-union organizations. The students' scientific society includes several thousand members. The sports club, which covers various forms of sports activities has a membership of about 8,000.

The *Komsomol* and trade-union organizations render assistance to the party organization and the professorial and teaching staffs in the political education of the student body, in the planning of instructional periods and students' independent work and in the organization of their leisure and day-to-day life. An important aspect of the Communist education of young specialists is the inculcation of communal-organization habits, initiative and conscientious self-discipline. One of the most important methods of developing these qualities is the evolution under the direction of the party organizations of various forms of student self-government.

At present, there are three principal types of student self-government: the student councils (soviets) in hostels, student academic councils in the faculties and student building-site committees.

Existing within the framework of the *Komsomol* and trade-union organization and linked with these by a common aim—the training of citizens for a Communist society—each of these bodies organizes and directs student initiative in a particular field and has its own specific tasks and functions. Such traditional organs of student self-government as student councils in hostels, for example, have the function of organizing the everyday life and leisure of the students living in the particular hostel.

Academic councils (soviets) which have not been in existence very long, are charged with co-ordinating the efforts of student organizations and rendering assistance to the faculty administration in the field of student instruction.

Finally, building-site councils and committees play a large part in the working education of students on summer building sites.

These student councils are divided into three different types on the basis of structure and composition.

Student academic committees, which were first set up in all faculties in the academic year 1963/64, play an important part in improving the success rate of students and in academic discipline.

The academic committees are co-operative organs of student self-government, formed from the elected representatives of the *Komsomol* and trade-union organizations and from the representatives of student leaders.

The main tasks of academic committees are:

*a)* to involve a wide range of students in the organization of the teaching-process and also in the struggle to raise the success-rate and to strengthen discipline;

*b)* to eliminate the previous duplication of effort in instruction provided by *Komsomol,* trade-union organizations, student leaders and the university faculty, and to co-ordinate their efforts in this field under the direction of the party organization.

Academic commissions and committees in their concern to raise the success-rate, to increase student-attendance at classes and to organize the independent work of students, also help students who have fallen behind.

They participate in drawing up programmes of work, in the preliminary examination of curricula and in questions of the suspension, re-admission and transfer of students.

The academic councils give considerable assistance to the faculty administration in drawing up and supervising examinations. They summon all students, whose academic performance is unsatisfactory, to appear before them and explain to them the reasons for their failure. They also offer their observations to the faculty administration on the suspension of students or their admission to the examination.

During the examinations, the academic councils run a duty roster, ensuring punctual attendance of students, issuing information on the course of the examinations and keeping order in the examination rooms, etc.

Although the final authority for any decision rests with the faculty administration, cases of reversal of decisions by the academic council are extremely rare and a summons for a student to appear before the academic council can be more unpleasant and more effective than a summons to appear before the dean of the faculty.

Although the functioning of the academic council system is not yet faultless, experience of the best councils (in the chemistry, physics, economics, philology and history faculties) have shown that the organs of student self-government can give considerable assistance to the faculty administration in the organization of instruction. In a number of cases it has been possible with their active participation to obtain an appreciable improvement in the success-rate of students (in the chemistry, philology, mathematico-mechanical faculties).

Special organs—the student soviets (councils)—are elected, in order to organize the everyday life of the students. The soviet is elected for a period of one year by the students of the particular hostel. The student soviet is concerned with the organization of the leisure, cultural activities and everyday life of students, and arranges communal service for the general good of the hostel. Every year, in conjunction with the warden, they allocate students to floors and rooms, ensure compliance with the internal rules of the hostel and take steps to prevent any breach of discipline. The student soviets are the oldest organs of student self-government.

With the improvement in the living conditions of the students and the increase in their cultural requirements, the role of the student soviets has been extended to cover the administrative organization and the aesthetic improvement of the hostel, the operation of student restaurants, the organization of lectures, concerts, excursions and other forms of cultural leisure activity for the students.

The student building-site soviets and committees are concerned with the organization of the work, everyday life and leisure of the students on student summer-building-sites.

These organs differ also in the content and range of their powers. The role of the building-site soviets and committees is of particular importance as they operate outside the higher education centre, where they are in a restricted sense the only authorized representatives of the VUZ on the spot. They have a greater potential impact in terms of carrying out measures of an educational character, since they hold in their hands not only moral but also material stimuli.

None of the three types of organs of student self-government, therefore, existing within the framework of the *Komsomol* and trade-union organizations, duplicate one another, but on the contrary each of them in its own sphere contributes to the realization of the common main aim—the Communist education of the students. A study of the experience of the working, functions, structure and composition of the organs of student self-government and also the defects in their operation is of great importance for their further improvement and for an increase in their role in the development in students of social, organizational and administrative attitudes and the inculcation in them of a sense of collective, communal responsibility.

The further development and perfection of student self-government is one of the main tasks in the realm of Communist education of the student body.

An important part in the formation of a Marxist-Leninist view of life and in the inculcation of organizational habits is played by extramural activities.

In this connexion a fundamentally new factor, which has had a decisive influence, has been the change-over to a five-day week.

The change-over to a five-day week has resulted in a considerable increase in the available free time of workers. The majority of workers have the opportunity of raising their cultural level by various means and of devoting much more time to their own chosen hobbies (reading, theatre-going, cinemas, concerts, engaging in various amateur activities and collective functions, sports, etc.).

A considerable contribution can be made by students at higher educational centres to the organization of the workers' free time. Their participation in this important field will be developed along the following lines: the propagation of political, scientific and aesthetic knowledge; the improvement of existing collectives and the creation of new ones for spontaneous activities among the workers; the organization of various types of Sunday courses and schools (for increased qualifications, entry to higher education or the public-service professions, and for individual interests); the wider participation of students in various types of duties (for example in schools, day rooms, childrens' nurseries at housing bureaux, workers' rest centres, green patrols, etc.).

Steps should be taken to prepare students to carry out these worthy tasks. In particular, a start should be made with the large-scale organization of training of lecturers, broadening of students' training for the public-service professions and the study of important questions in the fields of organization and administration.

It goes without saying that none of these activities should impinge upon the students' independent studies.

These are only a few of the questions which arise in connexion with the organization of instructional-educational work of Leningrad State University.

# Part II

# Scientific activity in the university and trends in its development

## 1. The problems of planning research work and criteria for evaluating its effectiveness in institutes of higher education

As is well known, there exist at least three basic conditions for a steady improvement in the qualifications of young specialists at universities and other educational establishments. First of all it is necessary to improve the qualifications of the lecturers, for this in particular determines the standard of the educational process and consequently the knowledge of the students. Secondly, connexions between the college and the national economy and educational establishments must be strengthened; such connexions must be not only in the form of help to production but must also contribute to the campaign for a high standard in the educational process ; as for the changing demands of science and the national economy, higher educational establishments can react more effectively if the teaching staff is closely connected with the future research workers. Thirdly, a factor which in our opinion predetermines a high standard for the two factors already mentioned, is a broad development of scientific research at universities. Moreover it should be emphasized that the broad development of scientific work at universities, which includes all the members from the professor to the students, is the only good basis for the preparation of highly qualified specialists, not to mention the fact that universities where research is carried out actively, attract, to a far greater extent, outstanding workers from science and industry.

The optimum combination of teaching and research and their interdependence, is the most important existing economic and pedagogic problem in the development of universities under present conditions.

It is not necessary to prove in detail that the idea of a conflict between research and teaching is meaningless, since the exclusion of research will lead inevitably to dogmatism in teaching and this in contradiction to the demands for the training of creative specialists. It is clear that to attempt to teach the student a certain amount of knowledge following a set programme is useless, as it is extremely difficult to predict which scientific-technological problems will confront the present-day student even in the present century.

Although a practical solution to the problem of combination of teaching and research is rather complex, nevertheless their rational combination has an important significance.

In determining the role of scientific work in the general scheme of activity of the university and in the fulfilment of its social functions, the university starts from the following basic assumptions.

1. The professor of the college and in particular of the university cannot be a proper instructor and educator of students if he himself does not carry out research work. Without this condition the academic instruction would become degraded to pure school teaching, and it would lead simply to the communication of a certain amount of information to the listeners.

2. An active participation by professors and instructors in research allows continuous improvement of the teaching process, its contents and form. A close and continuous association between teaching and research by the instructors themselves ensures the continuous enrichment of educational plans and programmes, and the incorporation in them of the most recent achievements of modern science. Proof of such an association is the constant inclusion of new courses in the teaching-plans that have developed from special courses directly stemming from the process of scientific research.

3. The link between teaching and research is not one-sided. The educational and teaching activity of university staff, in turn, has a favourable influence on research work. The interests of teaching at the present standard demands from the university lecturer a constant watch for all new phenomena and discoveries. Giving lectures helps to avoid narrowness of outlook and interests and focuses attention on general problems, questions connected with closely allied disciplines, etc. All this is reflected in the nature of scientific interests, in the formulation of problems for research, and in the determination of their range and depth.

4. Active participation of all professors and instructors in research produces the type of creative atmosphere which exerts a considerable influence on the training of the specialist as an independent worker capable of finding new openings and solving new problems.

5. The university fulfils an important function in the preparation of new research and teaching cadres, not only for itself but also for many other

higher educational establishments and scientific institutions, including the institutes of the Academy of sciences. Thousands of scientists graduating from Leningrad University work in the most varied types of research institutes, thus determining to a considerable extent the scientific progress of the country and developing, in these establishments, traditions and trends of university science. The number and quality of young scientists is determined largely by the conditions and standard of scientific research work at the university.

6. The development of Soviet science and the national economy require that a large proportion of university professors and instructors actively take part in the solution of general problems in the scientific and technological progress of the country. Therefore all university science is regarded as an important component of the whole complex of scientific establishments in the country.

Participation in scientific work is not regarded as the private concern of the professor or lecturer, completely dependent on his wishes and inclinations. The constant carrying out of research is just as important a responsibility of the professor and lecturer as is teaching. The lecturer who does not take part systematically in research work ceases to fulfil his obligations and as a general rule cannot remain a lecturer at the university.

The present scientific-technological revolution therefore stresses the demand for transformation of the universities into large educational and scientific centres where the training of cadres for science and industry is combined with intensive research work in the field of contemporary problems of scientific-technological progress.

Thanks to the continuous care and attention of the Communist party and the government for the development of scientific work in the establishment of higher education, the volume of research carried out in the higher educational establishments of our country is steadily growing. Apart from the laboratories attached to science faculties, a great number of specialized scientific establishments carry out scientific work at universities. At present at universities in our country there exist forty-one scientific research institutes, 320 laboratories for research and more than 300 branch laboratories, and in these 17,000 state engineers/technologists are working. The total number of research workers and teachers in universities in the country is approximately 300,000, i.e. 2.5 times more than in 1956. The range of research also grows continuously in the VUZy of Leningrad. As regards the high standard of the research and the importance of the subjects studied in the Leningrad universities last year, evidence of this is provided by the fact that one in eight of the subjects from the plan of the research work was among those classified as the most important throughout the country.

Much of the fundamental research carried out by qualified cadres of the VUZy is on a level with, or exceeds some of, the best world achievements. A large number of the university staff received the Lenin prize for solving some of the most important scientific-technological problems in recent years, which is evidence of the place of the university in the scientific-technological progress of the country.

In the post-war period there has been a wide development, not only of research carried out in higher educational institutions and financed from the state budget by the Ministry of higher and specialized secondary education, but also of research carried out by professors on a contractual basis with industrial enterprises and financed by branch ministries. In the country as a whole, expenditures on contracts are greater than financing from the state budget. This influences the character of research; research topics become more important. Direct links between higher educational institutions and industrial enterprises are much improved. The laboratories and material bases of higher educational institutions have improved because of money brought in by these contracts. The training of specialists becomes more closely linked with the demands of modern industry.

During the past ten years the volume of research work carried out by higher educational institutions on a contract basis has increased nearly ten times and now represents two-thirds of all contract research work carried out in the country.

About one-half of all doctors and candidates of science in the USSR work in the system of higher education. The situation is similar in Leningrad.

The rate of increase of personnel with the highest qualifications in educational institutions during recent years has also been higher than in specialized research organizations. The existence of a large number of highly qualified scientists and theoreticians—a big research potential—is the main peculiarity of higher educational institutions.

That is why an increase in the efficiency of research activity in higher educational institutions is of great importance both for the institutions themselves and for increasing the rate of scientific and technological progress in the country.

An important and indispensable advantage of higher educational institutions, especially universities, in comparison with any other research organizations, is the possibility of carrying out large-scale fundamental research due to the different fields of knowledge represented. They can carry out research in the junctures of different fields of knowledge, they have a permanent influx of young research workers, and they have the opportunity to choose talented youth. This facilitates the organization of research in new fields and in new directions.

121

Besides this, certain higher educational institutions can carry out work more economically because they can use graduate and undergraduate students as assistants in research work.

Taking into consideration the present scientific-technological revolution, which constantly demands advances in science for industry and theoretical and fundamental research with practical application, it is necessary to increase the part played by establishments of higher education in the development of scientific-technological progress. For this reason, particularly, the central committee of the CPSU and the Council of ministers of the USSR in a resolution of 3 September 1966, 'on measures for the improvement of training of specialists and improvement in the management of higher and secondary specialized education in the country' introduced measures for accelerating the research activity of universities and for their wider participation in carrying out research contracts with plants and establishments. For these purposes the necessary material, technical and financial means are provided.

A concrete programme for the future development of Soviet science was drawn up by the decree of the central committee of the CPSU and the Council of ministers of the USSR, on 24 September 1968 'on taking measures for increasing the effectiveness of the work of scientific organizations and the acceleration of the use of scientific and technological achievements in the national economy'. (In future we shall refer to this as 'decree on science No. 760'.) This decree marks the beginning of reform in the organization of scientific research in our country. In it is also stressed the demand for increased effectiveness in the research work of universities, for the improvement of the management and planning of research in the VUZ.

Scientific research in our country, as also in the whole national economy, is based on the principle of democratic centralization, which provides a rational combination of centralized management and local initiative. Given this principle we can distinguish several levels of administration of research. At the highest level, that of the government and state committee of the Council of ministers of the USSR for science and technology, the principal choice of themes is made —a choice which determines the balance between research and production, and between pure and applied research, and the establishment of budgetary policies. The governmental decisions on themes are the crucial ones and are subject to special control by ministries and universities. At the level of the ministry and the ministerial board, the specialization for each university, the distribution of assignments and the systems of interaction between universities, specialized research institutes and factories are decided. The rectorates of the universities decide how to choose the most promising projects, how to build up the organizational structure of the university and relationship between the faculties and departments, and how to stimulate the creative activity of research workers and teachers.

Although at present dependent on the ministries, universities in our country are increasingly using regional forms of co-ordination and planning.

In Leningrad, the north-western branch of the Scientific-Technological Council (STC) of the Ministry of higher and specialized education of the RSFSR, plays the role of regional co-ordinator. At the suggestion of Leningrad scientists, the present acting Council intends to change the branch from an advisory organ of the Ministry, which it was until recently, into one with precise administrative functions.

The STC branch is an organ of the Ministry of higher and specialized education of the RSFSR, which carries out through its expert commissions, co-ordination and planning of the most important governmental contracts for research work in universities of the north west. It co-ordinates work by research teams, supervises the carrying out of the most important research and its application within the national economy. It also determines the perspective and direction of development based on the needs of the particular branch of science and technological developments in the industry of the region, and participates in planning and development of higher education in Leningrad and the north west.

In the process of carrying out its tasks, the STC branch studies trends in the development of scientific-technological progress in the north-western region and formulates recommendations for long-term planning of research in the VUZ, draws up a co-ordinated plan for the most important research work, and organizes the co-operation of universities with industry, with specialized research institutes and with establishments of the Academy of Science of the USSR. It also hears reports from university leaders on problems of organization, planning and research results; organizes competitions for scientific work by students; organizes, together with social organizations, publicity concerning the most important research work completed, conferences, meetings, seminars and other activities; and draws up a combined plan for arranging local inter-university, all-Union and international conferences.

In order to carry out its functions the STC branch has access to material from universities connected with the organization, planning and co-ordination of research activity; can make recommendations to universities about the nature of their research activity; and recommends the investigation of certain important current problems, selecting the more important universities and departments to carry out co-ordination and scientific management of research. It can make recommendations to the Ministry on the distribution of assignments for the most important government work; it contacts branches of ministries and other government bodies regarding the centralized distribution of finance and the organization and planning of the most important research contracts, using the help of research teams.

The existence of such branches helps the Ministry to differentiate between regions, to take into account their specific problems and to direct the activity of universities.

It should be noted that these branches of the Council of the Ministry act on a voluntary basis. The scientists in the expert commissions of the Council do not receive any pay for their work. Recently, different methods have been used to attract a broader group of research workers to direct research projects. For this purpose continuous attempts have been made to find the correct balance between government administration and social organization.

At present at universities in our country, measures are being formulated for improving the planning of scientific work. These measures are mainly directed at eliminating duplication of research and wastage of effort and resources.

In recent decisions of the government on the development of science, the necessity to strengthen the centralized planning mechanism for research has been stressed. In this country it is the practice to make a long-term prognosis for scientific and technological work (ten to fifteen years and more) and five-year plans for scientific research work. Planning research right from the beginning through to the final results ensures scientific-technological progress. It is nevertheless very complex in nature.

The planning of research in universities is successful if one adopts as a basis suggestions on fundamental problems made by different co-ordinating councils, whose themes are in accordance with long-term prognoses and with the five-year plan. The final decision, however, is made after a detailed study of the proposals of different universities and departments for the solution of these problems.

Such a method of planning permits the carrying out of planned competitive projects and contracts. When necessary it is possible for several research teams to solve problems in different ways. In this way one can compare projects and also select at early stages of research the best technical and economic decisions, and after this the development of the plan can be handed over to that organization which will carry it out in the best way and at the lowest expense.

Intellectual competition organized in such a way is a guarantee against scientific and technological monopoly, which inevitably leads to stagnation of thought, and obstructs progress.

Such competition is not contrary to the specialization of scientific organizations, universities and departments. A favourable influence on the standard of planning and co-ordination of research work has been experienced by the main organizations dealing with basic scientific-technological problems and also in institutes of scientific instructors who may be responsible for the solution of a certain part of the problem. Thus every research organization is responsible for the development of one or several aspects of scientific-technological progress.

It should be stressed that centralizing the planning of long-term programmes does not entail the existence of detailed regulations as regards which practical problems must be solved within the scope of the programme. It is necessary to point out that too many detailed regulations in the planning of scientific investigations do not improve it but would make it difficult to adjust to the great variety and continuous change in practical demands.

A scientifically-based centralized planning of scientific research work will avoid making such regulations. It must determine general proportions, rate of growth and optimum relationships in the development of individual branches of science, but within the scope of each one of them must also decide the distribution of effort and resources for tackling the most important problems and programmes. The expanded centralized planning of scientific research in higher educational establishments (themes and measures to implement them) is important as it selects the most important problems for scientists from the social point of view and determines the rates of development of different branches of science and technology from the country's point of view.

The economic contracts carried out by departments for industry must fall within the framework of these long-term problems, and must put them into practice and work out details of them. This means that though there may be a great number of contracts, there will be no duplication or study of unimportant matters.

The right of departments of universities themselves to formulate the portfolio for economic contracts does not mean, in this case, that individual contracts must be drawn up with each client, although this has frequently been done. For large works such contracts may be made directly by universities with factory groups or even branches of ministries. However, fundamental theoretical work by universities must be financed by the government budget through the Ministry under whose control the university lies.

It must be stressed that the combination of several economic contract projects into one theme leads to a combined creative effort by workers of several departments, and in turn reflects favourably on scientific standards and the dates of completion of the projects.

Scientific work in universities is influenced by the fact that they are not only scientific establishments but are also higher educational institutions. Even small departments cannot concentrate all their efforts on tackling one particular narrowly specialized problem. No matter how the organization of the department is sub-divided, the interests of teaching require instructors specializing in different fields within the scope of the general subject and this determines the scientific interests of members of a department. Moreover, a high scientific standard of teaching demands that members of the department, as research workers, will be in different branches of the major discipline taking part in instruction in the department in question.

This enables a large number of scientific projects to be worked on at universities. However, in practice it causes conflict of interest because a large number of projects is a disadvantage in maintaining the standard of scientific work, and leads to dispersion of effort, and consequently to a lowering of effectiveness.

Taking these objective factors into consideration in the planning of scientific work, higher educational establishments aim to find optimum solutions which cannot always be expressed quantitatively. The solution to this problem is reduction in general number of projects, and concentration of collective effort on the solution of the more important problems.

One form of inter-departmental co-operation is the working unions or NII formed on the initiative of the Leningrad Polytechnical Institute, at the head of which are scientific councils made up of numbers of the most competent scientists from different fields and representatives of branch and industrial organizations.

One of the greatest achievements of such unions is the drawing up of a long-term scientific programme. All projects are now ranked according to their degree of importance and the basic orientation of scientific activity. The smooth planning of research work has also improved. The absorption into one project of several contract tasks appears to be advantageous, as the combined work of the members of several departments, particularly of theoreticians and re-searchers within the scope of the same project, enables the problem to be studied in depth.

At present much interest is being shown in the development of a system of planning, and in the statistical and accounting aspects of the development of science. This is understandable as a system of criteria and quantitative aspects can play an important role in elucidating the basic factors which influence the effectiveness of scientific-research work and in discovering methods to increase it.

A system of criteria and quantitative characteristics has been adopted to ensure reciprocity in the methods used to direct scientific-technological progress, since to carry out optimum plan assignments and determine the rates and proportions of the development of corresponding branches of science, it is necessary to know the practical state and dynamics of research, time taken, efficiency in carrying out research work and its application in industry.

A system of indices measuring the effectiveness of research activity in higher educational establishments must as far as possible be used both for the preparation of forms of statistical accounting at universities and for the planning of scientific work. It must seek to ensure maximum use of internal reserves and specific features of higher education.

Planning indices in faculties and departments must stimulate the following: the development and co-ordination of the most up-to-date theoretical and applied research; the raising of the level of qualifications of teachers and research workers by attracting a large proportion of instructors and also students of higher courses to take part in research; the combining of research on problems and reduction in number of problems and projects, in order to allow deep and varied treatment; the achievement of maximum practical efficiency in the use of results of scientific procedures carried out in the university; the reduction of time spent on research and processing; the attainment of a leading place in the particular field of science and technology and a standard of research comparable to the highest in the world.

The system of criteria for evaluation of efficiency of scientific work must ensure that the contribution of each team to scientific-technological progress is taken into account and that bottlenecks in the organization and planning of science in the university are detected. At the same time, the criteria must take into consideration the fact that the duties of universities do not include only the development of theoretical and applied research but also the improvement of the quality of training of specialists and the production of cadres with higher qualifications. Therefore emphasis should not be given, for example, only to that part of the scientific work of the professor-teaching section of the university that gives direct economic benefit; i.e. applied research. Such one-sided emphasis would have an adverse effect on the number of doctors and candidates of science, and the development of future theoretical research, which determines the standard of teaching as well as the economic potential of science. At the same time it is not possible to ignore economic efficiency in the universities. The scientific activity of workers at universities is not limited only to publications. In evaluating their results it is necessary to take into consideration the application of their scientific work. The more important and complex the work carried out by the scientist, the more important it is that the authors should participate in its application. The efficiency of theoretical and applied research in universities must naturally be carried out according to different criteria.

By 'criteria of scientific research work', we mean a definite way of measuring scientific research which is expressed by numerical parameters or quantitative indices able to reflect the effectiveness, including economic effectiveness, of such research.

The effectiveness of scientific research has a dual character. On the one hand, there is the quality of research work evaluated by its influence on the development of national output and of science itself, on the other hand, there is the productivity of individual scientists, their personal contribution to the development of scientific knowledge, and the extent of utilization of the possibilities, potentialities, working hours of scientists. Consequently, it is necessary to distinguish between the economic effectiveness of research in the national context and the economic effectiveness of research in the institution.[1]

In order to explain the basic factors influencing the effectiveness of scientific research, the corresponding criteria should take into account the two aspects mentioned above. One of the high priority tasks of economics is to work out a system of planned statistical and accounting indices for the development of science in order to evaluate the actual economic effectiveness of the practical utilization of scientific and technical projects and to determine whether scientific technological policies are correct. In order to elaborate optimal projects, to determine their pace and ratio with regard to the development of the corresponding sectors of science and technology, it is necessary to know the actual state and dynamics of scientific research, the time limits and efficiency in carrying out scientific and technical research.

At present, many economists are dealing with the question of criteria and indices which they consider to be one of the most pressing scientific problems for the sciences.

Many authors believe that the main, if not the only, criterion of effectiveness of research is the economic effect achieved by practical use of the results. In industry, this leads them to the conclusion that the productivity of scientists is defined by the economic effect of the work of one individual scientist[2]. Others consider it possible to measure the quantity of scientific production on the basis of the number of publications, inventions, volume of new information, etc.[3] The third concept, which comes closest to our own opinion, is that of working out a whole system of indices of effectiveness of science, taking into account the different fields of scientific activity, since it would be extremely difficult and perhaps impossible to establish one single index of effectiveness which would apply to all research work, there being differences in character (theoretical or applied), time limits for completion, etc.[4]

Therefore the field of application of economic effectiveness in science is rather limited. In the chain 'theoretical research—applied research—elaboration'

1. See B. Volgin, "Evaluation of research work", *Economic Journal* No. 18, May 1967; W. Shamin, "On Economic science", *Economic Journal*, No. 4, January 1968.
2. See N.D. Tyamshanski, *Basic indices of the work of specialized scientific research organisations*. Works of the Lenin Polytechnical Institute, 1963, No. 227, pp. 187-191.
3. See G.A. Lahtin, "Quantitative criteria of effectiveness of scientific research work". Collection "Effectiveness of scientific technical work", in *Nayka*, 1968, pp. 29-65.
4. See L.S. Blyakhman, G.M. Dobrov, etc.

only the last link refers to the utilization and to the economic effect. The final results of much theoretical research and other similar work cannot in principle be evaluated in economic terms only. Thus, the economic effects do not represent an evaluation of immediate scientific output, but an evaluation of the results of their utilization, depending to a large extent on factors which do not concern individual scientists and research teams (such as the scale of application and utilization of scientific ideas, the value of new output, etc.).

Furthermore, the integral character of scientific work complicates the measuring of the contribution of individual research, since every project contains a great number of ideas, decisions, and data taken from other sources, which are often not directly related to the work. The practical impossibility of determining the contribution of new research to the whole project, leads to exaggeration of economic effect. The economic effect represents in itself a function of time. Therefore the 'problem of long-term creative ideas makes the individual assessment of their effectiveness an insoluble problem. A useful action of scientific output is postponed indefinitely'[1]. This implies the non-identifiability of the variable of the economic effect and complicates its utilization as a quantitative criterion.

In any case, the economic effect of research does not lead to immediate material gain. It is also necessary to take into account the various indices, such as the increase in productivity, the improvement of quality of production, the reduction of material expenses, the improvement of working conditions and other factors, which are not subject to immediate quantitative evaluation.

All that has been mentioned up to now refers to a certain degree to scientific work at all institutes of higher education.

A system of statistics and indices for planning in higher education should take into account the need for an improved training of teaching staff as this is the basis for comprehensive fundamental research and demonstrates the interdependence of scientific research and the teaching process and of participation of large numbers of students and post-graduate students in research work.

Indices to measure the effectiveness of scientific research in institutes of higher education must meet the following basic requirements:

*Representativeness.* The number of indices must be sufficient to describe all the activities of the institutes, and every index must reflect actual activities.

*Additivity.* The indices should not be contradictory but mutually independent. That quality can be expressed in the following way: if the evaluations $V_i$ and $V_k$ correspond to the indices $m_i$ and $m_k$, it follows the evaluation $V_i + V_k$ should correspond to the total result $m_i + m_k$.

1. Strumilin, S.G., *On the methodology of the calculation of scientific work.* Edition of the Academy of Science, 1932.

In cases where the increase of one index $m_j$ implies logically the decrease of another index $m_i$, or if their simultaneous increase causes a decrease in the total, that use is inadmissible. A disturbance of the relationship leads to wrong results.

*Identifiability.* The indices must be expressed in terms which avoid any ambiguous interpretation in order to exclude the possibility of numerical errors.

*Comparability.* The indices must provide the means to make objective comparisons between the results of the work in institutes of higher education and subdivisions of different sizes and characteristics.

*Controllability.* In 1966 the Ministry of higher and secondary specialized education in the RSFSR introduced an accounting system of quantitative indices for institutes of higher education as an experiment. In 1968 that system was improved to some extent. It consisted of four parts: 'Teaching staff', 'Scientific research work', 'Educational process' and 'Other scientific work'. Let us consider the first two parts.[1]

1. Staff

— Number of chairs held by professors and doctors of science, as a percentage of the total number of the teaching staff (excluding the chairs for teachers of foreign languages and Russian, physical education, special training, art and graphic arts).

— Requirements of the institute for doctors of science.

— Number of theses defended during the year per 100 members of the professorial staff with the degree of 'Candidat' of science (post-graduate degree).

— Number of theses for the degree of Candidat of science defended during the year by teachers of the institute, per 100 members of the professorial and teaching staff without any academic degrees.

— Number of examinations for the degree of Candidat of science passed by teachers of higher education during the year, per 100 members of the teaching personnel without any academic degrees.

— Number of students with academic degrees or academic status leaving the university during the year and joining the teaching staff as a percentage of the total number of the professorial teaching staff.

— Number of 'aspirants' (post-graduate students preparing for the degree of Candidat of science) having finished their theses in due time and submitted them for defence, as a percentage of the total number of aspirants having finished the post-graduate course during the year.

— Number of aspirants assigned by the institute for special training at

1. Appendix No. 1 to the letter of the Ministry of higher and secondary specialized education in the RSFSR of 2 October 1968, No. 11-75.

another institution of higher education, as a percentage of the total number of the teaching staff without any academic degree or academic status.

2. Scientific research work.

— Summarized volume of scientific research work based on national plans and national budget (in 1,000 roubles), per teacher and scientific worker, (senior and junior scientific worker, senior engineer, engineer).

— Economies, achieved in the previous year in sectors of national economy as a result of the practical utilization of scientific research work, in terms of 1,000 roubles of the volume of work, based on the national budget and the national economic plan.

— Number of themes elaborated on the basis of decisions of the Council of ministers of the USSR and the RSFSR.

— Number of themes and volume of research work based on the national budget, per 100 members of the teaching staff engaged in that work.

— Number of themes and volume of research work based on the national economic plan, per 100 members of the teaching staff in charge of that work.

— Total number of publications, awards, prizes, patents, national medals obtained per year in every institute of higher education.

— Number of students engaged in research work, per 100 members of the teaching staff.

— Amount of student work received and mentioned in municipal and regional reviews; and works received for exhibitions on regional and national level, and honoured by medals, attestations and prizes, per 1,000 full-time students.

The system of indices adopted in 1968 by the Ministry of higher and secondary specialized education of the RSFSR is in itself an essential step forward as compared with the former system, and clarifies a great number of aspects of the educational and scientific activities and other scientific work of higher educational institutes and also of the work of the teaching staff.

A quantitative analysis of the development of scientific research in institutes of higher education was made in 1967 by the scientific technical council of the Ministry in order to determine the basic institute of higher education in accordance with the decisions of the central committee of the Soviet Communist party and the Council of ministers of the USSR of 3 September 1966.

In 1965/66 we elaborated and tested the complex system of criteria and quantitative indices for the evaluation of the effectiveness of scientific work in institutes of higher education, which now enables us to carry out a differentiated analysis of the most important theoretical and applied research projects.

## Indices of effectiveness in the field of theoretical and practical research

There are different points of view regarding the evaluation of effectiveness of theoretical research, which range from total disbelief in the possibility that effectiveness of fundamental research can be evaluated to methods put forward for the calculation of the economic effectiveness or even the economic feasibility of those research projects.

We consider the matter in neither so negative a light as the first group, nor in such an optimistic light as the second one.

It is true that at present there are no indices for the quantitative evaluation of the contribution of research teams to the development of fundamental theoretical research. In 1932 S.G. Strumilin, a member of the Soviet academy of science, wrote 'until now, strange as it may seem at first glance, science which essentially begins with measurement, weight and calculation has not been able to solve the problem of objective evaluation of its own achievements'.[1] S.G. Strumilin proposed as a solution to this problem the composition of *a scale of evaluation* of *the quality of scientific production* against which *specialists would determine the quality of their scientific work according to one of four ratings*. Despite the fact that the scheme proposed has not been put into practice, the idea of quantitative evaluation of the effectiveness of fundamental research by the comparative method appears to us to be extremely promising. In this connexion it is also very important to compare the level and scale of fundamental research projects with analogous indices in other countries.

At present, evaluation of the importance of fundamental theoretical research is carried out in this country by the National committee for science and technology, and the Academy of science of the USSR which is responsible for the guidance, control and co-ordination of fundamental research projects in the natural and social sciences carried out in academic and specialized research institutes and institutes of higher education. For that purpose the Scientific councils of the planning commission and the Academy of science of the USSR have been organized to solve complex scientific problems, and their staff is composed of scientists, experts from scientific research institutes, and institutes of higher education.

These councils analyse the present state of research with regard to corresponding problems in the USSR and abroad, define basic trends and the scope of scientific research and ways of practical utilization of their results. On the recommendation of the Scientific councils of the Academy of science of the USSR, outstanding scientific work, inventions and discoveries are honoured by gold medals and national prizes named after outstanding scientists.

1. S.G. Strumilin, publications.

The most outstanding scientific achievements of great theoretical value and importance for the national economy, which open up new prospects in scientific and technical progress and exceed previous world-wide achievements in the respective field of science, are after thorough discussion in public, honoured with the Lenin Prize, whereas other achievements in science and technology are honoured with national medals.

Thus, the number of scientists and amount of work honoured by medals may be considered as one important index of the contribution of research teams to the development of fundamental research. Let us underline, however, that this index shows the results of long years of work and cannot therefore be used for the daily evaluation of individual work of scientists.

An evaluation of the results of research work is carried out also in different kinds of scientific conferences, meetings, symposia and seminars. During the past years about ninety international meetings of scientists per month have been organized in this country.

Over the past ten years more than 500 inter-university conferences of national importance have been organized in this country; they were attended by teachers of institutes of higher education and scientists of the Academy of sciences, specialized academies, special scientific organizations and collaborators from industry.

According to data which is not yet complete, in 1968 institutes of higher education in Leningrad organised ninety-nine scientific conferences, among them twenty-five on national level, where about 8,000 papers were discussed; 2,000 papers were presented by scientists of institutions of higher education in Leningrad at conferences on national and international level. These conferences contribute to the dissemination and rapid utilisation of scientific achievements and thus facilitate the planning and co-ordination of scientific activity.

Another quantitative criterion which characterizes the level of theoretical research is the volume and importance of scientific publications. The economic effectiveness of scientific ideas is directly proportionate to the extent of its dissemination in time and space.[1] Publications, especially, guarantee the dissemination and the possibility to utilize ideas in practice. The volume of scientific and technical publications throughout the world is doubling every fifteen years, and that of technology every eight years.[2] Nevertheless, it is calculated in the United States that 10-15 per cent of work done in the engineering and research sector, at an annual cost of more than one billion dollars, duplicates previous work. If the necessary information were always

1. S.G. Strumilin, publications.
2. Collection "Technology and its place in the history of society", Moscow, 1965, p. 51.

available in due time, at least 20 per cent of similar research work could be avoided. From 50,000 to 60,000 applications and inventions registered in the Soviet Union per year, only 10,000 to 15,000 are considered as new ones, not repeating well-known results.[1]

The importance of information and publication as a criterion of effectiveness of scientific work refers especially to those institutes of higher education where monographs and articles are used as educational literature. In 1968 the teaching staff of institutes of higher education in Leningrad published more than 1,000 education manuals and monographs; a total volume of more than 8,000 pages, about 300 scientific cumulative volumes and 8,600 scientific articles and statements in periodicals at a total volume of 4,600 pages, thirty-four textbooks and monographs, were translated abroad, which is evidence of their high scientific standard.

The extension of press and publication activity at institutes of higher education, envisaged by the party and government in the field of higher education, will contribute to a further increase in the number of publications. In this connexion it is particularly important to improve the scientific level of publications, since according to experts a trend to 'water down' the content of scientific information has become more and more noticeable.[2]

Another part of scientific information activity, the field of inventions and patents, is also an important criterion of the effectiveness of scientific work. After the USSR joined the Paris Convention in 1965, the safeguarding of rights for inventions, trade-marks and samples was regulated, and there has been a growing demand for the 'purity' of published patents. 'We should take our proper place in the world market for licences. For that purpose it is necessary to set up a new and improved machinery and equipment in order to get profitable licenses. The purchase of foreign patent rights enables hundreds of million roubles to be saved on scientific research projects in the new five-year plan.'[3]

Let us state that acquisition of patents and inventions, as well as the other indices of the first group, cannot serve as the only criteria of effectiveness of scientific work. It must be stressed that many results of fundamental research cannot be patented at all, not to mention the fact that some authors, for instance, prefer publication to patenting, etc.

Scientific information in the form of papers presented at scientific conferences and symposia, as publications, patents or inventions, has today become of real economic significance.

Taking into account that the creation of information involves not only

1. Collection *Scientific technical revolution*, Kiev, 1964, edition 1, p. 17.
2. See G.M. Dobrov, "Science of Sciences", *Scientific thinking*, Kiev 1966, p. 68.
3. Mimeographed report XXIII of the Congress of the CPSU, 1966. Speech by A.N. Kosygin.

human effort but also material expenditure (e.g. for equipment, energy, amortisation of buildings, etc.), then information may be considered as a specific merchandise. This means that information is an inalienable product, since it is not damaged in transmission. Furthermore, the cost of newly created information contains only a part of the labour used for it, since the utilization of previously created information does not in most cases cost anything.

An important criterion of the effectiveness of scientific research work in institutes of higher education is the training of highly qualified teaching personnel (doctors and candidates of science). On their number and standard of training courses depend the effectiveness of investments in science; access to information on an international level; the fruitfulness of scientific research; progress in the field of applied sciences, and the time-lags for the practical utilization of new techniques.

In this country in 1966 we had in all 187,600 doctors and candidates of science, one half of them working in institutes of higher education. The training of highly qualified staff at institutes of higher education is faster than that in specialized research institutes. This is one of the most important criteria, on which, in our opinion, the evaluation of fundamental theoretical research carried out in institutes of higher education should be based. These criteria may serve for periodical evaluation (once every three years) of the effectiveness of scientific work, as envisaged by decree No. 760.

The current evaluation of the contribution of scientists at institutes of higher education to the development of science and technology may be based on the discussions and considerations of theoretical research results by specialized research councils (*problemnyje sovety*) and expert groups.

For an annual comparative evaluation of scientific activity in fundamental research in institutes of higher education, the author used the following indices: improvement of qualifications and training of scientific teaching staff (number of theses defended by candidates and doctors of science), amount of scientific publications, such as textbooks, monographs, scientific articles, etc., including translations; number of papers presented at scientific conferences, seminars and symposia, both on national and international level, patents and inventions. All these indices are calculated per 100 scientific teachers and the number of doctoral theses per 100 candidates of science.

## Indices of effectiveness in the field of applied research

Among the indices of effectiveness of applied research at technical institutes of higher education, economic effectiveness has priority (i.e. before application). The importance of this index will increase more and more under the present conditions of economic reform.

Bearing in mind that the efficiency of activity of any scientific institution or team, dealing with applied research, should in the long run have an effect on the development of corresponding sectors of national economy, it is necessary to carry out a systematic control of the actual economic effectiveness of scientific research, with which the expenditures for such work have to be compared. Therefore the second index for the effectiveness of applied research is the coefficient of effectiveness calculated as a ratio of the economic effect of its application to the corresponding expenditure.

The next index of effectiveness of applied research is the dynamics of the volume of scientific work carried out by institutes of higher education on the basis of economic contracts with factories. In 1968 the value of that work in institutes of higher education in Leningrad was more than six times that of the 1949 level.

Thus, the second group of indices evaluating the effectiveness of applied scientific work at institutes of higher education includes: the economic effect in 1,000 roubles per 100 scientific teachers, the coefficient of effectiveness of scientific research calculated as a *ratio between the economic effect and expenditure on the scientific work and indices for the dynamics of the volume of work based on economic contracts, also per 100 scientific teachers.* The very fact that industrial enterprises spend a lot of money to finance scientific research on a contract basis proves the importance of such research and demonstrates the high scientific standard of the higher educational institutes.

## Indices of the organization and planning of scientific work in institutes of higher education

As shown in an analysis, institutes of higher education with about the same number of scientific teachers and the same equipment, are often different as regards their effectiveness and the volume of their scientific research, and this is often caused by the difference in quality of organization and planning of scientific work.

In other words, the efficiency of the scientific potential of institutes of higher education characterizing the level of the teaching staff (A), the scientific information (B), the material and technical supply (C), and also the optimum of organization in the scientific system (D)[1] (see Table 13), depends not only on the size of each index, but also on the maximum proportions between these 'elements', their 'inside' structure.[2]

We assume that one part of the indices of the first two groups belongs

1. See G.M. Dobrov and others, "Potential of science", *Scientific thinking*, Kiev, 1969.
2. A. Tuschko, "Some elements of the scientific potential", Collection *Problems of the increase of effectiveness of the scientific research work*, Novosibirsk, 1962, p. 52.

to the sections A, B, C of the scientific potential, and at the same time, come also under section D, as do the indices for the quality of planning and organization of scientific work.

Indices of that level may be the following: complexity of research and importance of its subjects; correlation between theoretical and applied projects; participation of students in scientific work (in relation to the total number of day students) and the structure of teachers of higher education. The complexity of research subjects is characterized by the number of topics accomplished by two or more departments in relation to the total number of subjects, average cost of one subject based on economic agreements, the total amount of expenditure per 100 teachers, average number of scientific workers, carrying out the corresponding subjects. The importance of subjects may be evaluated according to the number and proportion of that subject included in the national and regional plans for scientific and technical progress. The character of the structure of the academic research can be seen from the ratio of teaching and research personnel, and supporting staff, and also from the proportion of staff having academic degrees.

There is obviously no need to deal in detail with the importance of these indices. The extent of the basic advantages of institutes of higher education over other scientific establishments depends on the complexity of subject-matter and the choice of correlation between theoretical and practical work. The participation of students in scientific work is an indispensable condition for the effective functioning of institutes of higher education as well as of educational centres.

The indices of the first, second and third groups should be applied in one operation. Each of them, taken separately, reflects only one aspect of the work, and may lead to wrong conclusions about its importance as a whole. At institutes of higher education, theoretical and applied research are closely connected with each other, therefore the effectiveness of the research work, subject to immediate practical utilization, enables us to a large extent to assess the efforts made by scientists at all stages of scientific research. The above-mentioned quantitative indices have to be supplemented by an expert appraisal as to the scientific level of research, the contents of publications, the importance of theses, the 'patent-earning capacity', etc. Among the factors considered particularly important for the evaluation of the effectiveness of fundamental research we would stress the potential (prospective) possibility of utilizing the results in the national economy, the level and scale of scientific work compared with that of other countries, the setting up of new rules, and the role of theoretical research in the cultural development of a country.[1]

1. See 'Bulletin of the Academy of science of the USSR', 1966, No. 7.

An analysis of the activity of twenty-two institutes of higher education in Leningrad during the years 1959-68, which we carried out on the basis of the above-mentioned criteria (see Table 13), shows that these criteria reflect with sufficient objectivity the quality of organization and planning of scientific work at institutes of higher education and may serve as a basis for recommendation to increase its effectiveness. Between 1959 and 1968 the rate for indices relating to the defence of doctor theses increased by 150 per cent, that of papers presented on conferences doubled, that of publications increased by four times, and the coefficient of economic effectiveness increased by 50 per cent.

TABLE 13. Scientific potential at institutes of higher education

| A | B | C | D |
|---|---|---|---|
| Teaching staff | Scientific information supply | Material and technical supply | Maximum value of organization of scientific system |
| Number | Inherent scientific 'surplus' | Financing, structure and dynamics | Maximum value of system, with reference to utilization of scientific potential |
| Qualification structure | (including theses of doctors and candidates of science, monographs and publications, patents etc.) | | |
| Age structure | | Material and technical supply | |
| Number of potential academic staff (including 'aspiranty' and candidates for a doctor's degree) | Dissemination of results on international level | | |

Let us state that certain indices of the first three groups characterize the dynamics of scientific activity compared with previous periods (relative indices for the defence of theses for doctors and candidates of science for the dynamics of work based on economic plans), others represent the level of scientific work comparable with special norms (coefficient of economic effectiveness, relative indices for patents, inventions and publications, etc.).

Some indices can serve only as an indirect measure of effectiveness, reflecting the standard of organization and of potential of the scientific team: the factorial indices. The legitimacy in using them for the objective evaluation of the effectiveness of scientific work, was investigated by us by means of the method of correlation.[1] We thus measured the proportions of factorial indices with the results of the scientific work of twenty institutes of higher education in Leningrad in 1960, 1965 and 1966. In many cases the dependence of individual evaluative indices on factorial indices—whereby that dependence is characterized by the correlation coefficient (C)—proved to be sufficiently essential. There is an inverse relation between the volume of work carried out and the indices of defence of theses (C=0.65). The increase in the volume of publications is in relation to the contribution of teachers with scientific qualifications (C=0.74). The increase in the number of doctors of science is in relation to the number of new doctor theses (C=0.51). At the same time, the number of teachers working on the same subject is in inverse proportion to the defence of doctor theses (C= −0.65) because of the individual character of the defence of theses; but in direct proportion to the share of applied subjects to the total number of completed projects (C=0.84). The increase in the number of complex subjects based on economic plans is proportionate to the number of applied subjects (C=0.51) and to the expected economic effect (C=0.69) and is in inverse proportion to the defence of candidate theses (C= −0.89). At the same time the increase in the proportion of complex subjects based on economic plans and of the expected economic effect per 100 teachers are proportionate to the increase of the quality of scientific work in institutes of higher education (C=0.69). It is obvious that the progress made by students is proportionate to the percentage of teachers engaged in scientific research (C=0.69). A negative influence is caused by the increase in the share of applied subjects to the detriment of theoretical research work (C= −0.59).[2]

On the whole the correlation method of quantitative analysis confirms many conclusions based on the qualitative examination of the single indices depending on the level and form of the organization of scientific work. At the same time this analysis showed again that none of its single indices may be used universally for the evaluation of the activity of an institute of higher education as a whole. Under the present conditions, no complex index can be found for the evaluation of the activity of research teams.

We investigated also the dependence of the effectiveness of scientific work on the factors of management and organization by grouping the institutes of higher education in Leningrad on the basis of the indices of the first three

1. See L.S. Blyakhman, A.P. Solovev, I.S. Minko, P.A. Rodionenkov, V.A. Bunkin: "On the indices of the evaluation of the activity of scientific and technical organizations", Collection *Problems of economy and planning of scientific research,* Edition Leningrad University, 1968.
2. Evaluation of the relations depends on the transition variable of the error, which is connected with the number of units of observation (20).

groups in 1967. This brought out the extremely important influence of those factors on the research activity. Thus, large institutes of higher education with more than 700 teachers gained the most importance with regard to the index and to the coefficient of economic effectiveness. It is obvious that the big research teams have certain advantages compared with smaller ones, since the realization of a great number of projects enables them to utilize the results of one research project when working on others, and to cover the expenditure for work having negative results at the cost of the work with high economic effect, thus creating a better co-ordination of work. At the same time maximum economic effect was reached in institutes where an average amount of contract work was done and having an average rate of growth of 25-50 per cent a year, which shows that there are maximum limits to financing contract research, and to the proportion of this research in the total. The fact that the relative indices of defences of theses and publications depend on the rate of growth of financing by contracts or the national budget and also on the contribution of teachers with scientific qualifications, is analogous to the correlations in the analysis. An essential increase in the economic effect calculated per 100 teachers is observed in connexion with the increase in the number and scale of the activity of different research laboratories, which are principally engaged in applied research. Finally, the complexity of subjects in higher in the group of institutes of higher education where the share of doctors of science and the number of working groups is higher. This means that the conclusions drawn on the basis of grouping coincide with the results of correlation proportions.

## 2. Scientific research at the university

We shall examine how far the above-described planning and assessment of research work are actually applied by the Leningrad University research organization.

Leningrad University, being the biggest training centre for specialists in various branches of national economy, state construction, culture and education, is outstanding also as one of the fundamental centres of research in the country. The professors and lecturers at the university have enriched their native country and the world by their outstanding achievements in science.

It was here that a start was made in many scientific ventures, subsequently developed by the collective efforts of various scientific institutions and teaching establishments.

Research, together with educating students, is looked upon as the most important work of the university and therefore, the level and quality of research work is considered as important as basic university training.

The organization of research work at the university is remarkable for its specific characteristics. Theoretical research dominates the majority of scientific problems at the university. This does not prevent scientists from developing themes of a practical nature.

The participation of university people in applied research is on the one hand a means of putting into practice the results of theoretical research; on the other hand it provides an opportunity to enrich and broaden the scope of scientific research by including projects of a technological nature. By means of applied research, the university establishes many links with its environment which are particularly necessary to the university, as indeed they are to any type of research institute.

Research at Leningrad University has certain special features. The main one being that this university has a whole system of scientific research institutes and other research stations, including: institute for mathematical and mechanics research, computer centre, observatory, institute for physics research, institute for chemical research, institute for biological research, institute for physiological research, institute for earth crust research, science institute for research in economic geography, laboratory for lake study, institute for social research.

The institutes of any scientific research establishment have at their disposal their own staff of assistants, although the degree of their autonomy varies. Some have their own budget and an account in the state bank (biological institute and laboratory of lake study), others have an estimated amount included in the total budget of the university (the institutes of physics, chemistry, physiology and others).

Some of these institutes have subsidiary establishments and undertakings, organized separately and operating on their own budgets (experimental workshops of the institute of physics, experimental workshops of the institute of mathematics and mechanics, etc.).

Although independent, all these establishments are subdivisions of the university from an organizational point of view and do not differ from other autonomous institutes.

However, the university institutes have their peculiarities, resulting from their status and role in the university. They organize, co-ordinate and combine not only the activities of their co-workers on research, but also that of all the professors and lecturers of faculties, of which they are members. In this way in each laboratory work is carried out by laboratory assistants as well as by the staff of professors, fellows, senior students, and lecturers of the particular faculty. This system creates a unity of purpose in the teaching and research work to be done, ensures that the directives from the department are followed in the interpretation of basic problems, and ensures continuity of scientific research.

The institutes are a part of the corresponding faculties, and the director of the institute is considered as an assistant to the faculty dean in research work. The only exception is the institute of social research, organized in 1965. The creation of this institute was prompted by the fact, that up to that time the study of man in society was fragmented and the various aspects of one social phenomenon, i.e. the economic, legal, moral, social, psychological, psycho-physiological aspects, etc., were investigated independently by respresentatives of various faculties. In order to combine these efforts and organize a complete study the institute was born. The institute is in no way a part of any particular faculty and by the nature of its work is an inter-faculty establishment.

Professors and lecturers in economics, philosophy, law and other sciences take an active part in the work of the laboratory and in the groups of co-workers at the institute, in addition to permanent staff.

## Planning of research work at the university

All research is planned. There are plans both for one-year and for long-term research. The research plan for one year embraces all subjects, all research workers, and all professors and lecturers engaged on research.

The long-term plan for research is for five or more years. It includes and names only the basic executives and leaders of the prospective work.

Long-term planning of scientific research plays a significant part in the development of Soviet economy.

Long-term planning by the university includes all the basic aspects of its activity; a highly significant portion of these plans is devoted to scientific research.

The preparation and realization of these plans provides the basis and main instrument for managing scientific activity at the university since they show the fundamental working trends and the necessary steps to be taken for their realization. Annual scientific planning, which is based on these plans, represents in itself a concrete programme of activities for the whole academic staff of the university and for each individual member. Whereas long-term plans determine more or less only the general outlook, the annual plans go into more detail. In this connection, modifications are made and specifications are inserted as new scientific problems emerge and changes take place in the academic staff structure, or as a consequence of the improvement of material and technical facilities, etc.

At the present time, the university has a long-term development plan for the period 1967-80 and a five-year plan for the years 1966-70.

The long-term plan for university development for 1967-80 makes no provision for concrete scientific topics or problems. It contains the basic factors of development, in general, and defines the leading problems of scientific-research development in the university during the period concerned. It likewise maps out new trends for future research work or widens the scope of the present research activity. Further development of the university structure is considered in accordance with the plan, i.e. the creation of new departments, laboratories and research institutes. Thus the plan provides for the organization of eight research institutes (economics, psychology, astrophysics, astronomy, etc.); sixty-three new departments (operational research, mathematical logic, kinetics and catalysis, virus research, labour psychology, physico-mathematical methods of geography, history of economic thought, languages of south-east Asia, etc.), some sections of which exist already; and over seventy new scientific laboratories.

In order to ensure the development of scientific work in general and in any given directions, the plan also establishes a range of indices for training scientific personnel, for the numerical increase of the national quota of scientific-technical and auxiliary staff, for creating scientific auxiliary institutions and a technical service for the development of libraries, and for the increase of university publications, etc. All these inter-dependent indices are defined with the necessary accuracy for development over a period of fifteen years.

The five-year plan for scientific research in the university for 1966-70 defines, in more detail, the same content of scientific work. It involves scientific research as a whole. Only highly significant problems and topics, more particularly complex ones, are formulated therein. The total number of these subjects, included in the five-year plan, amounts to 230 (out of 18,000 subjects studied every day in the university). The plan does not fix certain time-limits for the execution of any subjects studied but merely gives the general dates of their implementation. At the same time, it indicates the leading scientific establish-ments and departments interested in the practical utilization of the results of research.

The plan likewise contains instructions on the practical utilization of research results, the training of scientific personnel, the supply of technical equipment and the financing and capital investments.

All these indices enable senior authorities, in particular the Ministry of higher and secondary specialized education to co-ordinate scientific work in several establishments, to bring the development in higher educational institutes into line with the material and technical facilities and to submit the practical utilization of research results to the approval of the departments concerned.

In drawing up these plans the university takes into account the general level of national and world science as well as a whole series of factors emanating from this, such as: notes from the Academy of Science of USSR and other Soviet Union organs on the direction of theoretical and applied research spread

143

over this or that period; tasks received by the university from organs of higher standing, or taken on by agreement with other organizations; traditions and successes of the university, the schools of science and their trends; research capacity; material and technical possibilities and means.

The plan of scientific research work is confirmed by the academic council of the university and is presented either whole or partially to the higher authorities, who plan the development of science in the country, i.e. the Ministry of higher and specialized secondary education, its scientific technological councils including the branch of the scientific and technological council of the Ministry in the north west located in Leningrad; it is also submitted to the councils and committees of the Academy of Science of USSR, and from there to departments directly connected with university matters. These departments are called upon to tie up wholly, or in part, the work of the scientific establishments, draw up composite plans, plans for working out the most important problems and make corresponding recommendations. The plan contains two groups of subjects or two defined divisions: subjects included in the so-called thesis plan and subjects following the faculty, department or individual plans.

To the first category belong subjects dealt with on the instructions of the government, or government departments, when the university is consulted in solving these or other scientific or technical problems in the capacity of co-executive; then come the subjects concerned with developing the national economy; subjects included in the co-ordinating plans for solving problems of a scientific-technical nature and plans of the USSR Academy of Sciences; subjects dealt with and completed on the instructions of industrial undertakings, building, designing and other organizations in accordance with contracts.

As a rule, the subject-matter of this category is included in the plans made on the university's initiative, taking into consideration the facilities the university can offer in the way of specialization, qualifications of the co-workers and emerging trends of scientific research. The remaining subjects, which were not included in the first group, are included in the faculty, department and individual research plans.

The relative correlation of quantities of subjects of one or another scientific research group was as follows: in 1968 from the total number of subjects, 1,825, only 34 per cent belonged to the first group and 66 per cent to the second.

This means that one-third of subjects worked out by university scientists are connected with the work of other establishments and departments and are co-ordinated at various levels on the scale of government plans.

The funds for financing research by the university come partly from the national budget and partly from purely commercial contracts.

The major part of research work is financed through the national budget from funds appropriated for the specific purpose of completing clearly defined but most important tasks.

During the last few years there has been a large increase in the number of research projects undertaken by the university on a contract basis. Such contracts were entered into with building, designing and other industrial institutes. The work in such cases is financed by the clients.

The volume of contractual work has multiplied in the last fourteen years by more than twenty-five times. The great advantage of contract work is that with the money coming in from clients, the university can afford to employ, apart from their own staff, additional assistants. In 1968 this source of income provided salaries for an additional 1,060 assistants, of which 198 were scientists and 862 technicians and assistants. Over and above this, 1,000 professors, lecturers, laboratory technicians, fellows of faculties and students were drawn in to take part in this work at an additional salary equal to half the normal scale.

The volume of research work done under contract is not equally distributed between faculties, because the specific nature of the research is predominantly scientific and technical. The faculty of physics and the institute of physics handles more than 36 per cent of the contract work. The mathematics-mechanics faculty and its science establishments share 18 per cent, the faculty of chemistry and institute of chemistry 12 per cent, the faculty of soil-biology, the institute of biology and the institute of physiology 9 per cent, the faculty of economics 2 per cent and the institute of social studies 3 per cent, etc.

The total number of subjects dealt with and completed in 1968 under contracts amounted to 410. The incorporation of contract work into the research plan is done either on the initiative of the university, which would suggest undertaking research to a practical organization interested in it, or on the other hand on the initiative of the organization approaching the university to solve certain problems they are up against, or on the suggestion of government departments requesting the university and the organization to carry out together certain research work.

The assessment of costing the contract work is done by the university faculty concerned with the work and the organization, i.e. the clients who will receive the completed job.

The total of such work handled by the university amounts to 1,825. However, in assessing this figure, one has to take into account that a considerable number of subjects, which are a part of individual plans, are, in fact, a part of a larger subject.

The time taken to develop the subjects depends entirely on their character; but subjects can be grouped as follows: approximately 30 per cent are of one year's duration, 20 per cent two years duration and 50 per cent three years and longer. It should be pointed out that newly included subjects often represent an extension of an already developed theme.

The number of new subjects each year entered in the plan of scientific research, differs from year to year. On the average it can be taken as 30-40 per cent each year.

The volume of scientific research carried out by the university is expressed not only in the number of subjects, but also in costing. In this, the direct expenses such as acquiring equipment, materials, expeditions, etc., as well as salaries for teaching and research workers and auxiliary personnel, are taken into account.

Comparing these findings with the total number of scientific workers, the over-all university budget and the total number of theses, it is possible to obtain some relative indications, characterizing the university research work.

## Number of people engaged on scientific research work

What has been said above about the role and position of scientific work in the activities of the university, also determines the number of staff participating in carrying out planned science research.

Those taking part in it are: the staff of professors and lecturers, the regular scientific personnel of the science research institutes, laboratory supervisors and senior and junior assistants. The people fundamentally are research workers, and post-graduate students should also be included in their number.

The teaching and research personnel, whose duty is to carry out research, is 2,740 strong, excluding candidates of which over 900 are scientific co-workers in research at the institutes and laboratories, entirely devoted to scientific work. As a matter of fact, only about 100 persons, mainly young teachers busy on working out a curriculum of studies—teachers of physical culture, etc.,—do not take part in the annually planned scientific work.

In this way about 96-97 per cent of the university science teaching staff takes part in scientific research work.

All science teachers are divided in accordance with their science training, but not according to faculty or institute, in the following manner: physico-mathematical sciences represent 25.8 per cent of the total staff, chemical sciences 9.9 per cent, biological science 10.8 per cent, geology and mineralogy 4.7 per cent, geographical science 4.5 per cent, agricultural science 0.8 per cent, philological sciences 21.5 per cent, history 4.8 per cent, economic science 3.5 per cent, philosophical science 3.0 per cent, law 3.0 per cent, science of education 4.7 per cent, remaining, art and others, 1.9 per cent.

The high level of qualifications of the research and teaching personnel is an important factor in research work and indicates the effectiveness with which the overwhelming proportion of the scientific staff of the university was trained by the university.

Participants in scientific research, apart from the teaching staff, are the auxiliary technical and the auxiliary teaching personnel.

The number of auxiliary workers of various categories amounts to 2,800 persons.

The proportion of the research staff, i.e. those engaged in fundamental research work, to the auxiliary personnel is 1:1. But this proportion varies between the faculties.

In the humanity faculties where the need for auxiliary personnel is much less, their number is comparatively small, while in faculties connected with experimental research, the proportion is somewhat higher.

In assessing these figures it is necessary to bear in mind that a considerable proportion of the junior research personnel and junior scientific workers do not carry out independent research, and in this respect should be considered as an auxiliary force.

## *The participation of students in research work*

The involvement of students in scientific work, and the instilling of knowledge of research work, has posed a problem of teaching methods. The teaching plans of all faculties provide for such methods of teaching as test and diploma work for students in their final studies. A significant part of students' diploma work is of scientific interest and the results are published in science periodicals. Taking these circumstances into account, it is safe to say, that approximately one-fifth of the university, namely those in their final year, take part in scientific research. This form of activity includes students of all courses, i.e. full-time, evening and correspondence.

But apart from this form of participation, which is provided by the study plan, and compulsory for students, a whole system of student involvement in research work is practised at the university, starting from the junior courses.

The organizing of the scientific work of students at Leningrad University is based on the fact that this work can be fruitful only if it forms part of research carried out by research teams in the university. The whole system of guiding and organising the scientific work of students follows this principle. The organisation and guidance of students' scientific work proceeds, on the one hand, from participation of the professorial and teaching staff and the corresponding university and faculty authorities, and, on the other, from students themselves, their representatives and student bodies.

The existing system of organizing and guiding the scientific work of students in the university comprises the following elements.

147

Above all, it is up to every professor and teacher to encourage students to participate in creative work, since this is an inalienable factor in the training process of young university specialists. Hence the professor or teacher stands out as the prime organizer and guide of students' scientific work. The part he plays, as such, is not determined solely by his obligations towards his students. The interest of the professor's own research often acts as a magnet. Thus students often become his assistants and it is precisely this circle of collaborators that is the nursery for future scientists, post-graduate candidates and chosen pupils and heirs to the professor's own ideas.

University departments are a basic cell for organizing and guiding the scientific work of students. They accustom pupils, specializing in a given field, to scientific research, instil a taste for research, train the students' habits of practical work and acquaint them with methods and resources of research in any given field of knowledge. The university department thus also ensures the material and technical basis of students' scientific work (the assigning of working places in laboratories and the provision of the necessary equipment, etc.). The part played by the university department is decisive no matter what form of scientific work prevails in any given faculty.

Owing to a series of conditions, due largely to the specific character of scientific work in one field of knowledge or another, the scientific work of students in the university has been established in accordance with various forms of organization. These forms may be reduced to two, namely:

1. The participation of students in a scientific subject on which professors and instructors are working as members of a given department; in this case, the students collaborate in certain theoretical or experimental sections of the subject treated or perform these or other auxiliary tasks (calculation, treatment of material, etc.). The important part played by the department manifests itself in the organization of similar kind of work for students.

2. Participation of students in the activity of branches of the students' scientific society. The basic form of work, in this case, lies in the preparing of papers, original reports and their discussion at branch meetings. These branches are established in departments even when inter-departmental branches exist as well. The supervisors of branches are leading (or other) members of the department, i.e. professors or readers acting on its behalf. The senior member or secretary of the society is elected by those students who are active members themselves.

The initial form of organization for students' scientific work is to be found in the faculties of physico-mathematical and natural sciences, related to a large extent to experimental work; the second form is to be found in the humanities. It is necessary here to note that these forms are not incompatible. Indeed they are not infrequently associated. The results, obtained by students in the course of a general subject in a department, and the total number of experiments made by them are reported to the branches and, vice versa, the branch as a whole is sometimes induced to carry out some part of the scientific work of the department.

The academic council and dean of the faculty manage the scientific work of students at faculty level. For the carrying out of concrete work of students and for ensuring liaison with the governing body of the faculty, there exists a council of the scientific society of students in the faculty. The academic council, for its part, chooses supervisors for the scientific society of students from among the professors in the faculty.

The council of the scientific society is a student body. Together with the supervisor, it effects co-ordination of the activity in branches and other scientific work in the faculty, makes arrangements for students to take part in scientific work, organizes scientific conferences for students in the faculty and exhibitions of student work, holds competitions for the best scientific work done by students, and ensures the participation of students of the faculty in competitions and reviews on a general-university, city, urban, regional or national level as an important incentive to creative scientific work on their part. The scientific council of students and its supervisor look after the material and technical basis of scientific work and publication in scientific periodicals.

The best work performed by students has been published in a series of collections by the university for some years past. The usual channel, however, for publishing such work consists of the normal university editions or those of other scientific establishments. Hence the main bulk of work submitted by students, in keeping with the demands made on original scientific research, has been issued, not in special collections of student work, but in general scientific publications including the journals of the Academy of Sciences of the USSR.

At university level, the guidance of scientific work of students depends on the academic council of the university, the rector, pro-rector for scientific work, and the curator and the council of the scientific society of students at the university. The functions of the councils of the scientific society of students both on university and on faculty level are analogous.

The public organizations of students like the *Komsomol* (young communist league) and the students' union take an active part in the guidance of the scientific work of students.

During 1968, 3,100 students participated in scientific research, not counting students who were doing their diploma work, as part of their training course. Of course, the tempo is unequal, as some students work steadily while others more spasmodically.

In training specialists, the university's problem is to create an atmosphere for newly arrived students which will be favourable to training prospective research workers, rendering them capable independently of solving these or other problems likely to confront them in the course of specialized work.

In 1962 only 450 students were engaged in research work financed by the national budget while 570 worked under contract to organizations as compared to the figures in 1968, which were 1,100 and 800 persons respectively.

The university's efforts in this direction are further confirmed by figures showing student participation in various branches of scientific work.

In assessing the efficiency with which the work is done, other indices are also considered. Account is taken of the number of papers by students showing results of research completed. In 1968 university students took part in twelve science conferences for students, some of which were organized by the university; and 158 papers were read by students. Students are also drawn into the work of science seminars attached to the faculty. In three of the faculties alone (mathematics-mechanics, physics and chemistry) over 800 students took part in the seminars in 1968 with 10 per cent presenting reports and communications.

Competition is a great stimulus in the perfecting and widening of students' research work. These competitions are arranged on different levels, covering areas varying from the whole union, to individual republics, and towns, or even just a university. About 600 students participated in these in 1967 and 1968.

Prizes, diplomas, premiums and medals were awarded to 105 students.

The publication of 132 papers prepared by students indicates the maturity of their work.

## Indices of the level and efficiency of research work

The above-mentioned criteria of work by the VUZy are equally applicable to universities as a whole and for that matter to individual universities, faculties and institutes.

Let us quote some of the most essential indices illustrating the level of organization of scientific work and its efficiency.

— the participation of the teaching personnel in research work. On an average 96-97 per cent of the teaching personnel of the university take part in planned research;

— carrying out of approved plans of research. On average about 96-97 per cent of the planned scientific work is accomplished. About fifty to sixty theses per annum remain uncompleted due to personal and other reasons, beyond the control of the researcher;

— the total number of published articles in the scientific press per annum amounts to 3,000. More will be said later about the activities of the university editors;

— attendance by university scientists at gatherings, conferences, meetings, etc. In 1968 the professors and other members of the educational staff submitted over 1,000 scientific reports and communications. This index, about which more will be said later on, is evidence of an active team at the university and of the theoretical importance of results achieved in its research activities;

— the quantity and volume of contract research at the university steadily increases and in 1968 was over 4.5 million roubles. Of course, this index cannot be applied to analyse the activities of different faculties, the activities of the faculty of physics and that of history, for example, but a comparison with faculties and institutes of a similar kind is fully justified;

— the number of developments introduced and their effect on the economy by application in industry. This index is connected with the one above, but only in the sense that the themes already developed can be applied in other forms apart from contracts. To this category of indices belong contracts of creative co-operation with producing organizations, which unlike the former contracts do not offer any binding financial arrangement. The university has about eighty such contracts, under which it carries out some limited research. Over and above this the university gives about 3,000 consultations yearly free of charge;

— another pointer in assessing the work of the university is that it patents and registers completed research work in the form of inventions.

— to appreciate the contribution made by the university scientists in developing science in the country, it should be mentioned that the university was given both a state and a Lenin prize for outstanding scientific work. About fifty scientists received the state prize and nine the Lenin prize.

— the university considers it a duty to spread scientific knowledge throughout the population. This work has many aspects. To organize and co-ordinate lectures for the masses, the university has attached to it an All-Union society under the title 'Knowledge'. In the course of a year, professors, lecturers and research workers give over 4,000 lectures.

## 3. Training of research and teaching specialists

Together with teaching students, there is an important section of university activity, namely the training of science and teaching specialists, by means mainly of post-graduate courses. Out of 10,000 day students, there are more than 1,000 fellows and interns, who receive preparatory full-time training.

The planning of the post-graduate studies is as follows.

The university draws up a prospectus (five years duration) and yearly plans for training fellows, taking into account the available scientific staff, material, technical possibilities and the availability of suitable candidates amongst students in their final year. These plans are submitted to the Ministry of higher and secondary specialized education, which confirms the plan of intake of fellows each year.

The plan confirmed by the Ministry reflects the government requirements of science-teaching specialists, the prospective development of science and the network of science establishments and VUZy, and the university's capacity and tradition as a science centre.

After the Ministry has confirmed the planned acceptances, adjustments have to be made in the university's forecast for a number of specialists. The differences arising from this adjustment are in the region of 5-15 per cent, either cutting the university's estimates or increasing them.

The plan of admissions is set out for the university in the form of a cross-section of specializations. At the same time, when being put into practice, the plan undergoes some corrections, resulting from the fact that the faculty selects and recommends very able candidates for specialized studies for which no provision of entry was necessarily made. In all, at present, the university carries out training of science-teaching specialists by fellowships in 134 specialities.

Students are drawn from: (a) students recommended by research committees of faculties. The number of these students admitted reaches 35-40 per cent and in some faculties 80 per cent; (b) candidates for specialized fellowships directed to the university by colleges and scientific establishments. This category in the number of admissions represents 40 per cent and in some specialities 60 per cent; (c) persons who have a record of practical experience after leaving the VUZ. This category represents 26-30 per cent of those admitted.

All those who wish to be admitted take the preliminary entrance exams and submit a science paper.

A characteristic of admission to these courses in the last few years has been an increase in so-called 'special purpose' fellowships. The fact is that a large number of graduates or assistants from the different VUZy and scientific establishments, or even graduates of Leningrad University, are being sent to take post-graduate courses at Leningrad University.

After training, they go back to work in the VUZ which sent them, or in a science research institute. This arrangement has the advantage that the institute will know beforehand what kind of scientific worker it will get back, and often it is a local man. The role of these special fellowships is particularly important for newly opened colleges and science institutes; which are not fully manned with science teaching staff of high qualifications. Leningrad University played an important part in supplying the staffs to newly opened institutes in Siberia, as well as to the Far East. For the Far East University alone, fifteen to twenty fellows are trained every year.

The clear advantage of specialized fellowships has been one reason for their development during the last few years.

For instance, in 1960, twenty-four persons were given specialized fellowships; in 1964, eighty-five; in 1967, 133; in 1968, 144 persons.

There are 40-45 per cent of women amongst the fellows. The age groups are; under 30 years, up to 80 per cent; from 30 years of age to 35, 15 per cent, and over 35, 4-5 per cent.

Up to 30 per cent of those admitted to fellowship have either published scientific papers, or finished parts of a thesis.

The subjects of the research theses are approved by the department in the first year of the fellows' residence. In the majority of cases the subject of the thesis corresponds to science problems already being studied in the department and in this way the fellow becomes a researcher on the team of this or that department or laboratory, and does a part of the total scientific work. The exceptions are those who have a specialized fellowship with research subjects already fixed and approved by the establishments sending them to Leningrad University for science training.

During the period of work, the fellow receives a government grant, is assured of a place to work in the laboratory, makes use of its scientific equipment or is supplied with new equipment paid out of the funds of the department, and has the possibility of going on scientific missions, etc.

One of the members of the department, usually the professor, supervises the fellow's work, draws up reports about its progress. In addition the fellow has to attend faculty meetings regularly and give them progress reports.

During his stay, in the course of three years, the fellow has to pass exams and prepare a science research thesis, which has to be defended before the research council.

At the end of their courses, the fellows are despatched, in accordance with the state plan, to universities, scientific research institutes, design offices, works laboratories, etc. A considerable proportion of post-graduate students are kept on in a teaching capacity at the university itself: forty-two in 1963 (17 per cent of the total), fifty-three (18 per cent) in 1964, forty-five (14 per cent) in 1965, forty (12 per cent) in 1966, and fifty-seven (15 per cent) in 1967. Up to 70 per cent of the remainder go to work at universities, and 30 per cent to scientific research institutes and other establishments.

There is a post-graduate students' council at the university for discussing and solving problems concerned with instruction, culture and living conditions for post-graduate students; this council consists of representatives from the post-graduate students on different courses in different faculties. The council can approach the academic council or rector's department on matters requiring solution by them.

Post-graduate courses are an important source from which the scientific teaching staff of the university itself is augmented. In the past six years, about 300 of those who have completed post-graduate courses have been kept on as instructors and assistants at the university. At the same time there is a system at the university for improving scientific qualifications, by training candidates and doctors of sciences from the staff of the university.

This system of improving scientific qualifications is as follows.

Long range and annual plans for improving the scientific qualifications of the staff of the institute are compiled on the basis of proposals by the departments, and approved by the academic council. These plans are based on the prospects for developing research and teaching, the number of candidates and doctors of sciences in the departments and laboratories, and the prospects of individual members of staff. The plans also contain a number of measures for assisting those working on dissertations (assistance in acquiring equipment, travel within the country and abroad, publishing monographs, etc.). A proportion of teachers working on doctorate dissertations are made senior research workers, i.e. they may be released from teaching work for up to two years; at present there are sixty-three such cases. Some teachers are given leave for up to six months in order to complete the work on their dissertations. At this particular moment there are seventy-five of these. For a number of teachers, the teaching load is reduced by as much as 50 per cent.

As a result of all these measures, every year a considerable number of the university staff defend candidate and doctorate dissertations.

Between 1959 and 1968, 680 members of the university staff (assistants, junior scientists, engineers and laboratory assistants) defended their candidate dissertations. During this period, 209 members of the staff defended doctorate dissertations. The average age of those who defend doctorate dissertations has steadily dropped, from 47 in 1965 to 43 in 1968.

The great effectiveness of the entire system for training scientists and teachers and raising their qualifications is the result of the high standard of scientific research work at the university, and the truly creative atmosphere which is typical of the life of the staff. This has enabled the university to fill almost all the vacancies arising in its research and teaching staff from among its own students. It is therefore an extremely rare occurrence, usually of a purely personal nature, for scientists from elsewhere, from other universities, scientific institutes or industry, to join the university on a permanent basis. At the same time, the university itself provides large numbers of candidates and doctors of science for other universities and scientific establishments, including the Institutes of the USSR Academy of Sciences.

# 4. Scientific conferences, congresses, symposia and discussions

Every year the university holds many types of meetings, and considers this to be an important branch of its activities.

Addresses on the results of their research delivered by scientists at the university are aimed principally at acquainting all scientists with the results. In addition to this, discussion of the addresses by experts means that criticisms can be utilized in further work, and the lines followed by the research compared with similar research being conducted at other scientific establishments. Creative discussions, scientific conferences, symposia, etc., are a necessary form of scientific intercourse between scientists; they reveal new subjects, lines and approaches in scientific research work.

Great importance is therefore ascribed to the part played by university scientists in these discussions, also to their organization on a university basis.

The following figures indicate the part played by members of the university staff in scientific conferences, sessions, symposia, etc., organized in our country.

TABLE 14. Participation of university staff in national scientific conferences

|  | 1965 | 1966 | 1967 | 1968 |
|---|---|---|---|---|
| Numbers of congresses, conferences, symposia, etc. in which representatives of the university took part | about 300 | about 300 | 400 | 376 |
| Numbers of addresses and reports delivered at these by university scientists | 1 043 | 752 | 1 201 | 1 180 |

In addition to this, scientists from the university delivered addresses and reports at international congresses, symposia and meetings.

The university itself also organizes scientific conferences, symposia and sessions; representatives from many scientific establishments and universities in the country take part in these. During the past ten years, about fifty of these inter-university conferences were held. The number of scientists from other cities in the country taking part in the second inter-university conference held in 1968 was 148.

The different scientific seminars which are held are important to the scientific life of the university; these are seminars on an inter-department, institute, etc. basis, for departments and institutes at the university, and the results of individual research projects are discussed at them. No precise quantitative data regarding their activities are available. The following example gives an idea of the work done by these scientific seminars.

The seminar of the nuclear spectroscopy department of the physics faculty was inaugurated in October 1944, and since then has held regular weekly meetings (except during the holidays). It operates under Professor B.S. Dzhelepov, the head of the department and a corresponding member of the USSR Academy of Sciences. Since it was inaugurated there have been 780 sessions, at which 1,405 scientific addresses and reports have been discussed. Members of other departments and faculties at the university, members of the staffs of Leningrad VUZy and scientific establishments, members of establishments in other cities in the country, also foreign scientists visiting the university, have delivered addresses at the seminar in addition to the staff, post-graduate students and students of the department. Details of the work done by the seminar during the past three university years are given below:

TABLE 15. Work done by seminar of nuclear spectroscopy department, 1965-68

| | Total sessions | Attendance at sessions | Numbers of addresses and reports | Addresses and reports delivered by department staff | Addresses and reports delivered by staff of other university departments | Addresses and reports delivered by staff of other scientific establishments |
|---|---|---|---|---|---|---|
| 1965/66 | 31 | 40-300 | 65 | 29 | 10 | 26 |
| 1966/67 | 36 | 40-300 | 74 | 40 | 8 | 26 |
| 1967/68 | 29 | 40-300 | 70 | 41 | 7 | 22 |

An average of ten to fifteen students at the university have taken part in each seminar.

# Certain other aspects of the activities at the university

## 1. Administration of the university

The university represents a united teaching and research establishment; all its sub-divisions (faculties and institutes) are closely linked in all their activities. This takes a number of different forms and follows many different lines.

As regards teaching, this connexion takes the form of a number of the subjects at any one faculty being taught by the departments and teachers from other faculties, in compulsory laboratory work being carried out in the laboratories of another faculty, in students taking courses at other faculties, etc.

As regards scientific work, it takes the form of combined research expeditions organized by two or more faculties, the combined organization of scientific sessions and conferences, permanent participation by professors and teachers of other faculties and institutes in the work of seminars organized on combined and integrated analysis of a number of subjects, etc. In 1962, twenty of these combined subject analyses were carried out at the university; the figure for 1965 was nineteen, for 1966 it was twenty-one, and for 1968 it was thirty-seven.

The extension and widening of interconnexion between faculties and between institutes, and the maintenance and development of unity in all the activities of the university, are among the principal tasks for all the organizations of university administration, both faculty and general university organizations.[1]

All the work done at the university is supervised by the rector, who is appointed by the RSFSR Ministry of higher and specialized secondary education. The rector bears the full responsibility for the state of the university and its activities.

The rector is responsible for compiling the curricula and plans for research

---

1. The organization of the university administration is shown graphically in Figure 3.

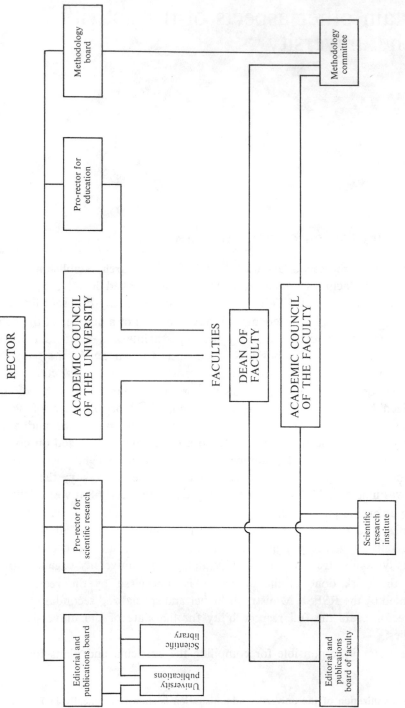

**Figure 3.** Organizational chart of the University administration

work, supervising ideological education, organizing entrance and final examinations of students and post-graduate students, organizing living accommodation for the students, etc. The rector has the appropriate powers to carry out the functions for which he is responsible; he can publish obligatory orders within his terms of reference, represent the university at all establishments and organizations, make agreements; open budget and other special university accounts in the banks; allocate staff and finance to the faculties and other sub-departments of the university, etc.

The rector delegates responsibility for individual fields of the university's activities to pro-rectors: a pro-rector for studies, a pro-rector for research work, a pro-rector for evening and correspondence classes, a pro-rector for administration and economics, and a pro-rector for capital construction (this last appointment has been included in the organization of the university in view of the large amount of new university construction work taking place in Staryi Petergof). Each pro-rector is entitled to decide all matters within his competence.

To enable him to supervise all the activities at the university, the rector presides over the academic council, of which he is chairman. Resolutions adopted by the council must be approved by the rector; while on many matters the rector can refuse approval, he only does so or alters a resolution if the procedural rules for considering a matter have been violated (awards of scientific degrees and titles, selection of heads of departments, etc.).

At present the academic council numbers eighty-nine. It includes the rector, the pro-rectors, the deans of faculties, the directors of the research institutes, the heads of the departments in the university, and other university scientists. The council includes sixty-six professors, of whom fourteen are academicians or corresponding members of the USSR Academy of Sciences and republican and specialized academies. The council also includes representatives from all the principal university organizations of professors, teachers and students, also from the party, trade union and *Komsomol* organizations. The members of the academic council which meets once a month all work at the university.

The academic council has an extremely wide range of functions, covering all the principal activities at the university. It discusses and approves the plans for teaching, education and scientific research, hears reports on the fulfilment of these plans, and takes decisions regarding the formation of new faculties, departments and laboratories; it submits its decisions for final approval by the RSFSR Ministry of higher and specialized education, approves decisions taken by faculty councils regarding the award of doctorates, selects the heads of departments on a competitive basis, awards professorships, appoints lecturers, and appoints senior research workers in accordance with recommendations made by faculties and the competition commission, awards annual university prizes for the best scientific work, puts forward the most eminent scientific

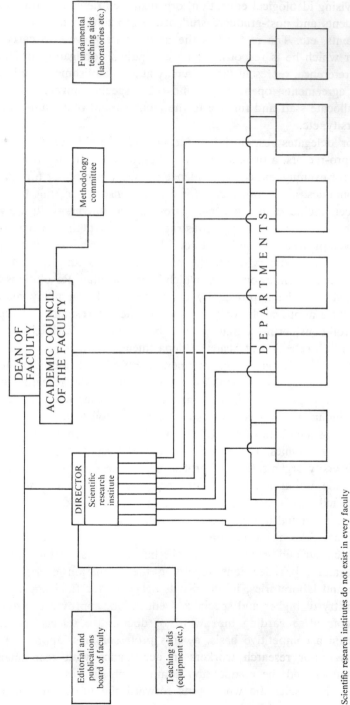

Scientific research institutes do not exist in every faculty

**Figure 4. Organizational chart of University faculties**

work for Lenin and state prizes, and puts forward candidates for membership and correspondent membership of the USSR Academy of Sciences, etc.

In order to consider and solve problems, not requiring approval by the council, in a more operative manner, there is an academic council presidium, which acts as a working committee and is formed of members of the council; these consist of the rector, the pro-rectors, the faculty deans, the directors of the institutes, and representatives from the social organizations.

The functions and activities of the council are defined by regulations for universities approved by the government, and by the appropriate documents issued by the USSR and RSFSR Ministries of higher and specialized secondary education, also by the Higher Attestation Commission as regards the award of degrees and titles and the holding of competitions.

Every year the council approves the plan for its work in the forthcoming academic year; in addition to current problems (the holding of competitions, the awards of degrees, etc.), the plan includes the most important and serious matters in the teaching and research activities of the university.

The initiative for deciding the matters to be discussed and resolved by the council, within its terms of reference, lies with the rector of the university, the members of the council, the social organizations, the faculty councils, and the RSFSR Ministry of higher and specialized secondary education; this applies both to deciding upon the work to be done in the university itself, and to general problems of organizing higher education and science in the country.

The activities of faculties are supervised by their deans. Deans are elected by faculty councils for three years, and are responsible to the rector and the faculty council for their work.

Each faculty has its own academic council, of which the dean is the chairman.

Like the university academic council, there are two faculty councils in each case. There is the council for awarding degrees, and there is also the council for submitting candidates for university titles, and for problems of teaching methodology and the election of teaching staff.

Public defence of dissertations for the degrees of candidate and doctor of technical sciences are held in the council for awarding degrees. In some faculties this council is in turn sub-divided into sections (for instance the council in the mathematical and mechanics faculty has mathematics, mechanics and astronomy sections). Each council includes all the heads of chairs, the leading scientists of the faculty concerned, also scientists from other organizations outside the university. From the scientific point of view these councils are highly qualified organizations including the leading experts in the city in the branch of science concerned. In 1967/68, the members of these councils in all the faculties amounted to 484; of these, 362, or about 75 per cent of the total, were professors. Among the members there were 135 (mostly professors) from other organizations. The organizations with representatives on the faculty councils include VUZy in Leningrad (the polytechnic, mining, technological, electrical engineering, engineering economics, finance and economics, shipbuilding, teaching and pediatric institutes, the timber academy, the institute of soviet trade, the institute of refrigeration, the institute of rail transport, the institute of water transport, etc.), Academy of Sciences' scientific institutes (mathematics, theoretical astronomy, physics and technical, silicate chemistry, high-molecular compounds, botanical, zoological, cytological, history, Russian literature, oriental studies, ethnographic, linguistic, etc.), regional scientific research institutes and establishments (geographical observatory, optical institute, institute of experimental medicine, national geological institute, geological survey institute, institute of exploratory geophysics, institute of psychology and neurology, institute of synthetic rubber, institute of petrochemical processes, and so forth), also other organizations and establishments (the Hermitage, the City court, the City prosecutor's office, the City newspaper editorial board, the north-western geological administration, etc.).

The inclusion of representatives from other organizations on the council means that problems associated with the awarding of degrees can be solved with the aid of better qualifications on a more objective and extensive basis, and that closer and permanent contacts are maintained with allied and similar establishments.

The second section of each faculty council is the council for submitting and awarding university titles and for teaching method problems; its size varies between thirteen and forty members in the different faculties, according to the size of the faculty and the complexity of its organization. These councils include the dean, his deputies, the heads of departments, leading scientists in the faculty, the head of the scientific library branch in the faculty, also representatives of the party, trade union and *Komsomol* organizations. Altogether these faculty councils include 373 persons, of whom 223, or about 60 per cent of all the members, are professors.

The principal task of these councils is to combine the efforts of the entire staff of the faculty concerned in the performance of the tasks with which the faculty is faced as regards the further development and improvement of its teaching, educational and scientific work. The functions of the councils include the following: considering draft curricula and programmes, reports on teaching methods, educational and research work done by faculties, reports on the work done by individual departments and members of the staff, solving problems concerned with organizing teaching and industrial practice for students, discussing the qualifications of candidates for post-graduate courses and classifying these candidates, holding elections for new teaching staff and faculty deans, etc.

We can see from the details given above that a large number of members

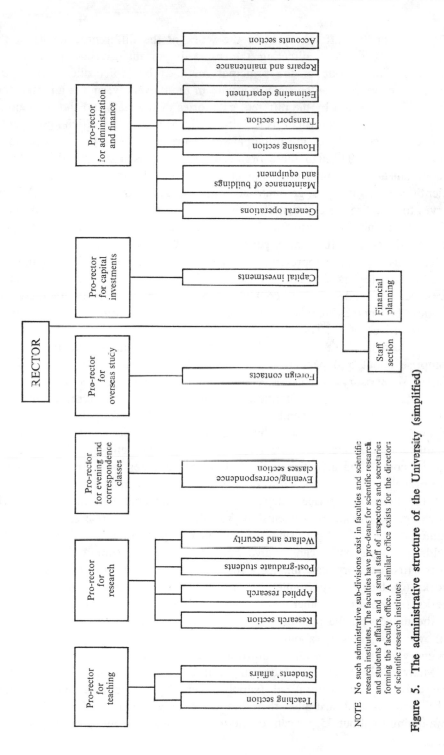

**Figure 5.** The administrative structure of the University (simplified)

NOTE  No such administrative sub-divisions exist in faculties and scientific research institutes. The faculties have pro-deans for scientific research and students' affairs, and a small staff of inspectors and secretaries forming the faculty office. A similar office exists for the directors of scientific research institutes.

of the university staff take part in the work of the different councils of the principal organizations directing the most important aspects of university activities. This is one of the principal methods by which the staff of the university can influence the state of affairs in the university, and is an important form of participation by the different categories of the staff and those attending the university in the control of its activities. This is assisted by official representation, on the councils, of the principal social organizations—party, trade union and *Komsomol*. Through these organizations there is a reserve link between the organizations administering the university and the masses of teachers and scientific assistants, post-graduate students, students and employees. All this serves to mobilize the entire staff of the university towards solving the problems with which universities are faced, and in particular those which are assigned to the university by the central government and the party organs.

There is no special representation, within the regulations, of any individual category (professors, assistant lecturers, junior teachers, post-graduate students, employees or students). The councils include representatives of all these categories, but not as representatives of the categories, rather as members or representatives of the social organizations.

The administrative staff of the university, its faculties and its institutes comprise about 500 persons. They can be sub-divided into three categories: (a) the supervisory administrative staff—the rector, the pro-rectors, the deans of the faculties and their deputies, and the directors of the research institutes and the other large independent sub-divisions of the university (the directors of the scientific library, the publishing house, the institute for improving the qualifications of social science teachers, etc.). Those employed in these categories control the activities in the individual branches of the university or its sub-branches, and are entitled to decide on problems concerning their activities; (b) the heads of services, departments and technical equipment (scientific, teaching, post-graduate studentship, supply, economic services, housing and domestic, etc.). In supervising the technical organizations in their particular fields, these personnel cannot give final decisions, but submit their proposals to the first category staff members responsible for them and under whom they work; (c) technical personnel in the services and departments (inspectors, clerks, secretaries and other employees). Taking all the administrative personnel at the university, the relationship between these categories is quantitatively as follows: first category about 13 per cent, second category 8 per cent, third category 79 per cent of all administrative employees.

Many of the functions of carrying out the teaching and research work at the university are centralized (supply, technical services, accounting, etc.). The faculties and institutes therefore have only small administrative staffs, amounting to about 35 per cent of the total number of administrative personnel.

## 2. The university libraries

A single library, the Gorki scientific library, provides the university with its library service. The organization of this library has been built up, for historical reasons and traditions, as follows.

There is a central purely scientific library, and there are branches of this library in the faculties and research institutes. There are fourteen of these branches; some of them serve several faculties at the same time, while on the other hand certain faculties have more than one branch. For example, the physics faculty has a faculty library and the library of the scientific research physics institute, while the social sciences library serves three faculties at once, the history, economics and philosophy faculties. Branches of the library differ greatly in size (numbers of books, numbers of readers, etc.).

When necessary, the branch libraries in the faculties and at the institutes will provide suitable books for organizing department libraries, and this may amount to several thousand books. These libraries are not, however, independent, being merely part of the branch library.

From the point of view of finances, staff and organization, the scientific library is a separate establishment, operating on an independent budget.

The nature and special features of the books held by the scientific library and its branches, the organization of the reader service, and the lines along which they are run, depend on the teaching, educational and research work to be carried out by the university. The general trend of work by the scientific library and its branches is defined by the academic council of the university, and the faculty councils, in accordance with their tasks.

Constant contact and links between the work of the library and university activities are maintained by means of a definite system of organization. In the scientific library there is a library council, approved by the university academic council; this library council includes professors and teachers at the university and the library heads. Similar councils also function in the branch libraries, and these also include representatives of the students. The library councils determine what books are to be added to the library, discuss the annual plans for additions, in particular foreign acquisitions and lists of periodicals being published, assist and consult the library staff in compiling and producing catalogues, hear reports on the work done by the libraries, etc. The inclusion of the director of the scientific library in the academic council, and the heads of branch libraries in the faculty councils, has helped to establish closer links between the libraries and the actual activities of the faculties and the university as a whole.

Every year, 120-140 thousand books are added to the scientific library and its branches; allowing for wastage, the library is increasing by about 100 thousand books a year. (Table 16.)

TABLE 16.  Annual increase of number of books in university library, 1961-69

(in thousands)

| 1961 | 1962 | 1963 | 1964 | 1965 | 1966 | 1967 | 1968 | 1969 |
|------|------|------|------|------|------|------|------|------|
| 3,466 | 3,509 | 3,594 | 3,658 | 3,728 | 3,867 | 3,965 | 4,058 | 4,165 |

In terms of value, library stocks are as in Table 17 (in thousands of roubles).

TABLE 17.  Value of library stocks

|  | Books | Periodicals | Totals | Foreign literature |
|------|------|------|------|------|
| Scientific library | 1 424 | 807 | 2 231 | 792 |
| Branch libraries in the faculties | 1 338 | 332 | 1 670 | 261 |
| In the exchange system | — | — | 264 | — |
| Totals | 2 762 | 1 139 | 4 165 | 1 053 |

These figures show the differences in the nature of the central scientific library and its branches. The amount of foreign literature in the scientific library accounts for over 35 per cent, while it is about 16 per cent in the branch libraries. The same applies to periodicals, the proportion of which in the scientific library is over 36 per cent, while it is about 20 per cent in the branches.

These differences illustrate the different basic purposes of the scientific library and its branches. The books in the scientific library are intended for the purpose of readers requiring scientific information. They therefore comprise a universal library of all published monographs and periodicals on the different subjects covered by the university, while foreign literature is also basically held in the scientific library. In most of the branch libraries the main work is that of serving the students, and most of the publications in these branches are therefore manuals and textbooks, which sometimes comprise 50 per cent of the publications in a branch library.

The numbers of copies of manuals and textbooks acquired by the branch libraries vary according to the curriculum, number of students taking a particular course, etc. On the whole, however, the number is quite large: the library tries to acquire an average of one copy of each textbook to every three students. In some

166

cases there are more students to each copy, but on the other hand each student is provided with his own copy of certain textbooks.

The high proportion of educational literature held by the branch libraries does not mean that they do not possess monographs and scientific periodicals. Bearing in mind the requirements of senior course students working on course or diploma projects, attending special courses or taking part in special seminars, these libraries also hold a small number of copies (one to three) of scientific books and periodicals on the subject with which the faculty is concerned.

The principal sources from which the scientific library and its branches acquire books are: compulsory purchased copy (all literature published in the country, in the Russian language, on the scientific subjects taught at the university is despatched to the library by the central collector for scientific regions in Moscow), the purchase of books in shops and bookstores in Leningrad, and subscriptions to the periodical press through *Soyuzpechat*. Over the acquisition of foreign literature in particular, the book exchange system is the principal source of supply. The library exchanges books with 756 libraries, scientific establishments and societies.

On 1 January 1969 the scientific library had a total of 26,629 readers. Every reader can use any of the libraries at the university. In general, the proportion of different categories of readers corresponds to the proportion of persons at the university: professors, teachers, scientific assistants, post-graduates and other staff—27 per cent; students—70 per cent; outside readers—3 per cent.

For the readers there is a system of reading halls and lending services in the scientific library and its branches. In 1968, 2,513,836 books and periodicals were loaned to readers, i.e. an average of ninety-three per reader per annum. Approximately a third of all the literature was taken home by subscribers, and two-thirds was read in the reading rooms.

The university scientific library is the methodological centre for all the college libraries in Leningrad. For this reason, it also carries out measures for improving the qualifications of employees at other libraries by means of a system of courses, seminars, etc.


## 3. Publications by the university

The publication of scientific works is the most general means employed for publicizing the results of scientific research performed by members of the university staff. By this means, the research results become public property, belonging to science in general.

The number of publications produced at the university can therefore be regarded as an important index of the effectiveness of its scientific work.

Taken by itself, of course, this index is relative, since it does not by any means in every case indicate the standard of the work, or its importance for the development of science. Nevertheless the number of publications is a direct reflection of the scientific activity of any particular team and its individual members, and, allowing for other data (assessment in reviews, translations into foreign languages, reprints, etc.), it is a qualitative index of effectiveness and scientific importance. Unfortunately the university does not possess quantitative data under these headings, but when the work done by individual faculties, institutes, departments, laboratories and persons is assessed, they are taken into account.

Figures for the past ten years have shown that the scientific activity of the university has become much more effective. This has, in particular, been reflected in the total number of publications. (Table 18.)

TABLE 18. Increase in scientific publications, 1959-68

|  | 1959 | 1960 | 1961 | 1962 | 1963 | 1964 | 1965 | 1966 | 1967 | 1968 |
|---|---|---|---|---|---|---|---|---|---|---|
| Number of works published | 1 753 | 1 922 | 1 978 | 1 968 | 2 013 | 2 394 | 2 392 | 2 715 | 2 939 | 3 276 |

These figures show that, over the ten years, the total increase in amount of publications has been 187 per cent; this has greatly outstripped the increase in the number of scientists working at the university.

The vast majority of published works are articles in scientific periodicals (about 90 per cent of the published works). The remainder are monographs, handbooks and textbooks. Scientists at the university ascribe great importance to the production of textbooks and scientific pamphlets, and their works under these headings make a great contribution to Soviet educational literature. In ten years, university scientists have published more than 450 handbooks and textbooks for universities, some of which have been reprinted several times.

The university staff have had their works published by a wide range of publishers. Most of them have been published by the university publishing house. About 35 per cent of all the scientific works written by members of the university staff have been published by this publishing house.

The Leningrad University publishing house is one of the largest in our country. Each year it publishes books, symposia, reports and periodicals totalling 1,800-1,900 printer's sheets. In 1968 the university publishing house published books and symposia under 177 titles, totalling 1,947 publishers' sheets. In 1967 it published twenty-three handbooks and textbooks, and in 1968 it published twenty-nine. In addition to this, the publishing house produces two periodicals:

*Vestnik Leningradskogo Universiteta*—twenty-four issues per annum of six series, and *Pravovedenie*—six issues per annum.

As a general rule, the publishing house only publishes works by members of the university staff, but it also publishes works by scientists, mostly educated at the university, working along the lines and in the traditions characteristic of the scientific schools at the university. It also publishes a small number of works by Leningrad VUZy which do not have their own publishing house.

The work of the publishing house is organized and planned on the following basis. The publishing house is an independent accounting establishment under the university. It operates on the principle of being self-supporting, and is not in any way financed by the university. The losses on publishing particular books (natural losses in publishing small editions of books on special subjects, for which the price is set extremely low by the state in the interest of the customer) are covered by the profits made by publishing larger editions of other books.

The publishing-house plan is prepared on the basis of proposals by faculties, which are considered by the editorial and publishing council. These proposals are usually 100-200 per cent above the publishing capacity of the publishing house, and this is the principal reason for the lengthy delays in publishing works written at the university.

The editorial and publishing council of the university, of which the rector is the president, and which includes representatives from all the faculties, approves the publishing house plan, and despatches it for final approval to the RSFSR Ministry of higher and specialized secondary education. This Ministry approves the publishing plan with the RSFSR Council of ministers publications committee, in order to avoid the duplication of publications, in particular handbooks and educational textbooks; it then incorporates the plan into the industrial finance plan and the plan for provision of materials.

The manuscripts of works included in the production plan are discussed by the departments and the editorial councils of the faculties; only on the basis of the recommendations of these bodies does publication go ahead.

# 4. International links of Leningrad University

Leningrad University has extensive scientific and cultural links with foreign universities and other educational establishments. In 1967 alone, Leningrad University was visited by about 450 scientists and specialists from thirty-three countries in the world, including 364 scientists from socialist countries, fifty scientists from capitalist countries, and forty-four scientists from developing countries, who read lectures and gave details of their experience and scientific data they had collected. During the same period, the Leningrad (Zhdanov) State University sent 305 professors, teachers, scientists, post-graduate students and students to different countries to read lectures, teach, carry out research work, study, and take part in international congresses and symposia.

On the basis of the scientific and cultural co-operation agreements described earlier, the university is continuing to develop lasting scientific contacts with the Karl Marx University at Leipzig, the Lorand Eötvös University in Budapest, the Oriente University at Santiago in Cuba, the Higher Economics College in Prague, the Monash University in Australia, and Stockholm University. In 1967, Leningrad University signed scientific co-operation agreements with the University of Iceland (at Reykjavik) and Khartoum University in the Sudan. In addition to this, agreements have also been concluded with universities in a number of other countries.

Scientific and cultural collaboration take different forms. Of these, the principal form consists of visits by scientists to read lectures, exchange of working experience, consultations on agreed subjects, the training of young specialists and post-graduate students under the supervision of highly qualified scientists, a wide exchange of books between university libraries, contacts between student organizations, exchange of artistic personnel, and exchange of sports teams.

Leningrad University scientists give a great deal of assistance to the universities in fraternal socialist countries. The basic form of collaboration, consisting of contacts between kindred departments and faculties in the plan for developing scientific subjects, preparing combined projects, etc., is being successfully developed on the basis of inter-university agreements and working programmes for scientific and cultural collaboration signed by university rectors.

Another important form of inter-university collaboration is that of unpaid practical work in industry in summer by students. Groups of students from the philological, geographical, physics, biological and soil, and psychological faculties at the Leningrad State University have visited Hungary, the German Democratic Republic and Czechoslovakia for practical work, and to acquaint themselves with the cultural life and famous places in these countries. In 1967, altogether 192 students of physics, history, art and philology from universities in socialist countries attended Leningrad State University. Altogether there were eleven groups of students.

Every year, firmer contacts are established between the party, trade-union and *Komsomol* organizations. There has been an exchange of trade-union delegations with Budapest University. The *Komsomol* committee keeps up a comprehensive correspondence and exchange of information regarding the most important events in the lives of universities, an exchange of literature, and photographic exhibitions showing the educational and sporting life at universities. In 1967 there was an exchange of teams of student builders, on an unpaid basis, with universities in fraternal socialist countries.

Leningrad University is developing international sporting contacts. In 1967 a team of sportsmen from Leningrad State University visited Krakow, in Poland, to take part in an international fencing tournament for the 'Barbakan' prize. In June 1968 there was an athletics meeting at Halle, in the German Democratic Republic, among four universities, Budapest (Hungary), Poznan (Poland), Leningrad and Halle. A selected team of forty students from Leningrad State University took part.

Leningrad University is successfully developing contacts with universities in the well-developed capitalist countries along the lines of exchanging scientific delegations, reading lectures, training young specialists, etc.

About 800 foreign students, post-graduate students and persons released from work for the purpose, from seventy-two countries in the world, are studying at Leningrad University. A great deal of work is done on training scientific personnel for fraternal socialist countries, also for developing countries in Africa, Asia and Latin America. In 1967 alone, 126 students from socialist countries and forty-three from developing countries received diplomas on leaving Leningrad University. In addition to this, twenty-eight foreign post-graduate students defended dissertations and were awarded the degree of Candidate of sciences. In 1967, twenty-two young specialists from socialist countries and about sixty young specialists from capitalist countries took scientific courses at Leningrad State University. They all studied under highly qualified supervisors, worked in the archives and libraries, also in the laboratories and the university departments.

Every year, month-long courses in the Russian language are held for foreign tourists visiting the USSR through the international youth tourism office *Sputnik*. Leningrad University is the teaching and cultural base for these courses. In 1967 and 1968, 200 tourists from the United States of America, France, Denmark, Sweden and other countries followed the course. In addition to practical work in the lecture hall, various excursions were organized, also meetings with writers, actors, composers, workers and young students.

The extensive international contacts made by Leningrad University are assisting in developing science and in cementing friendship between peoples.

# The University of Sussex

*by* Hywel C. Jones, Geoffrey Lockwood *and* Norman MacKenzie

# 1. Preface

This study forms part of a larger project entitled 'Planning the development of universities', initiated and directed by the International Institute for Educational Planning.[1] The idea of the project in the first instance was based on the hypothesis that in the rapidly changing kind of world in which we all live a university should have planning and managerial mechanisms, which enable the institution to respond sensitively to internal and external stimuli and which assist the institution's leaders to monitor and measure its performance within such a dynamic social context. There are very few studies of the process of change within higher education, and one consequence of this is a considerable confusion about terminology. The word 'change' is often used not only to indicate growth or modifications to an existing pattern; at the present time it also carries the more emotive meaning of 'improvement'. That is why the word 'reform' is often used as a synonym for change. But not all change is necessarily for the better. Some aspects of a university may be adversely affected by changes that effect improvements elsewhere. For example, a gain in efficiency may be secured by new procedures that can have a deleterious effect on staff and student morale. This is where the concept of 'planning the development' is significant. It is much closer to the idea of systematic 'innovation', which means purposeful variation in a system in order to achieve its specified goals more effectively. Higher education is now beginning to move slowly from a process of change in which individual components are varied for intrinsic reasons, such as the need to accommodate larger numbers, or to change some aspects of the curriculum, without studying their repercussions on the system as a whole, to one in which the interplay of changes is foreseen and appropriate planning mechanisms established to control

1. This study of the University of Sussex is based on the personal assessment of the three co-authors and does not necessarily represent the official attitude of the University or of its Chief Officers.

them. This shift in outlook may be discerned within individual institutions as well as within a higher education system as a whole. With this in mind, the Institute invited the Rector of Leningrad University and the Vice-chancellor of the University of Sussex to participate in a retrospective analysis of their own institutions from this point of view. In a sense, therefore, this has been a pilot study, designed to test the feasibility of such analyses. For, hitherto, the vast majority of universities have not possessed the means nor indeed the interest to conduct case studies of this kind.

The guidelines of the project laid down by the Institute asked the authors of case studies to analyse the ways in which their institution has adapted to changes in its environment by concentrating on the main problems which have faced the institution, how those problems were identified, how they were discussed and resolved and whether any 'critical' indicators were used to assist in their solution.

The age of the University of Sussex and the rapidity of development of the higher education system in the United Kingdom in the period since 1962 combine to present major difficulties in applying that kind of approach to this particular study, which is therefore concerned with the development of the University as a whole, rather than with any specific problem or programme within the over-all context. The University was founded only eight years ago, in 1961, and for the larger part of its history the problems encountered have been the normal ones associated with foundation and growth. Similarly, the development of the national educational system and the fundamental revaluation of it (witness the Crowther, Plowden and Robbins Reports) which has been taking place in the last decade have raised so many problems for each and every university that it is difficult to select the 'main' ones, though it is relatively easy to explain their 'identification' since they have in the main common origins at the national level.

In these circumstances, we have decided to concentrate our analysis on the development of the machinery of organisation and decision-taking within the University as a whole. It is more illuminating in this first instance to consider the changes made to the framework within which all problems have been and are being discussed, than it is to trace the handling of particular problems within that framework, though we hope to do this in a later phase of the project. In any case, since the development of this machinery has itself been one of the major 'problems' confronting the University—and one to which it has devoted much thought, time and effort—it can therefore be regarded as a case study in its own right of the University's attitude to the introduction of innovations and the resolution of critical problems. Moreover, we hope to illustrate the concern of the University from the outset to build flexibility into its total system so as to enable it to opt for or switch to new directions, as opportunities occurred. A description of many of the innovatory aspects of the University is given in *Innovation in the New Universities of the United Kingdom,* a report prepared for OECD by Professor H.J. Perkin of Lancaster University in 1969. The greatest difficulties facing universities which wish to develop flexible and responsive institutional structures are the belief on the part of their members that only marginal changes can be made, and the failure of members to think in terms of the institution rather than exclusively of their own department or particular interests.

The University of Sussex has paid considerable attention to its management and planning systems, especially during the past three years. It is now attempting to create an integrated system embracing the planning, control, operations and evaluation of its activities. To date, it has concentrated on building up an institutional atmosphere conducive to change and managerial innovations, and on the construction of a framework of structures and processes for participation and decision-taking. This is the base to which certain sub-systems and particular specialist techniques will be added, such as, for example, programme budgeting, computerised simulation models and an integrated management information system.

It is important to set the Sussex case study in its own historical context. It was written in the spring of 1969 during the first year of experiment with a newly-adopted planning process being applied to the University as a whole. The year 1969 was the halfway point in the 1967-72 five-year cycle (known as 'the quinquennium') over which government grants to universities for recurrent expenditures are phased. There are over eighty distinct units within the University, and during the academic year 1968/69 each of them passed through the process of defining their long-term and immediate objectives. During the coming academic year, 1969/70, the University's proposals for development in the period 1972/77 will be drafted. In 1970/71, the penultimate year of the current quinquennium, each of these units will have an opportunity to consider the draft proposals before the final version is prepared and agreed for despatch to the University Grants Committee (UGC), which has national responsibility for determining the financial allocation to universities. In the process of preparing the final document, the University will re-state its institutional objectives in explicit and operational terms. This will be the first time it has thoroughly reviewed and revised these objectives; in the period 1961-69 the aim of over-all university policy was to achieve the initial objectives set out when the University was established in 1961.

No case study of this kind can be divorced from an implicit evaluation of the qualities of leadership which have been shown by the institution. Sussex has had exceptional good fortune in its two Vice-chancellors, Lord Fulton and Professor Asa Briggs, both of whom have been deeply involved in higher-education policy discussions at the national and international level, and both of whom have seen in Sussex the opportunity to shape and mould an institution which could play a dynamic role in the life of the society in which it is located. Both, moreover, had the ability to delegate and to encourage their colleagues to be as fresh and creative as possible in their thinking about proposals for development. The three authors of this case study wish no more than that they fulfil the faith expressed in them by the present Vice-chancellor, Professor Briggs, in delegating to them the task of responding to the Institute's invitation to prepare this case study of the University of Sussex. It should, however, be understood that while care has been taken to reflect accurately the policy and actions of the University, the views expressed in this study do not necessarily represent the official attitude of the University or of its chief officers.

# 2. The national context

The particular history of the University of Sussex is an integral part of the more general development of higher education in the United Kingdom during the 1960s. Though this study cannot analyse in detail the national educational decision-making structure, we must describe briefly those aspects of the national machinery which seem especially relevant.

One of the major features of the British system is that the Universities, though nowadays largely dependent on the state for their finance, are autonomous institutions, established by charter, conducting their own affairs. In this respect, the universities are almost unique among British institutions financed from public funds in not being subject to any kind of direct ministerial directive.

The Government deals with the UGC. Except where individual ministries give research and development contracts for specified work, the government has no direct dealings whatsoever with individual universities. This remains true, though in the last year a Parliamentary Select Committee visited a number of universities to discuss current student unrest, and the Comptroller and auditor-general's department is now retrospectively reviewing university expenditures. The UGC's dealings with and allocations to individual universities are thus independent of direct government control. The Committee, whose chairman is a full-time official, consists mainly of university teachers, with some industrialists and administrators. It is the UGC which presents a case to the government for university development over each quinquennial period and for the building programmes required. It is the UGC which distributes the government grant among the individual universities, and it does so without reference to the government.

The UGC was set up as a new standing committee to the Treasury in 1919. Its terms of reference at that time were as follows: 'To enquire into the financial needs of university education in the United Kingdom and to advise the government as to the application of any grants that may be made by Parliament towards meeting them.' The UGC terms of reference were widened after the second world war by the addition of: '... and to assist, in consultation with the universities and other bodies concerned, the preparation and execution of such plans for the development of the universities as may from time to time be required in order to ensure that they are fully adequate to national needs...'

Successive governments, of whatever party, have consistently maintained, over the whole history of the relations between government and the universities, that there should be no direct confrontation between the government, on the one hand, and the universities on the other. However, the apparently passive function of the Committee as buffer or shock-absorber has changed with the times. In the course of the last few years, the changes have been more marked. This is not surprising in view of the recent rapid change in the universities, in number, size and complexity. The increase in the number of institutions on the UGC's grant list from 29 in 1963/64 to 45 in 1968/69 has imposed considerable pressure on the Committee to re-define its role and relations with universities.

But the explosion in the size of the student population and the increase in the number of universities were not the only reasons for change in the UGC's role. Universities are now regarded, and indeed regard themselves, as part of the spectrum of higher education available to qualified candidates. Society generally has become far more interested in what goes on inside universities, and universities in turn have had to relate far more to society's needs. As a UGC Report says, 'both inside each university and among the universities as a family, there has emerged a felt need for more conscious and deliberate planning, organisation and arrangement'. (Paragraph 561, UGC Development Report, 1962-67.) The same report, published in November 1968, adds the following significant policy statement: 'The sheer number of universities, their decreasing homogeneity and the correspondingly increasing variety of their offerings, together with national considerations ... demand some central appraisal if uneconomic duplication is to be avoided and a reasonable degree of differentiation of function is to be achieved ... A rational distribution of specialised functions seems to be not inconsistent with clear thinking or with a sensible distribution of the financial resources provided by the tax-payer. This is not to say that the Committee aspires, still less that it should rightly aspire, to a detailed planning of each university's development, or to a detailed oversight of such planning. But it is to say that in the increasing complexity of university affairs there should somewhere be a strategic picture. And it is today regarded as the Committee's responsibility to sketch that picture.' (Paragraph 568.) Consequently, it is the UGC's duty to ensure, by its advice to the government, that universities, as institutions, have at their disposal adequate funds for their total and continuing activities.

In terms of the national organisation of higher education in the United Kingdom, the publication of the Robbins Report in October 1963 may be regarded as a key date, since it was at that time clearly recognised that the expansion of universities and the growth of other forms of higher education had implications for each other, and should be regarded as a broad interlocking spectrum of opportunity for qualified candidates. In the light of the recommendations of the Robbins Report, the government decided to link the university sector, together with Science, to the department responsible for education at large. In 1964 the former Ministry of education was accordingly transformed into the Department for education and science, and ministerial responsibility for the universities passed to that Department. The Cabinet post of Secretary of state for education and science was created, together with three supporting junior ministers.

The guiding principle laid down by the Robbins Committee (paragraph 31 of the main report) was that 'courses of higher education should be available for all those who were qualified by ability and attainment to pursue them and who wish to do so'. By this, it was clearly intended to imply that all institutions of higher education, not merely universities, should be expanded and developed to meet the national demand for student places. The government, on the day following the publication of the Robbins Report, accepted this fundamental assumption in its own published White Paper; that statement represents the only clear formulation of national policy in higher education, and subsequent national policy has reflected this.

Indeed, university development in recent years is perhaps best measured against the recommendations of the Robbins Report. In 1963/64, there were 126,500 full-time students in Great Britain, with another 12,000 full-time in Colleges of Advanced Technology and the Scottish central institutions, which were subsequently to be given university status. The Robbins targets were 197,000 students by 1967/68, 204,000 by 1971/72, and 218,000 by 1973/74. The government then set a new target for 1971/72 of 220,000 to 225,000 —a minimum of 16,000 above the Robbins target. In fact, by 1967/68, the universities had nearly 212,000 students and it is expected that they will reach 220,000 by October 1969, thus arriving at the government target two years ahead of time.

The numbers of full-time students in universities in Great Britain, together with the numbers of undergraduate entrants (including entrants from overseas) and the latter as a percentage of the relevant age-group, are shown in Table 1 for each of the last ten years.

TABLE 1. Full-time students at universities in Great Britain

| Academic year | All students | Undergraduate entrants | Entrants as percentage of relevant age-group |
|---|---|---|---|
| 1958/59 | 108 534 | 30 657 | 4.8 |
| 1959/60 | 112 979 | 30 677 | 4.9 |
| 1960/61 | 117 379 | 32 420 | 5.0 |
| 1961/62 | 123 803 | 35 280 | 5.0 |
| 1962/63 | 131 474 | 37 597 | 5.0 |
| 1963/64 | 139 655 | 38 893 | 5.1 |
| 1964/65 | 154 401 | 44 448 | 5.6 |
| 1965/66 | 169 486 | 52 231 | 5.9 |
| 1966/67 | 184 799 | 53 575 | 6.1 |
| 1967/68 | 200 121 | 57 127 | 7.0 |
| 1968/69 | 211 750 | 59 550 | 7.7 |

SOURCE  Hansard 16.12.1968, Written Answer column 306.

NOTES  (a) The numbers for 1958/59 to 1964/65 include students at the former Colleges of Advanced Technology and estimates for the then Heriot-Watt College and the then Scottish College of Commerce.
(b) The numbers for 1968/69 were provisional.
(c) The numbers of entrants for 1958/59 to 1964/65 may have excluded some students taking courses other than first degrees and diploma courses.

The expectations on which fixed sums of money were provided by the government in 1967 and distributed by the UGC to individual universities were that by 1971/72 the following distribution of student numbers would be achieved by the universities.

TABLE 2. Estimated distribution of university students, 1971/72

| | | |
|---|---|---|
| Science-based undergraduates | 100 000 | |
| Non-science-based undergraduates | 84 500 | |
| Total | | 184 500 |
| Science-based graduate students | 20 800 | |
| Non-science-based graduate students | 17 800 | |
| Total | | 38 600 |
| Grand total | | 223 000 |

In fact, it is likely that universities will expand beyond 223,000 by 1971/72, without the provision of additional funding of the UGC, apart from any supplementary grants to meet any inflationary costs.

Mrs. Shirley Williams, Minister of state, Department of education and science, recently announced that even if the present proportion of the age-group proceeding to higher education remains the same, by 1981 some 650,000 places will be needed, more than half of which will be in universities. The

increased size of the age-group, the tendency to stay on to study, the raising
of the school-leaving age and the, as yet, unknown and unquantified effects
of comprehensive reorganisation in terms of larger fifth and sixth form opportunities, all indicate a likely numerical expansion of great magnitude.

An understanding of the national context is necessary for the Sussex case
study for three main reasons.

## A. Timing of the foundation of Sussex

A comparative study of the Universities of Keele (the newest of British universities prior to the establishment of the seven in the 1960s) and Sussex would
demonstrate the importance of the timing of the foundation of Sussex. Unlike
Keele, which was established in the early 1950s and at the beginning of a
decade of relative stability in education, Sussex was founded at the beginning
of a period of agreed expansion in the national system of higher education.
Its progression to an institution of at least 3,000 students within a few years
was guaranteed.

The growth and distribution of student numbers registered during the first
eight academic years are indicated in Table 3 and Figure 1.

TABLE 3.   Full-time students, 1961/62-1968/69

| | 1961/62 | 1962/63 | 1963/64 | 1964/65 | 1965/66 | 1966/67 | 1967/68 | 1968/69 |
|---|---|---|---|---|---|---|---|---|
| Undergraduates | 52 | 411 | 807 | 1293 | 1699 | 2133 | 2557 | 2686 |
| Visiting students | — | 5 | 6 | 6 | 24 | 28 | 23 | 27 |
| Research students | 31[1] | 26[1] | 85[1] | 115 | 207 | 331 | 400 | 358 |
| Graduate students | — | — | — | 68 | 160 | 271 | 253 | 386 |
| | 55 | 442 | 898 | 1482 | 2090 | 2763 | 3233 | 3457 |

1. Includes a few part-time students also.
NOTE  It should be noted that the University does not accept undergraduates for a first degree on a
    part-time basis.

The University's first undergraduates, fifty in all, came up in October 1961,
just as the Robbins Committee was beginning its survey of higher education
in the United Kingdom. The University naturally wished to plan its longer-
term development in such a way as to make the most effective possible contribution to the supply of places needed to meet the 'bulge'—a desire strengthened by the belief that the promise of rapid growth was necessary for a successful
start.

The original objective, conceived by the UGC, was that the University of
Sussex should grow to a total student population of 3,000 over a period of

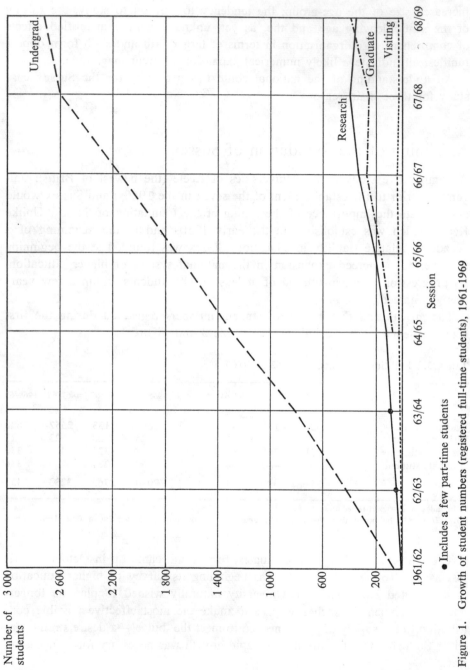

● Includes a few part-time students

Figure 1. Growth of student numbers (registered full-time students), 1961-1969

ten years. This proposed rate of growth was subsequently accelerated, following the government's broad acceptance of the enrolment figures proposed by Robbins. The University actually achieved the (1971) target figure of 3,000 by October 1967, thus completing in five years a programme of expansion earlier thought appropriate for a ten-year period. (The UGC Annual Survey 1965/66, together with other up-to-date figures provided by the UGC Secretariat, shows the growth of the group of new universities: see Figure 2.) This represented the most rapid development programme yet experienced by any university in the United Kingdom.

Sussex, it should also be noted, was the first university to be founded for a decade, and it was therefore a reasonable assumption that it would be able to recruit good members of faculty, well-disposed towards innovation because they had been experimenting with new ideas within existing institutions, or were anxious to experiment and had lacked the opportunities to do so. This may help to explain why, once the initial group of faculty had reached agreement on broad guidelines of policy, the earliest phase was more concerned with the working-out of the original concepts than with continual discussion of first principles. Sussex, that is to say, could benefit by the discussions about university structure, curriculum and teaching that had gone on elsewhere in the previous decade. Its new faculty members brought with them ideas that they wished to test out in the new context Sussex provided.

# B. Information network

Policy discussion about the national university system is highly concentrated; it takes place mainly in London, and involves a relatively small number of people. These are the members of those bodies or committees which co-ordinate or influence higher education, which relate higher to secondary education, and which link education to politics, industry, overseas aid policy, and economic and social development.

These closely-interlocked committees form a network which contains most of the information relevant to higher-education policy-making. The University of Sussex has been fortunate in having continuous access to it at a number of key points. Outstandingly, for example, the first Vice-chancellor and the first Pro-vice-chancellor (subsequently the second Vice-chancellor) between them were members of almost all the decisive committees or decision-centres on the network. There is nothing undemocratic about this situation: it simply meant that senior members of the University were constantly in touch with the evolution of national thinking, not least at the vital stage when opinion is forming but when no formal decisions have been reached. The first Vice-

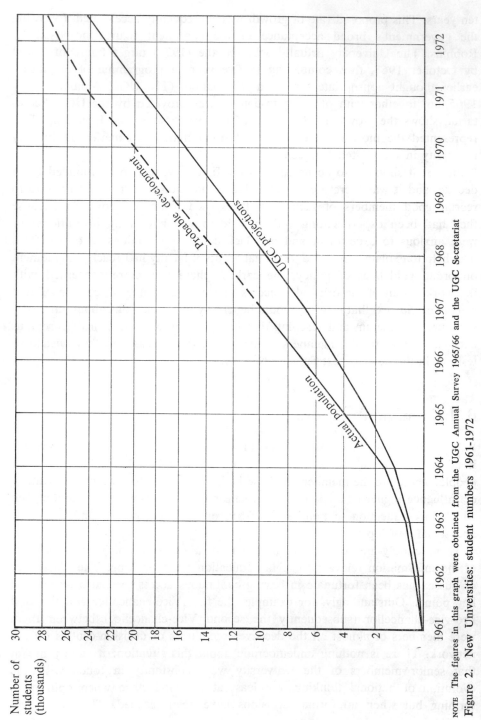

NOTE The figures in this graph were obtained from the UGC Annual Survey 1965/66 and the UGC Secretariat

Figure 2. New Universities: student numbers 1961-1972

chancellor was, for example, the first Chairman of UCCA (Universities Central Council on Admissions), the first Chairman of the National Society for Research in Higher Education, and Vice-chairman of the BBC: and the Pro-vice-chancellor was a member of UGC. They both were able to bring their national experience into the Sussex situation. This is especially evidenced by the location at Sussex of a number of research units or centres which were created in response to national need (e.g. the Institute of Development Studies and the Nitrogen Fixation Unit). Apart from these two most senior members of the University, there were others who, by virtue of the positions they held on national bodies such as research councils, were able to contribute formative lines of contact.

## C. The aims of the higher education system

Firstly, it must be appreciated that it is difficult to talk about 'a system' in the British context. The organisational structure of higher education has been the subject of widespread public discussion and modification since the founding of the University. It is only in recent months that the language of discussion in government circles has begun to move away from devisive terms (e.g. 'binary'—which distinguishes between the 'autonomous' universities and the 'public' colleges of education, technology, etc.) towards unitary concepts which regard the universities, polytechnics, Council for National Academic Awards (CNAA), colleges of education, colleges of technology, the Open University, etc., as parts of a complete spectrum of higher education. Nevertheless, at present, universities are still organised and financed quite separately from other institutions of higher education. This acts as a definite, though not insuperable, barrier to innovation. For it inevitably inhibits co-operation between universities and other institutions on such matters as an academic division of labour or attempts to rationalise the allocation of resources.

Secondly, it is implicit in the British system that there are no comprehensive official statements of its philosophy or practical objectives. It may perhaps be claimed that the Government's acceptance of the Robbins Report meant that it now adopted an implicit philosphy: that is, it was accepted that places for undergraduates should expand to keep pace with the demand from suitably qualified applicants. But there are no similar principles defined in respect of research activity, postgraduate training, re-training programmes, etc. Moreover, the Robbins plan in regard to the provision of places for undergraduates has been subject to criticism from some quarters ever since it was accepted. It has been argued that provision of places should be geared to the demand from the economy for the products of the system, not—as at present—to the demand from school leavers for places within the system. That line of criticism has not been generally accepted, partly for political reasons, and partly because no one knows how to estimate the manpower demand, or to regulate resources within universities with sufficient flexibility to ensure that they are kept in balance with changes in any skilled manpower needs that are determined. This is part of the price that is paid for autonomy in a university system, and ambivalences of attitude in this respect can be found in a number of official documents. We note, for example, the contrast between the UGC's *Memorandum of General Guidance to the Universities* in 1967, which was based upon applicant demand, and the *Dainton Report* in 1968, which was based upon the manpower planning argument.

Although no aims have been publicly stated, it is the case that similar conflicts of assumptions have been taking place over the past few years in relation to the research and postgraduate activities in universities. The details of these discussions are fascinating, but they are not entirely relevant to this case study. (They could well provide ideas and material for several special case studies.) What they illustrate is that the aims and nature of the system have been, and remain, in a state of debate and transition. In the absence of greater central control, and given the subtle interplay between various elements in the system, it is difficult to define a coherent national policy, and it is often the case that contradictory policies may be followed by bodies which ultimately report to the same government department, or at least to the government itself. Thus, with the exception of specific aims concerning the total numbers of undergraduates, the individual universities have had neither a set of national aims covering all of their activities against which they can formulate their own policies, nor formal aims against which they can check their performance. This fact is of fundamental importance in any examination of the internal planning of a university in the United Kingdom.

Thirdly, planned national aims and objectives are one way of providing external goals and assessments for individual universities. Alternatively, in their absence, a set of aims and objectives could be provided by a 'free market' economy in which universities would have to operate as educational firms. Although there are elements of a free economy in the United Kingdom situation, it is not sufficiently classical to be used for planning purposes. While the government, the UGC, the Research Councils, etc., do not specify aims, goals (or even timetables for policy discussions in some cases) they do control and adjust the supply of resources to universities to a large degree and in considerable detail (e.g. the UGC's procedures for controlling the expenditure of capital and recurrent grants, and its decision to concentrate certain academic fields in a few 'centres of excellence', etc.). Also, in regard to its products, a university is rarely judged as an individual institution. For a variety of historical reasons, the 'brand image' in the United Kingdom is accorded to the universities as a whole. Thus, provided a particular institution remains within a broad brand of competence, it 'sells' under that brand image. The academic and social 'pecking-order' which actually exists is largely *sub rosa,* or at least lacking formal acknowledgement, and its impact is felt in obscure and haphazard forms.

The above three points combine to illustrate that it has been, and remains, very difficult for a university in the United Kingdom to plan with reference to external and national goals and assessments. An individual institution may well gather information (particularly from the many reports commissioned by national bodies), and it will interpret, in its own style, the needs of the national environment. It can set its own targets. Even so, systematic response is vitiated by the procedures through which the university obtains its supply of resources. Unless it has made shrewd estimates, or lucky guesses, it may not be able to match its own plans to the resources it is given. If it has guessed wrongly, it still retains sufficient autonomy to devote some resources to its own favoured objectives, but it will find it increasingly difficult to enter upon new developments or continue old ones that run strongly counter to policies favoured by the agencies controlling funds, such as the UGC, the Research Councils, Foundations, etc. For while no specific national aims are formulated, there are 'filters' between the resource sources and the university and these 'filters' (e.g. an area sub-committee of the UGC or a subject sub-committee of the Science Research Council) impose their judgement of national needs upon the pattern of resource allocation (e.g. a Research Council will encourage applications for grants or fellowships in some fields and not in others). Since it is difficult for any one institution to foresee the decisions of dozens of such filters (operating without an over-all policy framework), it is impossible for the individual university to plan with accuracy, to select between alternatives or to evaluate its performance. It is also the case that the existing filter bodies consider and deal with separate units of each university; because they can give departments or research units special funds, their work may thus clash with the efforts of a university to strengthen the concept of internal corporate planning. Indeed, strong units within a university can and do use their access to these filter bodies to strengthen their own political and organisational position *vis-à-vis* units without such external recourse. Nevertheless, there are signs that the filter bodies are beginning to explain their objectives and relationships more systematically and are moving towards a more open method of planning which may eventually result in the production of more comprehensive aims and plans.

# 3. The foundation of the university

The history of the University itself needs to be borne in mind throughout this study, and some of the national factors bearing specifically on its establishment are set out briefly to explain the context of the University's early development. In particular, we stress the extent to which the University started from some nationally agreed assumptions, though, conversely, it should be noted that some of the founders of Sussex themselves contributed extensively to the shaping of national policy on the size, location and purposes of the new universities.

In February 1958 the Chancellor of the Exchequer announced the government's decision to establish a new University of Sussex, provided the UGC were satisfied with the plans as they were evolved and with the public support it might obtain. The UGC had previously (1956) recommended to the government that, on the basis of the future student population then envisaged, at least one university would be required at an early date and also that the Sussex plans were the only ones sufficiently advanced to make an early foundation possible. The local sponsors of the University of Sussex (primarily the Brighton Borough Council, with support from the neighbouring local authorities of East and West Sussex, Hastings and Eastbourne), had submitted a strong application for the University in June 1956. The Brighton Council's Finance committee had recommended that a site should be made available for the establishment of a university and promised financial support. Indeed, it is important to recall that Brighton had consistently pressed its claims for a local university since 1911, and this was clearly one of the deciding factors in favour of selecting Brighton as the first of the seven new universities to be established in the 1960s.[1] Local initiative and enterprise provided the initial inspiration and attractive sites, but national policy and national finance determined the decision.

1. A detailed and fascinating description of earlier proposals is given by Dr. W.G. Stone, the Chief Education Officer for Brighton at the time, in Chapter 10 of *The Idea of a New University*, edited by Professor D. Daiches (London, André Deutsch, 1964).

In determining the location of the new universities, the UGC was impressed by the conviction and enthusiasm of the various sponsoring groups. Most of the universities in this country had been established as the result of private or local initiative and the UGC was very conscious of the advantages which this brought. The interest of the local community is essential if a university is successfully to carry out its purposes; without such interest its full development could be frustrated; it can thrive only in a friendly environment. The UGC therefore looked for material evidence of interest and support in the form of financial contributions to either capital or recurrent expenditure. It attached importance to such practical support, not merely because it was an indication of local interest and commitment, but because it would enable the new university to develop more quickly and also to avoid complete dependence on central government funds.

The UGC Development Report for the period 1957-62 (paragraph 283) adds: 'In view of the growing importance of pure and applied science, we felt that the presence of industries in an area could provide a useful association and we therefore took account of the kind of industrial development in those areas which were claimants for universities and also of the existence of research institutions or organisations. On the other hand, we had the views of the Federation of British Industries; they regard it as important that a university should be part of a diverse civic community. The location of a university in a very large industrial centre might even have, in their opinion, some serious disadvantages; these included the difficulty of finding suitable residential accommodation for students and the tendency for such universities to attract an overwhelming majority of local students, living at home, educated at local schools and going into local employment after graduation. They regarded the cosmopolitan character of a university as one of its great educational and liberalising influences which could best be achieved away from the great centres, in the midst of well-established civic communities in which the university could play an important part. For that reason they regarded cities like Norwich or York as particularly suitable and did not favour the placing of new universities in the largest industrial towns'. The University of Sussex falls into this latter category. Nevertheless, its proximity to London and to the European continent has consistently been an important factor in attracting staff, students and academic projects to the University.

Once a suitable site had been pledged by the Brighton Borough Council and the UGC had provisionally arranged to reserve from its funds the amount of £1.5 million towards the foundation, an Academic Planning Board was set up in April 1958 to advise on the development of the new institution. The terms of reference of this Board were as follows:

(a) To consider the arrangements by which the universities may be assured of the maintenance of satisfactory academic standards at the University, on the assumption that the University will award its own degrees of Bachelor of Arts and Bachelor of Science.

(b) To consider the range of subjects to be studied at the University during the first year of its existence and the length and general character of the undergraduate courses.

(c) To prepare, in consultation with the local Committee, a petition for a Royal Charter for the University and a draft of such a Charter, and to select the persons to be named in those documents as the first governing body of the University.

(d) To select and nominate, in consultation with the local Committee, the first Vice-chancellor of the University and, with his advice, Professors of the principal subjects.

In sponsoring new university institutions the UGC had reached the conclusion that it was no longer necessary or desirable that they should be subject to the form of supervision which had held in the past, whereby an existing university retained ultimate responsibility for academic standards and granted its degrees through the agency of a new university college. This form of sponsorship had been adopted for the University College of North Staffordshire (now the University of Keele), but for the new foundation something different was desirable. The UGC therefore proposed that the new universities should be given degree-granting powers from the outset. This necessarily entailed the provision of certain safeguards for the maintenance of academic standards, since it was of critical importance that the new institutions should retain the confidence of the existing universities. The Academic Planning Board, set up by the sponsoring committee in consultation with the UGC, was seen as the necessary means by which the maintenance of academic standards could be safeguarded in the early years of the new institutions.

The Academic Planning Board for Sussex presented its first report to the UGC in June 1959. It suggested a first phase of development to begin in 1963 and reach 800 students after three years. In the same year it proposed to the Provisional Council the name of the first Vice-chancellor. The Limited Liability Company known as the University College of Sussex was registered in 1959; a Royal Charter for the University of Sussex was granted in 1961.

The UGC made certain other important assumptions, and these are set out briefly below, since they reveal the extent to which national policy attitudes were reflected in the original aims of the University, when established.

Firstly, it was felt that any new institutions should aim at not less than 3,000 full-time students as a minimum target, and some might rise to 7,000 or 8,000. This consequently implied a site of at least 200 acres, if all the buildings of the institution were to be on a single campus. In the early 1960s, particularly prior to the publication of the Robbins Report, there was an important school of thought which considered a 3,000 student population to be an ideal target figure for a university in the contemporary world. It should be noted that a figure of 3,000 represented a sizeable growth factor for many of the existing universities.

Secondly, the need to accommodate the increased number of students in the '60s and '70s was by no means the sole reason for the foundation of the new universities. The government, and the UGC in particular, and many university teachers felt the need for more experimentation in the structure of degree courses, in the content of curricula, in methods of teaching and learning and in university organisation and government. The decision to allow the new universities to award their own degrees from the outset consequently left them relatively free to innovate in all aspects of their development, and the members of the Academic Planning Board had been selected with a view to encouraging such experimentation. The first of Britain's new universities in the 1960s, Sussex consequently set out from the start to innovate not for the sake of novelty, but because the time seemed ripe for new thinking about the content and role of university education.

The UGC's interest in experimentation lay mainly in two directions. In the first place, it felt that the normal pattern of University government required adaptation to modern circumstances. It thought that, for national institutions, there was still too great a tendency to look to local rather than regional or national sources for lay help in the higher levels of university government, such as the Court and Council; that some of the higher bodies, particularly the Courts, could be reduced in size and their sphere of influence diminished; that staff representation on Senates and Council was still too hierarchical, and greater provision should be made for the representation of non-professorial staff on these bodies. Secondly, on the academic side, the UGC had declared that it wished to encourage the general broadening of the undergraduate curriculum, the breaking down of departmental organisation and the strengthening of the relationships between teachers and students.

In anticipating the possible demand for various types of graduate, the UGC had reached the conclusion that existing institutions were able to produce an adequate number of doctors, dentists, agriculturalists, foresters and veterinary scientists. It was expected by the UGC that the earliest developments in the new universities would be in the fields of arts, social studies, pure science and possibly at a later stage, in the applied sciences. Consequently, there were important limits placed on the academic areas which the new universities could attempt to cover.

# 4. The three phases of development

The history of the University's development may be broadly divided into three phases, and these are crudely summarised below.

## A. The first phase (1961-64)

In the first few years after it was founded, the University was essentially influenced by two factors: the concepts of the curriculum and teaching methods on which it was based; and the need to push ahead with the provision of the necessary buildings, scientific equipment, library resources, and social facilities.

The academic aims of the 'founders' rested on two basic assumptions: Schools of studies embracing a variety of disciplines should replace the traditional departmental structure, and the tutorial method (i.e. a tutor with two, three or four students) should be the heart of the teaching-learning process. The curriculum map was deliberately designed to give equal weight to arts and social sciences and the natural and applied sciences and to provide courses which combined specialist education with the kind of general education which sets specialist studies within common frames. (See fold-out Chart I between pages 200 and 201.) The organisation of the undergraduate curriculum on a School-of-studies basis was intended to emphasise the links between subjects. Each School embodied a pattern of studies, the distinctive character of which was determined by both its major subjects and the contextual or supporting subjects. The Schools were to help the student by giving him both an intellectual and a social centre. The undergraduate reads one major subject; he also reads other courses (contextuals) related both to his major subject and to the distinctive theme of the School. All undergraduates in the School take these contextual courses (not always exactly the same ones); the idea was for them to learn together and to let their common work support their major subjects. Because of this arrangement, a student sees much more of tutors and students in his own School than of those in other Schools. He shares with them a certain range of intellectual interests, and should not be lost in an undifferentiated crowd. The design of the original curriculum map is best described by a direct quotation from a chapter by Professor Asa Briggs, the present Vice-chancellor of the University, in *The Idea of a New University*.

First, greater stress was laid on the linked nature of the undergraduate curriculum. In each of the Schools, undergraduates were to combine study of a specialism in depth with common studies in which all the different specialists within the School would share. The specialism was to be the major subject. The common subjects were designed to set the different specialisms in their intellectual frame and to relate them to each other. In the language of the early discussions, the specialism was thought of as the "core" and the common subjects as the "context". Second, the Schools were envisaged not as super-departments, to which "subjects" were attached, but as centres of linked studies, some of which would be shared with other Schools. Certain subjects —for example, history and philosophy—could be studied as major subjects within the different contextual frames of different Schools; certain contextual papers would be common to more than one School.

The basic pattern, however, was clear enough. The familiar antithesis between "specialised" and "general" education was rejected: both specialisation and general education were seen as essential parts of a balanced university education. An undergraduate would be expected not to study a multitude of unrelated subjects side by side or one after the other, but continuously to relate his specialised study by impinging and overlapping studies. Thereby, it was felt, he would become not only an educated person, but potentially, at least, a better specialist. He would know about the bearings of his specialism as well as about its content. The contextual studies which would be common to different specialists in particular Schools would always include a critical evaluation of concepts and procedures, preferably comparatively, an examination of historical perspectives, and an exploration of contemporary issues and problems. In the School of English and American Studies and the School of European Studies emphasis would be placed on the unity of a civilization: in the School of Social Studies emphasis would be placed on the interdependence of different social studies in the contemporary world.

It followed from this conception of "general education" that the degree structure would be the same for all undergraduates. There would be no internal status distinctions. A Sussex graduate, whatever his School, would be given the kind of education in three years which would make it possible for him to compare, to relate and to judge. It would be a broader education than he would have received had he followed a conventional single-subject course or even a combined subjects course. At the same time, those graduates, necessarily a minority, who wished to go forward to research or to academic life would have been well grounded in their specialisms and well prepared to pursue them further. Within the teaching of the major subjects it was agreed that there was to be as little reliance as possible on sweeping survey work and as much as possible on learning "in depth" how to use the skills of the specialist. It was envisaged from the start that there would have to be fourth-year work, mainly of a specialist kind, for a larger number of students than had been conventional in the past. The development of such fourth-year work would not imply, however, that the three-year curriculum was less "complete" in itself than any other three-year undergraduate curriculum of a more conventional kind in other universities.

The main interest was in planning not for present change but for future change. There are likely to be immense rearrangements in the map of learning during the next fifty years—in the biological sciences, for example, where there is remarkable intellectual vitality, or in such fields of study as Asian history and civilization, which will pass from the domain of a small intellectual élite to a far broader section of the academic population. There is also likely to be a revolution in communications which will make the changes in the communications system over the last fifty years seem like an unsophisticated prelude. We knew, therefore, that a university curriculum which did not allow for far-reaching future growth and change would be doomed from the start. We also recognised our own limitations as surveyors of the intellectual world. As Graham Wallas once put it in relation to only a part of that world, 'every general survey of our social heritage must start from the vision of a single mind. But no single mind can see more than a thousandth part of the relevant facts or even a section of that heritage'. If only for this reason we were more interested in establishing conditions for growth than in plotting a map of learning for the 1960s.[1]

These academic aims essentially represented 'the Sussex ethos' (as it was frequently called at that time and from which all else was to follow); the elaboration of more detailed objectives from these broad aims and the construction of academic and administrative working procedures were the main concerns of all members of the University in its first phase of development. Sussex, like any other new institution, could not begin *ab initio* with a problem-centred approach. Until an institution actually exists, it has problems only in abstract. It can engage only in contingency planning, and the real weight of problems is not felt until those plans encounter the practical difficulties involved in applying them. At that point it becomes realistic to talk of problem-identification, and to shift the balance of administrative effort from concern with the original concepts to the actual modification that experience has shown to be

1. David Daiches (ed.), *The Idea of a New University,* op. cit.

necessary. Thus it takes time to develop both the awareness of problems or the machinery for dealing with them systematically.

Many problems emerged at Sussex during this first phase. In retrospect, however, they seem to have been mostly of a *procedural* kind: the *how?* and the *where?* rather than the *why?* The problems were dealt with in running order and within a clear framework of reference, but without the use of sophisticated planning machinery. An important area for future study would be the degree to which decisions about curriculum patterns, on the one hand, and physical resources on the other, are matched—or have common criteria—in the planning of new institutions or the development of old ones. There is considerable evidence that this is seldom done systematically, and the form in which recurrent and capital grants are made in the British system makes it difficult to achieve this type of congruity in planning even when there is a will to do so. Yet this may be one of the most vital elements in any attempt to make university academic aims, admission policy, capital investment and general policy more adaptive to changing social needs.

# B. The second phase (1964-67)

In this period of rapid expansion, when the student population rose from 1,480 to 3,200, problems emerged as more and more of the foundation 'map' was completed (the last four of the nine existing Schools of studies were established during this period), and as members of faculty and administrators gained experience of the machinery of the institution. But such problems, for the most part, were manageable: because the University was expanding rapidly, it was possible to meet problems by devoting fresh resources to them—of staff, funds, buildings, etc. The continual growth of revenue, and much flexibility in the ways it could be used, permitted the University to switch resources from one growth area to another as need appeared to dictate. Expansion also assisted organisational flexibility, and it was possible to add new structures, units, courses, etc. to bypass difficulties, since the expansion of existing units could also be catered for. It was therefore possible in this period for most problems to be met either on the basis of a consensus amongst the decision-taking groups, or by providing resources which satisfied all the competing claims sufficiently so that acute conflicts about priorities could be avoided. Again it may be said, the main efforts of the University were concerned with implementation rather than with design or evaluation during this period. Two comments may be made on the decision-making habits developed during this period. One follows from the fact that resources were broadly adequate to meet the demands of most major claimants: this tended to blur sharp conflicts about priorities, and encourage the attitude that everyone could have a reasonable slice of the available cake. The second is a related point. For similar reasons, it too often happened that implicit commitments for the future—which only fell due for implementation at a later date—were often made without sufficient awareness of the likely cost and other implications.

## C. The third phase (1967-    )

In this third period, which will probably last up to 1972 (the end of the current quinquennium 1967-72), the University was faced with a four-year period of relative stability in terms of the expansion of student numbers following the previous phases of rapid development. The University had already achieved its initial targets in terms of size, physical development and curricula. It has been faced in this reflective period with evaluations of its performance to date, and with increasing pressures to consider the priority allocation of scarce resources.

The most significant influence in this respect was the creation of academic momentum towards continuing expansion of specific subject areas. It becomes politically difficult to arrest this momentum later, and to redress the balance in favour of newer subjects when the decision-making bodies are largely staffed by earlier arrivals who have both vested interests and the political power to protect them. At striking example can be found in the need to achieve a fair formula for the allocation of limited funds for scientific equipment between the four Science Schools. Two of these were established much later than the others, but when they sought to buy equipment on the scale necessary to set up their laboratories they found themselves in competition with the two older Schools, who by then had a need for money to replace their obsolete equipment and buy more to support their continuing development. This kind of situation highlights the need for development planning. If projects are started without forward allocation of new resources to meet all their implications, critical shortages will arise. Now that the University is considering its expected burst of development in the 1970s, it has become essential to review its organisational structures and techniques, prior to that further stage of development, in order to avoid serious but unforeseen conflicts generated by claims on resources which are brought about by an undifferentiated enthusiasm for expansion. The first years of this period have therefore seen the transition towards new planning and organisational machinery, designed to meet the problems of innovation within an institution in which ongoing commitments inevitably claim most of the available people, plant and funds.

# 5. The organisation of the university

The analysis of the changing organisation of the University is divided later into two sections, one on structures and the other on processes. More detailed descriptions of these structures and processes have been included as appendices.

The experience of the last eight years has continually emphasised the importance of one critical decision about the organisation of the University which was taken in its first year. It was then agreed that the organisational structure should be reviewed annually. Here again it is necessary to understand the national context. English Universities are founded by Royal Charter, and Charters are historic, legal documents which require the governmental structure of the University to be explained in constitutional detail and language; and they are documents which are difficult to amend, other than through very slow-moving legal channels. This form of foundation has the considerable advantage that once the Charter has been granted, external constraints upon the University's internal methods of organisation are removed. However, it does impose upon universities a rather static and legalistic concept of government in comparison with business enterprises or even national government agencies; some claim, for example, that because the University Grants Committee's existence originally stemmed from an easily-rescindable Treasury resolution, not from a formal Charter or an Act of Parliament, it has probably been easier for it to modify its attitudes and policies in the light of changing circumstances.

The decision taken at Sussex in 1961, that the University would review its organisation annually, was therefore a basic one, in that it established the idea of continuing change and adaptation. This revisionist climate soon became familiar to all members of the University: though some members of the University complained that changes were indeed too easy and too frequent, they were in a minority. Why was this decision taken in the first place?

Firstly, the Charter had to be drafted and approved before the University

199

could become a legal entity, and the document had therefore to be based very largely upon the Charters of existing universities, not least because the Privy Council had indicated that any radical departures from traditional constitutions might mean a serious delay in the approval of the Charter. (It is an interesting example of the ambivalence of national bodies concerned with higher education—a point we noted earlier—that in its 1962-67 Development Report, the UGC complained that the new universities had failed to experiment sufficiently with their Charters.) Thus the Sussex Charter did not closely reflect much of the new thinking which had gone into the actual work of the University, or the ideas which germinated after the first members of the academic faculty had been appointed and begun to put plans into practice. It was therefore necessary to devise an organisational structure which, without violating the formal terms of the Charter, was considerably different both in spirit and in its detailed interpretation.

Secondly, it was realised at the very beginning of the University that its organisation had to be modified as its size and nature changed. It was foreseen that since the University would double in size every year for several years, and that it would be constantly widening the range of its activities, there would be a need to revise its organisational structure to match the breadth of its activities.

It is impossible to say which of these two reasons was the dominant one, but together they created a dynamic rather than static attitude towards the organisation of the University, and led to an emphasis on practical rather than formal and constitutional thinking. It would be true to say that, in a general sense—and because it was a new foundation—the University was task-orientated from the outset, even if some of the tasks were not clearly or fully formulated in the early years.

The fact that the organisation of the University had to be reviewed each year, in a sequence which involved the participation in some way or other of most members of faculty, clearly demonstrated that the concept of organisation was one in which the units, complexes and areas were not to be segmented and fixed; they were to be related and their boundaries and the structure of their inter-relationships were to change, though patterns would be fixed for one year at a time for reasons of organisational efficiency. The effort was continually to find points of overlap, connexion and co-operation between units, rather than to stress the formal jurisdictional frontiers between them.

In general terms, most senior members of the University took a view similar to that expressed by Everett M. Rogers of Michigan State University, who wrote:

> A modern university is a social system in equilibrium with all of its parts in functional inter-relatedness...tinker with one part and you cause consequences

Chart I

| UDIES | | B.Sc. DEGREE COURSE | | | | |
|---|---|---|---|---|---|---|
| | | SCHOOLS OF STUDIES | | | | |
| EURO 1961 | SOC 1961 | A.S. 1965 | B.S. 1965 | M.P.S. 1962 | M.S. 1964 | COURSES |
| | | | | | | Preliminary (15%) |
| | | | | | | |
| | | | | | | |
| | | | | | | |
| | | | | | | |
| | | | | | | |
| | | | | | | Structure & Properties of Matter |
| | | | | | | Mathematics |
| | | | | | | Optional Course |
| | | | | | | Supporting Courses (20-25%) |
| | | | | | | |
| | | | | | | |
| | | | | | | |
| | | | | | | |
| | | | | | | Arts/Science Scheme |
| | | | | | | MAJORS (60-65%) |
| | | | | | | |
| | 1965 | | | | | |
| 1966 | | | | | | |
| | | 1966 | | | | Automatic Control |
| | | | 1966 | | 1966 | Biochemistry |
| | | | 1965 | | | Biology |
| | | | | | 1962 | Chemistry |
| | | | | | 1964 | Chemistry, theoretical |
| 1962 | 1961 | | | | | |
| | | 1965 | | | | Electronics |
| | | 1965 | | | | Eng. Science, Elect. |
| | | 1965 | | | | Eng. Science, Mech. |
| | | 1968 | | | | Eng. with Op. Research |
| | | 1966 | | | | Eng. with Soc. Studies |
| 1962 | | | | | | |

in many parts... one way that such a system insulates itself from the possible dangers of such unanticipated effects is to institutionalise its functioning...but they become formalised in a way that impedes innovation and this need not be so...[1]

The hope at the University of Sussex in 1961 was indeed that sectionalism could be avoided. The secondary and beneficial implications of the decision to institutionalise annual reviews were that the organisation of the University had to be clearly described and explained to all members once a year and that discussion about the organisation had to be concentrated into one structured sequence each year, thus saving the time and risks involved in consideration throughout the year of specific proposals for change in isolated areas out of the context of the review of the inter-related whole. When, in 1967/68, it was decided to conduct a major organisational review with the help of a firm of management consultants (McKinsey and Co.), it was possible to handle that review in the same way as other annual reviews: it was an open process. What is more, the established habit of annual reviews and changes made it much easier to use consultants for such a review than was the case in some other British universities, where strong opposition to a move of this kind was encountered.

In this context it is essential to recognize that there is normally a gap between the real situation and the constitutionally described one when one discusses university organisation. At Sussex, however, the power structure has so far been closely linked to the Committee structure. This linkage was strengthened by what may be called a system of 'informational democracy', whereby full public account of proposed changes is given to faculty, and many opportunities are provided for discussing them.

The Organisation of University Business document is the result of each year's annual review. The documents produced in 1961/64 were relatively simple statements of the Senate Committee Structure. In 1965/67 they were extended to cover the Council Committee Structure. In 1967 they began to include the Management Structure, and in 1968 the Planning and Budgetary processes became part of the series. An historical review of these documents and associated papers would reflect the increasing complexity of the organisation and also the way in which all aspects concerning organisation have been seen increasingly to be inter-related. A study of the series of annual documents illustrates the continuing adaptation of the University's organisational system to meet its changing needs and nature.

The Organisation of Business document consists of four parts: The Nature

1. Everett M. Rogers, *Diffusion of Innovations,* New York, Free Press of Glencoe, 1962.

of the organisation, the Committee structure, the Officer structure and the Planning process. The first part provides an outline of the organisation. The remaining sections describe different aspects in detail. The Committee structure states the terms of references and memberships of each committee; the Officer structure describes the method of appointment, length of tenure, role and reporting relationships of every officer of the University, and the Planning process sets out the planning and budgeting systems of the University.

# 6. Organisational structures

The term 'organisational structures' embraces both units of organisation and the pattern of relationships which govern their activities. This study is concerned primarily with the patterns of their relationships (i.e. the machinery of government and management) rather than with the composition of units.

The committee and management structures in 1963/4, 1967/8, and 1968/9 may be studied in fold-out Charts II and III (between pages 208 and 209).

It is assumed that readers will be aware of the limitations of two-dimensional tree-charts; such charts can only select the main operating relationships from the mass of cross-links and inter-relationships which necessarily exist. Neither do they signify levels of status.

The main trends demonstrated by the charts are:

(a) that considerable change has taken place. The charts over-simplify the changes in the sense that it is easy to overlook the fact that a change of line or location represents a major shift in the duties, existence or authority of a unit, an officer, or a committee;

(b) the increasing complexity of the structures as the institution has grown in size and scope. The 1963/64 charts illustrate a clear pattern which became confused by 1967/68: in that year a major review was undertaken with the help of outside management consultants and the 1968/69 charts illustrate that a clearer pattern on a larger scale emerged from that review;

(c) the changing determinants of the boundaries. The 1963/64 pattern was based upon boundaries which are traditional in most English universities (divisions between 'academic' and 'financial' responsibilities, the separation of 'academic' and 'administrative' duties); the basis of the boundaries can be seen to be changing in 1967/68 and to have changed fundamentally by 1968/69 to an 'area' basis; and

(d)  the closer relationship between the committee and management structure. In the 1963/64 and 1967/68 charts the patterns of committee and management structures do not mirror each other, whereas by 1968/69, their bases are almost identical.

Since this section deals mainly with the patterns of inter-relationships, we need to indicate briefly the ways in which the University has used the design of units to anticipate problems, to foster internal change, or to stimulate the development of the institution in a particular direction. The units themselves are shown on the charts. Since its foundation, the main academic units of the University have been the Schools of studies. These multi-discipline, inter-disciplinary and overlapping Schools were designed by the University to reflect its teaching and research philosophy. Their nature and size makes them more flexible and 'open' than the normal basic academic unit (i.e. the single-discipline department) and allows the University to develop through cellular growth. In the foundation phase of the University's history, the problems could be met by developing the Schools, but in the phase of rapid expansion new problems emerged. The need to co-ordinate groups of Schools led to the creation of the Arts and Science Deans' offices; the need to ensure the effective development and integration of the technology of education into the teaching processes across Schools led to the establishment of the Centre for Educational Technology; the need to promote and organise research in areas not synonymous with the boundaries of Schools led to the introduction of a range of research centres (e.g. Social Research Centre, Science Policy Research Unit, Centre for the Study of Multi-Racial Societies); and the need to co-ordinate and focus the efforts of the various sections of the University on the life of the local community through the agency of a Continuing Education Programme. The University's ability to create new units, often of an innovatory nature in the context of the United Kingdom, to meet new problems or changing circumstances, remains evident in the third phase of its history. The concept of the Vice-chancellor's office as the key co-ordinating and initiating unit was introduced in 1968, with the intention of helping to focus the philosophy of the University as a corporate entity on its activities and problems. The merging of what had been a rather traditional Library with the unit responsible for audio-visual teaching aids into one Learning Resource complex took place in 1969, and provides yet another example.

*The design criteria of the structures*

The charts of the committee structure illustrate that the early committee structure of the University rested on three main and related assumptions, and these are described in some detail, with an analysis of their evolution until 1969.

The first assumption was that there should be a committee responsible for each aspect of the University's work. This approach stemmed from the concept of the University as a self-governing body of scholars, and the desire to involve all members of faculty, through the representative principle, in some activity of the University in addition to their own teaching and research responsibilities.

At this point it needs to be stressed that the distinctions traditionally drawn between professorial staff and non-professorial staff have been very much less at Sussex than has been the case in most other British universities. This is largely due to the decision to make a School rather than a department the key unit in its structure. The lack of distinction is reflected by the fact that no special provision is made for 'young' teachers in the committee structure; it is also exemplified by the fact that the non-professorial staff refused the UGC's official invitation to have separate discussions with them at the time of the UGC Visitation in 1966 (a normal UGC procedure) on the grounds that the non-professorial/professorial division was irrelevant to them in the Sussex context.

The results of the application of the principle of one-committee-one-aspect may be seen in the complexity the committee structure had developed by 1967/68. Changes had been occurring prior to 1967 (e.g. committees responsible for ceremonials, public lectures, etc. had been disbanded and the organisation of those activities made the responsibility of one member of faculty appointed by the Senate and reporting annually to the Senate). In 1967, however, when the major organisational review was undertaken, it was decided that the number of committees should be reduced. This decision arose from an acceptance of the view that, although a few major committees must accept collective responsibility and faculty must be kept informed of discussions and decisions, it is inefficient and wasteful of faculty time to have sub-committees responsible for every activity of the University. Such a system reduced the ability of individual 'managers' to take initiatives and also allowed inefficient 'managers' to rest upon the concept of committee responsibility, thus causing a great deal of frustration by the resultant inefficiency of the decision-making/taking procedures. Consequently, many committees were disbanded in 1968 (e.g. catering, bookshop, library, academic services, health service).

Secondly, it was assumed that the academic, social, financial and physical aspects of activity could be considered separately. This belief followed logically from the traditional division of responsibilities between the Senate and the Council, but it was carried through into the Senate substructure. For example, while the Academic Board discussed academic developments, these then had to be re-discussed by the planning committee because the Academic Board was not authorised to discuss the resource implications of proposals. The fact that the Academic Board, the planning committee, the finance and general purposes committee and the building committee were all of equal status with separate reporting relationships to the Senate or the Council, led to considerable confusion and overlaps. It also contributed to one of the constant factors in the history of the University, namely the great authority of the Vice-chancellor and the then Pro-vice-chancellor, since they were the only senior officers in a position of authority on all six of the major committees. The system was viable only because of the role of the Vice-chancellor and the co-ordinating function of key administrative officers, though not all of these attended the four key committees. It became unworkable, or intolerable, not through the increasing scale of activity, but on account of the introduction of systematic planning and resource allocation mechanisms. These mechanisms began to relate forward budgetary estimating to faculty-student numbers in each course of study, and finally to building and space requirements. These were constructed through the planning committee, and by 1967 that committee had become the dominant decision-centre. The major organisational review in 1967 confirmed this dominance by making the planning committee the executive committee of both the Council and the Senate, by abolishing the finance and general purposes committee and the Academic Board, by changing the buildings committee into a body to which the planning committee referred physical planning issues after the critical policy decisions had been taken, and by channelling all information to the Senate and the Council through the planning committee. The principle of division of committees by 'expertise' was therefore abandoned during the 1967 review, and replaced by the 'area' principle, described in Part One of the Organisation of the University. The three principal sub-committees of the planning committee (i.e. arts and social studies, science, social policy) are responsible for all aspects of activity in their areas (planning, finance, physical facilities, functional development).

Thirdly, it was thought possible that, beneath the main committees referred to above, there should be division into specialist 'topic-based' committees and general committees. The Academic Board had sub-committees on admissions, graduate studies, research, etc., responsible for those specialist activities across all Schools and subjects, yet the Schools themselves represented a parallel sub-structure having the right to discuss any topic relevant to their activities. Similarly, there had existed in the 'social' area, specialist committees (e.g. catering) and area committees (e.g. Falmer House committee) even though their responsibilities overlapped.

Gradually, linking committees emerged between these two types of sub-structure (e.g. arts and science sub-committees under the Academic Board, social policy committee in the social area) and it was those committees which were given additional responsibilities following each annual review, until finally they were made the dominant ones under the planning committee in the 1967 review.

The charts of the committee structure illustrate that there was a clear pattern up to 1963/64 and that the pattern became confused and complex over the next three years before a new and more coherent pattern was created in 1968/69. As explained earlier, the latter pattern has been emerging during the period of confusion. The bases of the new structures may be summarised as follows:

1. The number of committees should be kept to a minimum. This restriction stemmed partly from a general feeling that the committee system was using too much faculty time, partly from the need to reduce overlapping responsibilities, and partly from the cost of servicing committees. However, the main reason was the recognition that standing committees are not the most efficient mechanism in all stages of decision-taking. These various stages are listed below, together with crude summaries of the attitude towards them, formulated by the University in 1967/68.

(*a*) *Information collection:* This function is better conducted by offices or officers (e.g. the planning officer in regard to institutional self-knowledge; the information officer through internal journals in regard to the opinions of members of the University; the planning officer in regard to information on the national context and trends).

(*b*) *Information assessment:* This function can be performed by offices and officers in regard to routine information. If assessment requires joint discussion by representatives of groups or skills then a temporary working party or a consultative group can perform this function rather than establish a standing committee.

(*c*) *Decision-taking:* Clearly major policy decisions in a University have to be taken by representative committees and, as far as possible, they should be taken by committees having a wide range of responsibilities in order that each decision can be seen in its widest context. However, many minor decisions need not involve a committee, they can be taken by an individual to whom responsibility has been committed (the original meaning of the word 'committee'), who could be either a faculty or student representative or an appointed officer.

(*d*) *Communication of decisions:* This function can be performed by officers (e.g. the information officer through internal journals, the Vice-chancellor through regular general meetings with the faculty or students).

(e) *Implementation:* Committees are not very efficient devices for implementing decisions. If they appear to have responsibility for the implementation, or for the management of activities, and services, it detracts from the responsibility of the individual 'managers'.

(f) *Evaluation:* The evaluation of the results of decisions requires specialist skills which should be provided by individuals or research teams rather than by standing committees.

Thus, the analysis along the above lines in 1967 of the work for which committees had hitherto been responsible led to a reduction in the number of committees and the strengthening of the management structure and the communications processes.

2.  The management structures should be strengthened and the patterns of the management and committee structures should reflect each other. In summarising the structures of the early history of the University, little mention has yet been made of the management structures. The summary indeed is true to the attitude of that period, since the organisation of the University was always described and discussed in terms of committees. The entrepreneurial role of the Vice-chancellor in relation to the University, and of Deans in relation to the Schools, was an observable fact, but its existence was explained in terms of the authority they derived from the chairmanship of committees. The management structure, had that term been acceptable or the concept comprehensible, would have been taken to refer to the structure of the permanent administration. However, over the period 1964-67, the structure emerging from the chairmen of committees and the administration were brought more and more within one management framework under the Vice-chancellor.

The administrative structure consisted of the permanent professional administrative staff. In 1961-63, it was unified under the Registrar, though the specialist branches emerged into separate offices as the range and amount of work increased. By 1968 the Registrar, Bursar, Finance officer and Data processing officer were responsible for separate offices, reporting to the Vice-chancellor; the Appointments officer, the Accommodation officer, the Business manager and the Private finance officer had emerged as virtually independent officers; and the Planning and Information officers had formed the nucleus of the Vice-chancellor's office. In addition, 'area' offices, which had commenced with

Chart II

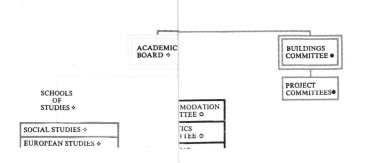

ACADEMIC
BOARD ✧

BUILDINGS
COMMITTEE ●

PROJECT
COMMITTEES●

SCHOOLS
OF
STUDIES ✧

MODATION
TTEE ○

SOCIAL STUDIES ✧

EUROPEAN STUDIES ✧

ICS
I TEE ○

Chart III

OFFICE OF THE

DEANS OF 3
ARTS SCHOOLS

NIOR
TOR

STUDENTS'
UNION

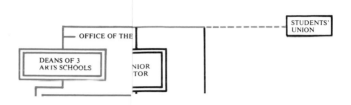

the establishment of the office of the Arts Deans in 1963, had developed in the arts, science and social policy areas with operational independence from the central administration and with responsibilities which cut across the specialist divisions of central administration. These 'area' offices also blurred the boundaries between the work of professional administrators and members of the academic faculty undertaking administrative duties. One of the results of these two trends, increasing specialisation at the centre and increasing devolution of responsibility to area offices, was the need to strengthen the Vice-chancellor's office in order to achieve co-ordination of administrative effort, particularly in the planning sphere, but also in the resolution of problems which crossed administrative boundaries.

Another significant facet of the management structure emerged from the duties of chairmen of committees. The Vice-chancellor derives most of his operating authority from the Senate and the Council. The Vice-chancellor has always devolved some of his authority, and the pattern of devolution has been remarkably constant, although two Vice-chancellors have by now held office. There have always been key officers responsible for arts, science and social policy on behalf of the Vice-chancellor: in 1963/64 the Pro-vice-chancellor acted as the 'deputy' Vice-chancellor and was responsible for arts and social studies, the Dean of physical sciences was responsible for science and the senior tutor for social policy. In 1967/68 the Pro-vice-chancellor (planning) was responsible for the arts and social studies Schools, the Pro-vice-chancellor for the science Schools and the Senior tutor for social policy. In 1968/69, the devolution to the chairman of arts, the chairman of science and the Senior tutor was formalised (the Pro-vice-chancellorship at that time became a 'ceremonial' office; and the newly-created Deputy vice-chancellorship has not been filled).

# 7. Critical organisational questions

Rather than describe the charts in detail, and the changes illustrated by them, we prefer to look at them from the point of view of the major questions relevant to university internal government over the past few years. In doing so, we hope to show the ways in which the organisational structures of the University of Sussex have changed to meet changing circumstances and how the consistent objective has been to encourage all members of the University to play a part in its development by creating the kind of framework within which this would be possible.

## A. The role of lay (external) members

The existence of Royal Charters has guaranteed the independence of universities in England and their freedom from interference in their government by external bodies. However, Charters have normally required lay members to be given a majority voice in the major financial decisions within the University. In the modal (or standard) system, the Council of the University is the governing body which has the ultimate power, although the Senate is recognised as the major academic authority. Charters usually require that lay members form a majority of the Council; this originates from the period when the majority of university income was not derived from the national government and when academic salaries were not the subject of national negotiations. External sources of finance, such as education authorities, industrial firms and local philanthropists, were therefore regarded as keepers of the University's purse-strings. The Sussex Charter follows that traditional pattern and the 1963/64 committee structure chart illustrates the role of Council and its separate sub-committee structure, in which lay members predominated.

The situation has now changed since that type of pattern was first devised.

The majority of University monies are received from the national government, salary scales are fixed nationally, controls on University spending are set by the University Grants Committee and are scrutinised by the Public Accounts committee of Parliament, and academics are heavily involved in financial decisions as advisors to the government or to industry. There is therefore less need, both in terms of control upon expenditure and lack of internal expertise, for the controlling role of lay members. Indeed, in many universities, the lay members may now be less qualified controllers of expenditure (and therefore of planning decisions) than almost all other representatives of the various interests concerned with the work of the University. These environmental changes have been reflected in changes in the organisation of Sussex University since 1961.

In summary, the sequence of changes in the committee structure was that joint Senate-Council committees were established in common areas, Senate committees began to undertake work which might otherwise have been conducted by a Council committee (e.g. the planning committee gradually increased its scope *vis-à-vis* the finance committee), until finally in 1968 the Council sub-structure was abolished and a minority of lay members placed upon the key committees (e.g. planning committee, social policy committee). In terms of the management structure, the trend has been one of increasing the authority of the Vice-chancellor and decreasing that of the senior lay officers (e.g. treasurer, chairman of Council), who no longer have separate Council machinery to operate but now work within an integrated management system.

Moreover, while the changes have reduced the collective role of lay members, they have increased their participation (though not their authority), because they are now placed upon certain key committees and each of them is associated with a particular academic unit (e.g. a School of studies). This represents a more positive and integrated approach, permitting the University to benefit from the relevant experience and skills of inidvidual lay members, in contrast to the old model which meant that one segment of its business was controlled by a group of lay members whose knowledge, experience and influence often derived from extraneous and irrelevant circumstances. Once again we note that the ability to introduce small changes each year from the outset enabled the University to make major changes of this kind over a period of time without serious disruption, and with a general consensus that the changes were for the better.

It is too early to say whether the above changes have increased the University's potential to adapt. The hope is that the association of internal and external members in a more meaningful relationship, and the more definite assignment of responsibility for the future of the University to its internal members, will enhance that potential. The association of individual lay members with Schools and Units, for instance, should lead to a more outward-looking approach on their part than might usually be the case. A modern university needs lay members less for financial control than because they are distinguished national or local citizens who are often able to act as 'go-betweens' for the university and the community at large—not least, its local community. In many universities, there has been a tendency in the past to fear the intrusion of lay members (especially the Chancellor) into the decision-making of the university. Through the much tighter and explicit relationships established at Sussex, it should be possible for lay members to play a more creative role in forging a link between the University and the outside world and for them to be treated as full and equal members of the University rather than as assessors or decision-makers with more than equal authority in certain spheres.

## B. The role of students

Questions concerning the role of students in University government and administration have been raised forcefully, both nationally and internationally, in recent months. It is of great consequence for the future that some answers to those questions have begun to be formulated through national negotiation. The immediate desire on the part of many universities in the United Kingdom to agree on a common line of response to such pressures may turn out to represent more significant intervention (in a practical rather than a constitutional sense) in the internal affairs of individual universities than any recent action by the government or the University Grants Committee. For instance, it can be argued that the Committee of Vice-chancellors-National Union of Students 'concordat' in 1968 on the role of students is much more serious in its implications for individual universities than is the more criticised action of allowing the Public accounts committee of Parliament to scrutinise the finances of individual universities.

In June 1968, the editor of *Universities Quarterly* wrote to the Registrars of all British universities, asking them to provide the present and the projected numbers of students on all their main university and faculty committees. The most striking fact to emerge from the replies about student participation was that there is still astonishingly little of it.

From the outset Sussex University has tried to create ways in which students could be creatively involved in the life of the University. The first Vice-chancellor of the University, Lord Fulton, wrote briefly about student policies when the UGC made a special visit to the University in January, 1966. He wrote:

We have always felt that a university founded at this time must, if it is to enjoy the whole-hearted support of its students, foster a new set of relationships between the generations in which the younger plays a more active part than has been usual in the past; and we believe that we have gradually succeeded in giving this ideal a workable form. Students now sit with faculty in about equal numbers and with equal power on all the University's main non-academic committees. As a result, co-operation between the Union and the Senate has now become easy, intimate and effective so that we believe the risks too have been greatly reduced, even with increasing size, of our declining into those attitudes of "we" and "they" which disturb the mutual trust required by the tutorial system.

Subsequently, the University has unequivocally expressed its intention to petition the Privy Council in due course for the revision of its Charter and Statutes to provide for student representation on both the Council and the Senate. However, until such a revision takes place, two representatives of the Students' Union are being invited to attend all meetings of the Council and to take part in its discussions, and seven representatives of the Union are similarly being invited to attend all meetings of the Senate. There is no statutory bar to students being members of University committees, and the Students' Union has full representation on many of the major University committees.

The planning committee (29 members, including four students), is a joint committee of the Senate and Council, responsible for making recommendations on all aspects of University planning. Students are also represented on the following committees: the social policy committee and its various sub-groups, which include the health service, the appointments service, the arts centre, the sports centre, and the accommodation group, etc.; the discipline committee; the bookshop and library groups; the buildings committee. The students are members of certain important working parties, e.g. the working party considering the revision of the preliminary and final examinations, the provision of counselling services, etc. In addition, each of the nine Schools of studies has a School joint committee, consisting of up to 12 members (half faculty, half students) which discusses and makes recommendations on any matters relating to the Schools. Moreover, there is a small joint committee, consisting of four faculty and four students, which is empowered to discuss any matter affecting the University and make recommendations to the appropriate body.

The degree of membership varies: in general the student members represent between 40 and 50 per cent of the total membership of committees concerned with social or welfare matters, between 5 and 15 per cent of the membership of committees dealing with major academic and organisational issues, and 50 per cent of the committees specially established for consultation in specific areas of activity. On all of the committees listed, no distinctions are drawn between students and faculty in regard to their rights and responsibilities as members.

It can be seen from the above list that students are members of the decision-taking bodies in all areas of University life, including curriculum, course content, teaching methods, major organisational and planning matters, finance, building, appointments, etc. The only major exceptions relate to the academic assessment of students' performance and faculty appointments and promotions.

The history of the role of students in the organisation of the University must be seen against the background of the University's teaching and social relationships. The reliance upon tutorial or small-group teaching ensures close and regular contact between students and faculty in work situations; that alone guarantees that a student has personal relationships with between ten and fifteen members of faculty during his course. In addition, each student has a personal Tutor, who remains constant throughout the student's course of study and whose job it is to give advice and friendship to the student. The tutorial system, coupled with a highly developed admissions policy, is designed to ensure that each student takes the combination of courses best suited to his interests and needs.

A further factor which has to be taken into account is that many of the University's policies are based upon what can be termed *a concern for the individual student*. This policy is reflected in the disciplinary code, the work of the health, appointments and accommodation services, the procedures which safeguard the student from arbitrary decisions about his academic future and the low attrition or wastage rate. It also has to be noted that the social policy of the University operates on the principle that wherever possible distinctions should not be made between students and faculty. Further, the Students' Union, to which all students must belong, is itself responsible for organising large areas of the University's social, cultural and recreational life, and many members of the faculty are associate members of the Union.

Against that essential background, the University's policy regarding the role of students in the government and administration of the University rests on two approaches. Firstly, a deliberate effort has been made to underpin any formal arrangements by the use of informal mechanisms. The Senior Tutor and his assistants are in daily contact with student representatives to resolve minor problems or to discuss approaches to major topics; every week the Senior Tutor and the President of the Union hold a joint informal meeting with 10 to 20 students and members of faculty to discuss issues which are emerging as likely problems. There are regular meetings of the administrative officers with student representatives; the editors of student newspapers and journals are regularly given full information on items of business currently being processed by the University; and the Vice-chancellor has meetings with the President of the Union, with the executive committee of the Students' Union, and with the general body of students. The managers of services (e.g. catering, library, health) are required by the Senate to establish and announce forms of consultation with faculty and students. These and other informal mechanisms are in many ways more important than the formal arrangements; they help create an atmosphere of mutual confidence within which differences can be resolved. These mechanisms have been in existence since the first year of the University and have contributed greatly to the relative lack of friction in, and over, formal arrangements.

In some senses the Senior Tutorship has always been the most important expression of the University's commitment to the principle of integrating students in all facets of the University's life. Though his responsibilities recently have been more concerned with the social and extra-curricular life of the University, in the period 1961-66 he was also expected to act as central guardian of the tutorial system. The Senior Tutor, who is and has been a chief officer of the University from the start, provides the focal point for all liaison between students and other sections of the University. He has had the responsibility for thinking systematically about student relations and for bringing forward recommendations for improving or adapting existing organisational patterns in this respect. Since 1965, the Administration has also provided a full-time member of staff to work with the Senior Tutor and facilitate the handling of all questions relating to the social life of the University.

Secondly, formal arrangements concerning students and the organisation of the University have developed pragmatically; organisational planning, in common with resource planning, has not taken the form of ideal model building, it has been done on the basis of previous experience and regular marginal changes. Clearly those officers most concerned with the total management of the system have models in mind when pressing for marginal change (i.e. it is a controlled process which has aims and goals), but the ultimate conception is not a fixed one. The history of the formal arrangements has had one constant. The joint committee, which consists of equal numbers of students and faculty under the co-chairmanship of the Senior Tutor and the President of the Union, has been the ultimate committee safety-valve; it has the authority to discuss any matter of concern to faculty and students (whether it be of an academic, social or financial nature) and to make a recommendation direct to the Senate. The fact that this machinery has not had to be used for several years is testimony to the efficient operation of the other formal and informal mechanisms.

The other formal arrangements are summarised in the charts of the committee structure: the trend has been to involve students increasingly in the formal machinery of government. Participation began in 1961 on committees concerned with social services and has been extended each year until by

1968/69, students were represented on the governing bodies (Senate and Council), on the key resource allocation committee (planning committee), on academic bodies (e.g. Schools of studies) as well as on the social, disciplinary and welfare committees (e.g. social policy committee). Another trend as the University has grown in size has been the devolution of student participation in the organisation of the University to units within the University (e.g. each School of studies is required to have a joint committee of faculty and students, and students in each School elect a student Speaker as their chief representative). As with the informal mechanisms, the aim of this devolutionary trend is not to replace the University-level mechanisms but to take some of the weight off them by the earlier resolution of problems and issues at the 'local' level. It cannot be over-stressed that the extension of student involvement has resulted from experience. If it had been suggested in the period 1961-64 that students should be members of the major financial and planning committees, it is likely that the suggestion would not have been accepted. Yet by 1968, students enjoyed membership of those committees because they had proved the value of their membership to the University by their contributions to subsidiary committees. Thus again, the ability to achieve major changes in small steps by the process of an annual review is clearly illustrated.

The role of the students in the management structure is largely confined to the management of the activities of the Students' Union, although the President of the Union plays a significant part as an advisor to many University Officers and the student Speakers perform a similar function within the Schools of studies. The only students who are appointed as officers of the university itself are the student disciplinary officers, who are directly responsible to the Senate for disciplinary matters affecting the University.

In 1966/67, a scheme was introduced to extend the academic courses of certain Union officers. This extension, granted to the President, Secretary and Student Treasurer of the Union, allows the officer concerned to devote the greater part of his time for one year to his Union duties. The grants for the year are paid jointly by the Union and the University. The Presidents of the Union have invariably played a key role in the development of close co-operation and participation between faculty and students. The University has regarded the President as a responsible University officer and it is fair to say that the student population has generally responded by electing a most responsible candidate. In terms of the newly developed planning process, the Students' Union now has the annual opportunity to submit its unit plan, containing recommendations for changes in those areas of University activity which affect the Union and its members.

Whether or not the involvement of students in the government of the University has increased the ability of the University to adapt to changes in its environment is difficult to answer. It can be stated that student involvement has been beneficial to the University in an inward-looking sense. Many decisions were beneficially affected by the active involvement of student representatives, ranging from the design of the disciplinary code to methods of academic assessment, from the wording of guidebooks for prospective applicants to the physical layout of the library and in the selection of special projects which involve the local community. Indeed, the fact that an institution would benefit from the representation of the largest constituency within it hardly needs proving. It is anticipated that in the next year or so, there is likely to be a switch from considerable involvement regarding the extra-curricular activities of the University to more participation in discussions about curriculum design and renewal. Recently, student representatives have played an important role in focussing on major teaching and learning problems in the University, and they have participated in preliminary discussions regarding ways of institutionalising improvements in this area.

# 8. Organisational processes

The main feature of the University's methods of problem indentification, discussion and solution is the increasing use of *processes* which underpin its organisational structure.

Most universities arrange for participation, decision-taking and control through their committee structures or occasionally in terms of management structures. Although, as we indicated earlier, such structures can be flexible, it nevertheless remains the case that they must contain fixed elements. In this University, processes have assumed a greater role year by year and they now carry much of the weight of participation, decision-taking and control. The processes are still a long way short of the fully-fledged systems of project programming and programme budgeting which have been developed in industry and some governments in recent years, but they represent significant steps in that direction. They lack some of the sophistications of the industrial systems, but they probably add a dimension of participation, normally unknown in industry.

In common with the trends in the committee and management structures, the early history reveals the separate developments in the planning of student numbers and other academic fields (in the Registrar's office and through the planning committee) in forward budget planning (in the finance office and through the finance committee) and in campus planning (by the consultant architect through the buildings committee). Those processes were not the subject of regular review. They depended upon initiatives, expertise and assessment by individual administrators. In the period 1964-67 logistical planning in the academic sphere developed rapidly, partly because demand pressure at the national level was leading to student numbers becoming the base of much national planning. In the University itself, the planning and allocation of student numbers became more closely related to the planning and distribution of academic faculty posts, and those two elements were used as the bases for ratios controlling the amount and distribution of technical support, secretarial and clerical services, and school funds. The construction of such inter-related ratios eventually covering approximately 60 per cent of University expenditure necessitated closer integration of academic and financial planning. It was the identification of the need for an integrated academic planning and resource allocation system which contributed significantly to the major organisational review of 1967. The seeds of the outcome of that review were sown in the initiatives taken in academic planning in the period 1964-67.

The results of the review are referred to below and are described in the appendixes on the planning process (Appendix A) and its subsidiary budgetary process (established 1968/69) (Appendix B), which demonstrate the integration of financial and academic planning now achieved and the ways in which these processes reflect and underpin the committee and management structures. In reading the appendixes, it needs to be borne in mind that the new comprehensive processes are still in their trial first year and that they are subject to annual review, together with all other aspects of the organisation of the University. The planning and allocation of physical plant and space is not yet adequately built into the processes, partly because of the different national procedures, and time-scales for recurrent and capital allocation; however, the revisions to the processes prepared for 1969/70 as part of the current annual review should correct that inadequacy.

The reasons for the introduction of processes and for the greater reliance upon them are complex and inter-related. There were three main reasons.

Firstly, a few key members of the University pressed for their development. They believed that the structuring of problem-solving and planning into a continuous process, requiring all parts of the University to produce plans, combining these into a University plan and re-evaluating them each year, would reinforce the view of the University as an entity which consists of interdependent rather than independent parts. It was anticipated that this would increase the University's ability to change and would optimise the University's opportunity to change. Throughout this study the examples used relate primarily to the economics of resources. It needs to be stated that the changes affect and were caused by other types of development, such as the recognition of a learning as well as a teaching process and the changing technology of education. The creation of an effective planning process was seen as the pre-condition of an effective problem-solving system, for other aspects of the University's work, such as curriculum revision, changing teaching methods and the revision of logistic balance. This is why so much emphasis has been given to it in the University and in this study.

Secondly, the increasing complexity of the University's problems of resource allocation, as the University moved from a situation in which the amount of new resources at its disposal was temporarily much greater than existing commitment or stock to one in which new resources were only marginal to the size of existing commitment or stock. In theory, the procedures and techniques for resource allocation in these two situations should have been little different, but given human frailty and the sociology of an institution, attention became focussed upon such procedures and techniques only when competing claims considerably exceeded the new resources available. It was inevitable in such a situation that interest groups should begin to question the efficiency of the distribution of existing stock, press for procedures which would ensure an equitable distribution of the scarce new resources, and enquire about the availability and disposition of resources in the future.

Probably the most decisive reason, however, was the changes in the external environment. The indirect and direct pressures from governmental sources for efficiency within universities have increased considerably in the period since 1963. These arose in the main from increased public concern with university problems, and from the rise in the percentage of public expenditure devoted to higher education. The rising importance of this factor was not unique to the United Kingdom. In *The Managerial Revolution in Higher Education* in the U.S.A., Rourke and Brooks stated: 'One common theme runs through a majority of the explanations which university officials give for their recent budgetary reforms; either an outside state agency required the change, or else the University decided that it should alter its procedures in order to compete more effectively with other institutions in the quest for public funds'[1]. In the context of the University of Sussex the latter explanation is much more the case than the former.

The pressure manifested itself in many ways. The UGC changed the format of the statistical returns required from universities in order that the Committee might have more relevant 'management' information (e.g. the use of academic faculty time and the unit costs of various categories of students). A host of fact-finding national surveys were mounted to ascertain information on specialist aspects of universities (e.g. space and plant utilisation, the feasibility of year-round courses). The UGC and the universities were placed within the terms of reference of the Public Accounts committee of Parliament; it was widely reported that the expensiveness of universities was one of the main reasons for the controversial 'binary' policy towards higher education; (even though statistics comparing the two halves of the binary system were not available, such an assertion placed further pressure upon the universities). External pressure was not always linked to the question of resources; the creation of the Universities Central Council on Admissions, the rush of appointments of information

---

1. Rourke and Brooks, *The Managerial Revolution in Higher Education,* Baltimore (Md.), The Johns Hopkins Press, 1966.

officers in universities and many other changes within universities may be seen to reflect the response to external pressures of other kinds.

Moreover, university personnel were becoming more aware of modern management techniques employed in industry and commerce (e.g. computerisation of administration, programme budgeting, cost-benefit analysis, operational research, project programming, critical path analysis, standardised building techniques, corporate planning, etc.). It is interesting to note in passing that the development of many of these techniques owed much to university faculty in certain related disciplines and that many faculty in those disciplines had been using such techniques in their own research work for some years. The use of any of these techniques for institutional purposes within universities, however, came late and largely on account of external pressures. The signs that universities are beginning to adopt them are partly the changes now emerging in individual institutions, and partly the creation of *ad hoc* co-operative agencies, e.g. the mushrooming since 1965 of regional University Organisation and Method units and the creation of collaborative machinery since 1965 by universities using identical computers for management purposes (e.g. the I.C.L. 1905 Users Group).

The reasons for the introduction of the processes have been given, but the methods by which they were introduced also require some explanation. In this context, it has to be stressed that planning systems in the University have developed pragmatically, and deliberately so, and they have been designed and implemented by generalist administrators working through faculty committees. It would have been possible for the University to have called upon the skills of theoretical planners and operational research specialists on its faculty to construct sophisticated planning models. This did not happen and it may be of interest to consider why development took a more pragmatic form.

The techniques and the value of model-building for educational institutional planning were not proven and were, indeed, unknown to many faculty and administrators alike. The techniques appeared to be at a level equivalent to those employed in the strictly economic models produced with unsatisfactory results for the under-developed countries in the 1950s. In other words, they may have been sophisticated but they were on narrow fronts. Equally the criteria were in dispute; Mark Blaug in his article 'Approaches to Educational Planning' in the *Economic Journal* (June 1967) summarised the situation:

> In these circumstances what is the planner to do?  Should he act on a man-power forecast?  But what if the forecast were to prompt action exactly opposite to that suggested by a projection of private demand or a calculation of the social rate of return on investment in education?  We are back to the problem with which we started.  Are we any nearer a resolution?  Planning

has been defined as the process of preparing a set of decisions for action to be taken in the future. Since it is orientated to the future, planning partakes of all the difficulties analysed in the theory of sequential decision-making under uncertainty. Educational planning is, as we have argued, particularly prone to uncertainty about the future, since even the present relationship between the supply of qualified students and the demand for educated people from industry and government is little understood. In the circumstances, we are always better off if we can build into the system the kind of flexibility that allows it to adjust automatically to bottlenecks and surpluses. In short, educational planning should largely consist of action designed to move the real world closer to the right end of the continuum, characterised by a multiplicity of alternatives in producing and utilising educated manpower.

A time of rapid change in the national educational system, during which the first initiatives were taken towards national planning processes and models, evidenced in particular by the establishment of a planning branch in the Department of education and science, was not an appropriate time for an individual institution to construct sophisticated models, the bases, the criteria and the future of which were all highly uncertain. It was also thought that the initial costs involved would be too high a price to pay for uncertain returns. It was appreciated that it might have been possible to meet the costs of the specialists concerned from research monies, but the system required in order to make use of any sophisticated models would involve the University in considerable expenditure.

The most important reason, however, was the feeling that planning could not be developed in isolation from the rest of the organisation of the University. There was little point in developing planning models which went beyond the capabilities of the University to implement their results; after all, planning has to be understandable by the majority of members of faculty and has to be worked by existing administrative staffs. It thus had to arise out of *their* experience and to be seen as relevant to *their* problems. The gap between models created out of the professional and research interests of skilled groups, and needs felt by the faculty and administrators responsible for an institution, is normally considerable. At Sussex it was decided that effective results could be best achieved by building upon those needs through an educative process involving the mass of members of the University. The University was in the early years of a long life; given that perspective it decided to integrate planning on a firm basis even though it would take several years to develop the appropriate means to a sophisticated level. In fundamental terms, it was a recognition that planning in a small-scale society should, where the two are in conflict, reflect the needs and understandings of the society rather than be imposed by the enthusiasm or convenience of the planners. The members of the society have to be given the opportunity to absorb the techniques and knowledge which will allow them to participate in the planning. That is what the Sussex planning process is all about; if it fails, then less participative methods may have to be adopted. If it succeeds, then the data systems which are now being built up and the experience which is being gained can be used by the key officers and the planning specialists to create more sophisticated models with the agreement and understanding of the members of the institution.

Before turning to the details of the processes, we need to provide a brief outline of the national framework for resource allocation within which the University has to operate. The University receives approximately 70 per cent of its recurrent income from the University Grants Committee and a further 12 per cent approximately from government-supplied research funds. Of the remaining 18 per cent of recurrent income, approximately 8 per cent derives from student fees and is therefore general income which the University has freedom to allocate, and approximately 10 per cent is received for research purposes. That latter 10 per cent, together with the 12 per cent received for research from government sources, is provided for specific research investigation.

Under present arrangements grants towards universities' recurrent expenditure (other than the statutory payment for local authority rates; these local taxes are financed separately) are determined by the UGC for periods of five years at a time. Towards the end of each five-year period there is a general review of university finances, on the basis of detailed submissions from all universities for the next quinquennium, and grants are then determined for a further period of five years. Supplementary grants have been made during the course of a quinquennium to meet increases, approved by the government, in academic salary scales. Supplementary grants may also be made to meet increases in the level of general (non-salary) costs, as measured by the Brown (formerly Tress) index of university costs; and to meet new national needs such as a major increase in the number of students for which the government wishes the universities to provide. The UGC announces the monies allocated to each university without discussion with the university and with no explanation as to how the specific sums were arrived at, other than an indication of the student numbers which the UGC has assumed for the university for the last year in the quinquennium (an assumption which the university is not bound by) and some generalisations on the national issues taken into account by the UGC.

This system has the advantage for the universities of giving them a firm basis for budgeting and for planning their expansion and development over a period of five years; it has the disadvantage that the forward planning period diminishes each year of a quinquennium—a handicap that has led some to suggest a rolling rather than a fixed five-year budget period. It has the advantage for the govern-

223

ment of defining the limits of their commitment for five years and of excluding attempts by either the Committee or the universities to re-negotiate the grants; this is the case for the fixed five-year period. The system also avoids the constraints which are normally involved in the system of annual Parliamentary Estimates. Each year's grant is paid out to universities in equal monthly instalments. But it does not have to be fully spent in that particular year and any unspent balances do not have to be surrendered. In this way, subject to the rule that expenditure in the last year of a quinquennium should not exceed income for that year, universities have flexibility in planning their expenditure within the quinquennium.

Recurrent grants to universities are given in the main as block grants without strings, the internal disposition of the grants being determined by each university itself as a matter of its own internal budgetary autonomy. Earmarked grants in practice represent a very small proportion of the total grants; and they are rolled up into the block grants as soon as practicable. In a few cases the UGC have felt it desirable to 'indicate' that special financial provision for a particular purpose had been made in the allocations. But these 'indications' were not mandatory and the amounts were not earmarked. The block grant principle has long been regarded as necessary to ensure a reasonable measure of academic freedom and to avoid the 'management' of the universities by the government or by the Committee.

In practice the freedom of universities is subject to certain qualifications and restraints. Expenditure on academic staff salaries, which accounts for about 40 per cent of the total expenditure (excluding expenditure from research grants and other specific income), is controlled to the extent that national salary scales for the various grades of staff are fixed by the government and that there is an agreed convention governing the proportion of senior to junior posts. It is for each university itself to decide how, within the over-all ratio, the proportions of senior to junior staff in individual faculties or departments should be determined.

In its Development Report for 1962-67 the UGC sets out its view of its relations with universities in this respect:

> More generally, the universities take their decisions within a frame-work of national needs and priorities on which it is our responsibility to give them the fullest and clearest possible guidance. Universities, as they assured the Government in 1946, fully accept the view that 'the Government has not only the right but the duty to satisfy itself that every field of study which in the national interest ought to be cultivated in Great Britain is in fact being cultivated in the university system and that the resources which are placed at the disposal of the universities are being used with full regard both to effi-

ciency and to economy'. Our allocations of grant are based on the estimates and development plans submitted by the universities; our views on their development plans are made known to the universities; there is a well-established convention that no major departures from the lines of development that have been discussed should be made without consultation with the Committee; it is customary for a university which is considering an offer of outside financial support for a development which may eventually become a charge on its general funds to consult the Committee; and universities are aware that unwise developments are liable to prejudice their claims in the next quinquennium. The Committee regard it as their business to set the general strategy, and to help universities to plan their own development by giving them as much information as possible on national needs, including changes in potential student numbers and in the need for graduates in particular fields; on developments in other similar institutions; and on the Committee's own thoughts about the general development of university education in the coming years. Universities are then free to plan their own development in the light of their particular circumstances and needs, but within a national pattern and strategy that are known to them.

It was in this spirit that the Committee accompanied their allocations of grant for the 1967-72 quinquennium with a memorandum of general guidance and with separate notes on particular points relating to individual universities. The memorandum of general guidance concluded with the following paragraph:

> The Committee hope that universities will find it helpful to have the considerations mentioned in this memorandum before them when they come to decide their own development policies and priorities for the quinquennium. Each university is free to determine the distribution of its annual block grant in the light of the guidance general and particular, which the Committee have given. It would, however, be in accordance with generally accepted convention that the Committee should be consulted before any major new developments, outside the framework set by the universities' quinquennial submissions and the guidance contained in this general memorandum and in the individual allocation letters, are undertaken.

Over 90 per cent of the University's capital expenditure on buildings and equivalent is received from the University Grants Committee. The division between capital and recurrent monies is a totally inflexible one, for the University has no opportunity to switch the monies received from the UGC between the two headings. The provision of capital funds is on a different basis and time-scale from those for recurrent funds; the University submits its capital plans for a year, three or four years in advance, and the monies are allocated for that year by the UGC two or three years in advance; in general, the monies are allocated for specific items rather than in the form of block grants and the UGC has developed control systems which require the University to work closely with the UGC at several stages in the planning and erection of each building.

# 9. The planning process

The planning process developed at Sussex is an abbreviated title for the complex of systems which contain the strategic and operational plans, the budgetary system, the control mechanisms and part of the information, records and statistics systems of the University. The basic elements of the planning process existed in the University prior to 1968 and the aim of the 1968 review was to build upon those foundations in several ways:

(a) To improve the co-ordination of plans by combining academic and financial plans, social and building plans, in each unit, and by processing the plans collectively through the committee structure;

(b) To systematise the production of plans by asking each School, Subject or other Unit to prepare a plan containing a statement of its objectives, its recommendations for changes and ideas for improvement;

(c) To improve the timetabling of planning and make it continuous;

(d) To increase participation in planning. All members cannot participate equally and very few will be able to participate in the total process, but the aim has been that everyone should have the opportunity to contribute to some aspect of the planning, especially where it affects the interests of the individual faculty member, and that all aspects of the planning should be open to comment by representatives of all sectors of the University;

(e) To make planning more effective by improving the mechanisms controlling implementation and by increasing control reports which allow the University to measure progress against the plans;

(f) To strengthen the flow of information related to planning, e.g. the national and international data and statistics required by units for the preparation of plans.

Since the process is a complex of systems with a cyclical pattern it is extremely difficult to describe simply. However, the five main *elements* of the process are as follows:

(i) *Strategic plans.* Strategic planning is seen as the setting of objectives and the selection of strategies to meet those objectives; its primary focus is to identify major long-term issues and point to major decisions which will change the fundamental character and direction of the enterprise. In the context of the University as a whole, it involves such issues as the long-term rate of growth, the balance between arts and science, the balance between undergraduate teaching, postgraduate training and research, the establishment of new Schools of studies, the sizes of Schools, the relationships of Research centres to the Schools.

(ii) *Operational plans.* Operational planning is seen as the translation of agreed objectives and strategic plans into specific action programmes over the short term (i.e. one to four years). In the University context, this involves such issues as the numbers of faculty and students, curriculum changes, or re-allocation of space.

(iii) *Budgets.* The budget is seen as the financial/numerical expression of the operational plan for one year ahead (e.g. financial budget, manpower budget). The budget at Sussex consists of a grid linking spending programmes and spending units.

(iv) *Control reports.* For example, the finance office produces regular control reports and statements of expenditure for each unit showing performance against budget, and for the major committees at stated frequencies throughout the year. Other offices produce similar reports (e.g. establishments office in regard to manpower, the admissions office in regard to student numbers).

(v) *Information.* It is essential that the process should be understood by members of the University and thus reference works on detailed aspects of the process are being made available (e.g. a Guidebook of financial procedures, a description of the University's records and statistics systems, etc.). Unit plans cannot be efficiently constructed unless information about internal and external factors and trends is made available; thus an information network is being erected along which information can flow to and through the planning officer from and to the persons concerned with teaching, research, admissions, examinations, appointments, health, accommodation, finance, space, educational technology, social policy, etc. It is also partly for this reason that institutional research is being conducted through the Vice-chancellor's office and the University's records are being computerized in order to build up an integrated management information system.

As at 1968/69, the University is structured hierarchically into four main levels (a chart of planning units will be found in Appendix C):

1. The University itself, represented by the Council, the Senate, the planning committee and the Vice-chancellor.
2. The University is then divided into four main planning areas: arts and social studies, sciences, social policy, and general.
3. Each of the four main areas consists of units (e.g. five of the Schools of studies belong to the arts and social studies area).
4. In turn there are sub-units of these units (e.g. Subjects are sub-units of the Schools, the admissions office is a sub-unit of the administration, etc.).

Each of these areas and units is required to produce a plan with the assistance and guidance of people external to the unit, principally the planning officer. The *annual planning cycle* is the flow of the elements of the planning process through these four main levels. In October each year the planning officer, with the Vice-chancellor, produces revised versions of the elements of the planning process (strategic plans, operational plans, budgets related to each other by various formulae). The assumptions built into those revised versions are critical in that they provide the framework which the ensuing discussions take place. The *annual planning assumptions* are then considered by the planning committee and the Senate before being sent to level four, from whence they proceed by timetabled discussions through levels two and three to reach level one again by March. After the Senate and the Council have approved them in March, they then flow back down through levels two, three and four. They flow back in this way because built into the process (particularly the budgetary system) is the ability of each area, unit or sub-unit to make further adjustments at its own initiative; indeed incentives to do so are an important part of the over-all process. The *quinquennial cycle* is derived from the annual cycle. In essence, the University's strategic plans have to be formally converted into a quinquennial plan every five years because of the national system of financing universities.

The co-ordination of the planning process is the responsibility of the planning officer. Four observations are relevant about this post. Firstly, it is sited in the Vice-chancellor's Office, and is the only one of the four chief administrative officers of the University (the others are the Registrar and secretary, the Bursar, and the finance officer) which is sited in that office. Secondly, the planning officer is also responsible for the staff work relating to the organisation of the University; thus, the relationship between planning and institutional organisation is reflected in the post and to some extent safeguarded by that fact. Thirdly, there is no planning office or team; the planning officer has to work with and obtain support from the administrators in the field, (e.g. secretary of science) and with the administrators in specialist branches (e.g. data processing officer). Fourthly, the planning officer is a generalist administrator rather than a specialist in planning techniques as such.

The role of the planning officer is succinctly expressed by John Argenti in his article on 'Lessons of Long Range Planning' in the October 1968 issue of *Management Today*. He says:

> Some companies are known to have appointed corporate planners who are little more than operational research scientists without experience of management at any level. Companies who have made this mistake are presumably under the impression that corporate planning is a management technique which can be 'applied' by anyone with a maths degree. Corporate planning is concerned with examining the innermost soul of a company, with deciding what sort of company it is to become, how it is to behave towards its employees, its customers, the government, the local community, what threats it faces, what opportunities there may be to exploit, whether its R and D department is good enough, how to strengthen the product range, what changes in the organisation structure are required. A corporate planner must be numerate, since he will have to use some fairly advanced tools, but he must be experienced in the ways of business, a generalist rather than a specialist, forward-looking and in tune with the rate of change of the modern world. Perhaps above all, he must have an acceptable personality, for, if he is going to examine the soul of the company on behalf of the chief executive, the other directors and senior executives are bound to resent his wide brief and to fear that he will criticise their departments behind their backs; this is the centre of the problem of introducing LRP into a company. It is the kernel in a nut which consists so largely of human relations problems; only the husk round the nut consists of problems of a technical nature.

The new relationship between planning and budgeting created in 1968 requires explanation. In simplified terms, prior to the introduction of the planning process, budgeting was the responsibility of the finance and general purposes committee of the Council. It took the form of traditional line budgeting generally used in public administration accountancy, and was largely built up through bilateral discussions between the finance office and the individual units; budgetary control was highly-centralised. It was, in short, dominated by accountancy. The budgetary system which was introduced in 1968, as part of the planning process, marks a significant step away from those attitudes and towards the idea advocated by Alan Williams in his booklet *Output Budgeting and Contribution of Micro-Economics to Efficiency in Government* (H.M.S.O., 1967):

Unfortunately, thorough-going cost-benefit analysis is not immediately feasible in many important fields of social policy, because of sheer lack of understanding as to what the relevant dimensions of the output are, because of difficulty in getting adequate data to measure them even where they are understood sufficiently or because of the inadequacy of our present evaluative techniques in attaching convincing money-values to them. It is, however, possible to move part of the way towards comprehensive cost-benefit analysis by tackling a rather more restricted task, that of setting up an output budget for governmental activities.

The basic idea of an output budget is to relate all cost items to broad functional objectives, by constructing a framework within which it is clear what resources are being devoted towards what end and with what results. The new budgetary system is described in appendix B. In essence, it allows the University to allocate monies to areas to meet the targets and standards set by the plans, but also encourages flexibility and provides incentives to areas and units as the main approach to efficient use of the monies. It is an experiment in controlled devolution.

We need at this point to mention more specifically the network of logistic ratios used for planning and budgetary purposes. If a more sophisticated planning model is developed, this network will probably be its basis. The chart in Figure 3 which uses the Science Area as an example is almost self-explanatory. Only one of the ratios shown on the chart is externally imposed (i.e. the ratio of senior to other faculty); the remainder have been developed internally. The first ratio to be established was the one relating staff and student numbers in 1961, and faculty numbers have remained tied solely to student numbers since that time; other derivative ratios were added to that primary one year by year. They provide the main bases for the calculation of the planning and budgetary assumptions. In other words, they help create a logical and easily understandable framework within which discussion can take place. Since student numbers are the main currency of planning and resource allocation, it is necessary to describe briefly the way in which they are planned.

The planning committee approves projections of student numbers, by total, by categories and by areas, for five years ahead on a rolling basis. The numbers contained in the projections are termed the *logistic student numbers:* they are the numbers upon which all resource allocation decisions other than academic faculty numbers are based (e.g. school funds, allocation of space); they represent minimum rather than fixed targets, since within certain limitations the arts and science areas may accept higher numbers of students provided that extra resources are not thereby requested from the University. In the determination of academic faculty numbers, not all categories of logistic

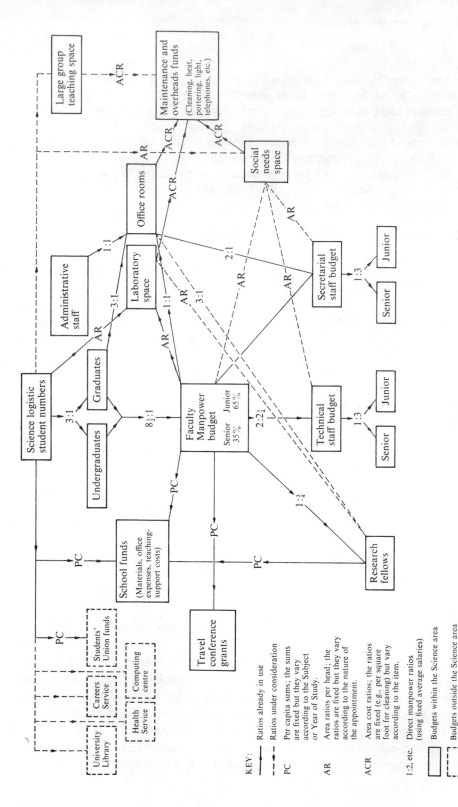

Figure 3. The inter-related ratios used for planning and budgetary purposes. The diagram represents those ratios in the Science area

students are included in the calculations; the student numbers used for this purpose are termed the *ratio student numbers,* and they consist of the logistic undergraduate and advanced course numbers plus the logistic numbers of first-year graduate students.

The use of the projections for resource allocation purposes may be summarised under two headings: firstly, this varies according to the distance ahead of the projections. The projections for the full five years do not represent fixed plans; they are reviewed each year and they are simply the best estimates available of future logistic numbers and their distribution. As such, they are used as the main base of the projections of resource allocation (e.g. budgets, faculty logistics, etc.) embodied in the University's operational and strategic plans.

However, once the annual process of review has been completed in March of each year, the elements of the projections become fixed plans until the next annual review, and other elements become alterable only at the margin. Thus, when the present projections were approved in March 1969:

(a) The 1969/70 ratio and logistic numbers contained in them were used for the final resource allocation decisions for that year. The budgetary academic faculty, space and other allocations were based upon them and will not now be altered even if the logistic numbers are under-achieved.

(b) The 1970/71 ratio and logistic numbers contained in them will be used as the basis of the budgetary assumptions for that year, as the basis for the calculation of provisional faculty numbers for that year and by the admissions office as the provisional intake targets for October 1970. Thus, although the 1970/71 numbers do not represent fixed plans, they are capable of only marginal alteration during 1969/70, since some actions will have had to be taken using them as a base. For example, faculty appointments for 1970/71 can only be marginally altered, since the admissions selection for October 1970 will be largely completed before March 1970; the admissions office will have used the provisional 1970/71 numbers for that purpose.

Secondly, the question as to how and when the actual number of students affects the projections and resource allocation requires explanation. It has already been stated above that the overshooting of ratio and logistic student numbers by units has no effect upon the use of the projections as the base for resource allocation. Such gaps between actual and logistic numbers are only taken into account in the framing of the Quinquennial Submission and in the resulting Quinquennial Development Plan at the beginning of each quinquennium. However, the under-achievement of logistic numbers is a different matter; it is taken into account through a procedure which allows marginal under-achievement without any corrective action (2 per cent to 5 per cent dependent upon the category). This spreads any necessary alterations over a period of time sufficiently long for the unit to make the necessary resource adjustments, but takes away resources from an area if it fails to meet its targets by a significant amount. The central admissions office is the main control agent in the field of student numbers; it monitors changes in the national pattern of demand, analyses the performance of the University against that pattern, contributes to the determination of the targets, organises the selection process and controls the numbers of offers made to applicants. The admissions office is thus a key post of the planning mechanism.

In this chapter, we have attempted to analyse some of the organisational processes and the reasons for their introduction. The question remains as to what effects the deliberate introduction of such processes has had on the institution. They have clearly achieved several of their goals (e.g. the involvement of faculty in planning, a better understanding of the ways in which the University works and the limits within which it has to operate, a clearer relationship between planning and finance, greater devolution of initiative and responsibility to areas and units). Have they, however, led to better forward-planning, to more efficient use of resources and to developments which reflect national needs and priorities? It is definitely too early to judge the effects of the new planning process in such terms. The first annual cycle has just ended. It has been a successful first cycle with every one of the eighty or so units producing reasonable plans and with the operational plans for the next three years now having been agreed. Also the mechanics of the process have functioned smoothly and according to schedule. However, although it may be too early to evaluate the new process, we feel that the preliminary results bode well for the future. They have certainly led to better forward-planning in certain areas, and they appear to have led to a more equitable distribution of resources. For instance, for historical reasons the staff-student ratios in science and arts had got out of alignment over the period 1962-66 (they were 7.5:1 and 9:1 in science and arts respectively) yet by 1968 they were back in balance. They have led to a more efficient use of resources; for instance, the percentage of University income spent on items directly related to the teaching and research programmes rose significantly in the period 1966/68. They have led to developments which reflect national needs and priorities; for instance, the science area agreed to cut back its allocation of resources to some stable subjects, such as chemistry and physics, in order to provide resources for new subjects high in the list of national priorities, such as biochemistry, polymer science, and automatic control. They have led to the areas using the initiatives and incentives given to them in beneficial ways; for instance, the student number targets have been exceeded by over two hundred students, which not only provides an education for more students but also reduces the unit costs of the University and therefore improves its chances of further development.

The innovations in procedures introduced in 1964-67 increased the University's ability to change and its opportunity to change. They are the pre-requisites for planning; plans are useless if the University is not able to change and to change in time for it to be effective. Many of the devices created in the period 1964-67 were designed to that end. For instance, on the resignation of a member of faculty the post reverts to a pool, from which it is re-allocated on the basis of priority need, rather than remaining within the subject or School of its previous holder. Similarly both planning and the ability to change are ineffective if the University does not have the opportunity to change; in the United Kingdom context that opportunity arises mainly (but not solely) by keeping its unit costs low, its standards high, and its activities relevant to national needs. Although the new planning process is fundamentally concerned with these two pre-requisites, it has moved beyond them; it aims to progress from logistic planning to a re-definition of the role of the University. The move is from means-orientated to ends-orientated planning; that is why objectives form the basis of the new process; that is why the process is a continuous rather than an occasional one, that is why it is participative rather than closed to all but a few key officers; and that is why it is linked to the organisational structure.

Finally, in this section it is appropriate to indicate the next major development we have under consideration. The processes outlined above are macro-processes and we now are considering micro-processes. Here we move from planning to the implementation of plans. Under the term 'projects process' we are thinking of ways of identifying projects at the end of a planning cycle and appointing project leaders and teams to implement and evaluate each project in accordance with an agreed timetable; thus when the planning process results in a decision to put up a new building, to introduce a new subject, to extend the computer facilities, etc., the implementation of that decision would be the responsibility of a project team rather than a standing committee or a permanent officer. The implications of this idea would be far-reaching on the organisational structure (i.e. the structural framework could be reduced to a minimum), and the nature of the involvement of individual members in the government and administration of the University; it would add a new dimension in flexibility.

The earlier sections represent a mixture of factual description of the structures and processes and our analysis of them. Clearly, we are in favour of the main trends outlined. Equally, it should be recognised that there are critics within the University, and we thought it desirable to list some of the criticisms which are made by members of both the academic and administrative faculties. Before doing so we need to reiterate two facts:

(a) All of the details of the structures and processes have been approved each year, after a review which involves all of the units and the major representative bodies of the University.

(b) All members of faculty are involved in some way in both the structures and the processes; thus they have both knowledge and experience of them.

The main criticisms which we have found are:

*The changes have increased conflict and acrimony within the University.* It is certainly true that conflict has increased, but this resulted mainly from the need to settle priorities for the allocation of scarce resources. However, it is probably true that the structures and processes have contributed by increasing the number of people involved in the discussions and by switching the discussion from means to ends (there is always more conflict over the latter). Our view, whilst not welcoming conflict, is that those who are very concerned about it have failed to realise that innovation and conflict are inseparable; also they still believe that it is possible for individuals who take decisions on committees to divorce themselves from their vested interests. In other words, they see the University as a collection of altruistic individuals rather than a political society.

*The planning process takes too much faculty and administrative time.* This criticism represents the opposite side of the coin to participation; it is made mainly by those in 'middle-management' positions, and they have voiced it more frequently as participation has extended beyond them.

*The amount of written material generated by the structures and processes is too great to be absorbed by any individual.* This criticism results from the openness of the system and the policy of disseminating information. It represents a genuine problem.

*There is too much change, and the University needs a period of stability.* This criticism is a plea common to many walks of life, but there is little evidence that the University is changing too rapidly in relation to external and internal needs.

*The structures and processes are concerned more with the mechanics of planning than with planning itself.* This is an understandable criticism at the end of a year when we have been testing the mechanics of the new long-scale process.

*Participative government and planning leads to equity or 'fair shares for all' being the main basis of resource allocation rather than priorities being selected on objective criteria.* This criticism is a crucial one and it is too early to

236

judge whether or not it is a justifiable one. We see signs that it is not justifiable, but we may be over-optimistic.

*In order for them to be effective, the structures and processes require a level of management skill which is not possessed by the heads of units or areas within the University.* This is another crucial criticism. The fundamental question which faces all universities is how to improve the level of management and leadership ability.

*There is too much organisation and planning, which diminishes respect for the University's main job of teaching and research.* This criticism is directed against the complexity of the modern university.

These are some of the criticisms which have been mentioned in conversation; no criticisms have yet been put in concrete form by any unit or committee. In the next few months the faculty will have their first opportunity to comment on the new process in the light of their experience of it.

# 10. Measuring performance

One of the prime aims of the International Institute in this project has been to establish whether or not it is possible to construct 'critical indicators' of University performance so as to measure how far institutional objectives are being achieved. It has to be said at the outset that the terminology and methodology involved in the use of 'critical indicators' in the context of institutional planning in British higher education are relatively unfamiliar. The systematic maintenance of comprehensive records and statistics for evaluation or planning purposes is a recent development in most British universities, largely occasioned by increasing national pressures. In any event, the lack of available and relevant indicators at the national level has resulted in a subjective use of indicators by individual institutions. The national data, for instance on research activity in the various subject areas, tends to be dispersed and unco-ordinated. Equally, within many institutions there has been a tendency for indicators to be used in strictly compartmentalised situations rather than for across-the-board planning; this is especially true of campus and space planning, particularly where the internal administrative structure of the University is split on the traditional academic-bursarial axis. One of the main reasons undoubtedly lies in the lack of any training for University leaders and administrators.

As implied earlier in the study, there was limited need for any sophisticated use of 'critical indicators' during this University's periods of foundation and rapid growth. This should not imply complacency. The University is now attempting to develop an institutional research programme, integrally linked to an embryonic management information system, and a new post of research and development officer has been established in the Vice-chancellor's office to work with the planning officer to this end. The University has consistently collected the kind of information required to construct indicators, and it has used this information in a rather generalised way as the need arose. Since the results were generally seen to be favourable (e.g. applicant demand, faculty recruitment, wastage rates, research income etc.) the initial mood of confidence of the University was reinforced by such evidence as emerged from scrutiny of the rather crude indicators available. There is little doubt that if the University had suffered any serious setback in an important aspect of its development, this mood would have been shaken and there would have been an earlier search for more precise indicators and more systematic and critical evaluation of its performance.

It is our thesis that the role of individuals, in interpreting to the University changes in the national environment and in conveying the judgements of national bodies to the University, has probably been the most important factor in determining the University's attitude to change. Many of the University's major policies have resulted from external stimuli or incentives, which have been transmitted through key individuals, or via national agencies or committees in which senior University faculty have participated.

## A. Recurrent resources

The University's progress has of course depended upon the availability of adequate financial resources for both capital and recurrent purposes. No recurrent grant was received until the first undergraduates were admitted in 1961, and the grant for that year (£40,500) was very small. A quinquennial grant was then received from the UGC for the period 1962-67, based on a yearly cost per student. It was reasonable that such a method of financing for the University should be based on the expectation that the annual cost per student would fall as numbers rose. The University had to keep a careful watch from year to year on recurrent costs. No 'passenger' or 'teacher-intensive' subjects were introduced, and as a result the University was able to build up certain subject groups, such as mathematics, physics, chemistry, history and philosophy, which are already within the top ten or even five in the United Kingdom so far as size is concerned. In the last two years of the first quinquennium (i.e. 1965/66 and 1966/67) the cost per head rose on account of the introduction at that stage of the most recent Schools of applied and biological sciences.

It should be noted, however, that the plans in 1963/64 for accelerated expansion were costed and it appeared that, while the total amount of recurrent funds available over the quinquennium as a whole was likely to be sufficient to sustain the over-all rate of projected growth, the amounts allocated by the UGC for particular years would lead to surpluses in some years and deficits in others. In particular, the programme for the last year of the quinquennium could only be achieved by carrying forward substantial sums from earlier years. Fortunately the UGC agreed that, in view of the special circumstances of this University, this could be done; it was therefore possible to set aside for this purpose a sum of £40,000 in the accounts for 1963/64 as a contribution to a Quinquennium Equalization Account.

Unlike the previous quinquennium, which was a period of rapid growth, this quinquennial period (i.e. 1967-72) was evidently to be a period of consolidation and the submission made by the University to the UGC was based on a bid for limited growth of student numbers to approximately 3,500 by 1971/72. In fact, the grants allocated were not only based on an even smaller student target, but provided a very much lower amount per student than had been allowed for in the submission. Like most other universities, Sussex was forced to face a period of austerity with minimal funds available for new developments. It was clear, indeed, that if any worthwhile new developments were to be provided in the latter part of the quinquennium it would be necessary to make major savings on existing commitments in the early years. By the exercise of strict economy it proved possible to set aside £65,000 from the income for 1967/68 to make provision for this subsequent development. The outlook was also improved when, as a result of representations from the University, the UGC agreed to increase the grant for 1968/69 by £50,000.

Table 4 shows the percentage of University expenditure and income under the various heads of account in 1967/68 compared with some previous years.

TABLE 4. University income and expenditure, 1962/63-1967/68

|  | 1962/63 | 1964/65 | 1966/67 | 1967/68 |
|---|---|---|---|---|
| *Income* | % | % | % | % |
| Parliamentary grants | 74.6 | 79.6 | 71.6 | 67.6 |
| Fees | 8.6 | 8.3 | 8.0 | 8.2 |
| Research grants | 4.2 | 8.0 | 16.2 | 19.9 |
| Other income | 12.6 | 4.1 | 4.2 | 4.3 |
|  | 100.0 | 100.0 | 100.0 | 100.0 |
| Total income for year (£) | 331 184 | 1 176 364 | 2 268 117 | 2 955 464 |
| *Expenditure* | % | % | % | % |
| Administration | 15.1 | 12.7 | 9.2 | 7.8 |
| Academic | 51.0 | 58.3 | 67.6 | 70.9 |
| Library | 7.9 | 8.7 | 5.8 | 4.7 |
| Premises | 14.3 | 14.7 | 12.4 | 12.2 |
| Other expenses | 11.7 | 5.6 | 5.0 | 4.4 |
|  | 100.0 | 100.0 | 100.0 | 100.0 |

The most significant single fact disclosed by Table 4 is the continued decline in the percentage of University income coming from the Treasury. From a peak of nearly 80 per cent in 1964-65 this had fallen by 1967/68 to less than 68 per cent. In fact, of the increase of nearly £690,000 in income over the previous year, more than £300,000 came from sources other than the UGC.

A small part of the increase arose from the controversial increase in overseas student fees imposed on all universities by government policy. Even the fact that Sussex University had more than the national average of overseas students did not rebound to its financial advantage, as a national equalization fund was operated to share the 'additional' income between all universities in proportion to their receipts of recurrent grant. In order to alleviate the effects of the fees increase the University made available funds to provide bursaries for overseas students who might otherwise have been prevented from pursuing their courses here. A much more important reason for the declining proportion of total income coming from grants was the dramatic increase in the value of receipts for research purposes, which totalled over £580,000 in 1967/68 compared with £360,000 in the previous year. This figure illustrates not only the University's success in raising outside funds to supplement UGC grants but also the growing importance of Sussex as a major research centre.

An indication of the increasing public importance of University finance came in the government decision to subject the accounts of the UGC and the individual universities to scrutiny by the staff of the Controller and Auditor-General. Sussex was one of the first universities to be visited. While it was evident from the course of the audit as well as from public statements at a national level that the emphasis was placed on efficiency rather than academic policy, this could well prove to be an important development in the relationship between the universities on the one hand and Parliament and the government on the other.

Table 5 has been calculated from numbers given in the recently published UGC statistics for 1965/66, and illustrates the unit costs of this University in comparison with the national average.

# B. Capital resources

Capital or non-recurrent grants from government sources for buildings, equipment, sites and professional fees were insignificant before the second world war. Indeed, University building was almost entirely dependent on private benefactions, endowments and local authority grants up until the end of the war. It was in 1947 that the government accepted its responsibility to make grant provision for University accommodation on an entirely new scale. A comparison of the actual government expenditures on capital grants between the last two

TABLE 5. Departmental expenditure and student loads, 1965/66

| Subject group | | Expenditure (£) | Undergraduate load | | Graduate numbers | | Unit cost (£)[1] | |
|---|---|---|---|---|---|---|---|---|
| | | | FT | PT | FT | PT | A[2] | B[2] |
| Arts | GB | 11 591 460 | 31 681 | 802 | 3 823 | 1 121 | 321 | 287 |
| | SX | 188 376 | 610 | — | 111 | 9 | 260 | 225 |
| Social studies | GB | 9 345 805 | 27 429 | 720 | 3 804 | 1 615 | 291 | 257 |
| | SX | 129 677 | 321 | — | 51 | 13 | 345 | 301 |
| Education | GB | 2 069 672 | 494 | 145 | 5 261 | 1 767 | 324 | 324 |
| | SX | 28 530 | 15 | — | 34 | — | 582 | 582 |
| Physical sciences | GB | 19 319 039 | 31 361 | 470 | 6 373 | 1 005 | 505 | 374 |
| | SX | 383 811 | 700 | — | 148 | 17 | 559 | 330 |
| Biological sciences | GB | 6 266 675 | 6 637 | 53 | 1 385 | 367 | 768 | 561 |
| | SX | 61 810 | 32 | — | 11 | 2 | 1 408 | 909 |
| Applied sciences | GB | 18 919 450 | 23 208 | 969 | 5 157 | — | 1 292 | 923 |
| | SX | | 43 | — | 5 | — | 2 098 | 1 500 |
| All groups | GB[3] | 87 284 007 | 139 025 | 3279 | 28 428 | 7 939 | 510 | — |
| | SX | 831 442 | 1721 | — | 367 | 43 | 395 | — |

1. To derive the unit costs, 3 part-time=1 full-time.
2. Unit cost A assumes undergraduates and postgraduates are of equal weight. Unit cost B weighs undergraduates as 1 unit, education postgraduates as 1 unit, arts and social studies postgraduates as 2 units, and science postgraduates as 3 units.
3. Figures do not total since disciplines not taught at Sussex, such as medicine, have not been included.

quinquennia, 1957-62 and 1962-67, is given below to illustrate the remarkable increase in government income for this purpose.

|  | Academic years | |
|---|---|---|
|  | 1957-62 | 1962-67 |
|  | (£000) | (£000) |
| Building and fees | 75 748 | 203 134 |
| Sites and properties | 6 498 | 12 732 |
| Furniture and equipment | 16 814 | 79 606 |
|  | 99 060 | 295,472 |

Plans for the first stage of this University's building programme were initiated early in 1959, following the UGC's agreement to make available a capital grant of £1.5 million to meet the cost of the University's first non-residential buildings. The architect, Sir Basil Spence, undertook to have two of these buildings (Falmer House, the social centre, and the physics building) completed in time for October 1962 instead of October 1963, as had been originally intended. Early in 1960, the College was invited to discuss with the UGC the possibility of revising its building plans in the light of the government's desire that more University places should be made available nationally during the next decade. The Vice-chancellor then prepared a plan which envisaged a student population of 3,000 by 1970, and this was approved by the UGC. The new plan necessitated a re-examination of the first stage of the building programme (i.e. up to 1963) and it was finally decided that four more major buildings should be commissioned, each of which would be somewhat larger than had been originally contemplated. In view of the heavy and increasing pressure on university places, the Sussex Council decided to try to accelerate its programme even further, and to accept some students as early as October 1961. This involved using temporary accommodation in Brighton, and in turn meant that the first intake could be for arts students only, since science students would require specialised laboratory facilities.

In November 1963, the University was asked to respond to the proposals for expansion of student numbers, recommended by the Robbins committee. The University offered to accelerate its original timetable, which had envisaged a student population of 3,000 by 1970, so as to achieve that figure by 1967, and the offer was accepted by the UGC. In consequence, the University had a large building programme on hand, although the capital grants asked for could not be made available in full during the period of consolidation which would follow (i.e. 1967 72). The University agreed to go ahead on this under-standing. Very substantial grants of £1.58 million for 1964 and £1.18 million for 1965/66 were made towards permanent buildings, together with a number of temporary buildings, to be replaced once the financial position permitted.

In 1965/66 the government announced deferments of building starts, for national economic reasons. This involved a six-month postponement of building starts in most fields of public spending, and University projects totalling some £15 million were delayed in consequence. Some part of this deferment was made good in 1966/67. Despite these inconvenient delays, Sussex has been able to construct the necessary core of permanent buildings and the present quinquennium (1967-72) is providing the opportunity to add further stages to existing buildings (e.g. arts, biology, chemistry, library). The single building which has consistently been deferred is the administrative centre, temporarily housed in a hall of residence, though it now appears that this will be included in the building programme for 1970, following the government's recent decision (announced 29.1.69) to provide additional capital funds in the last two years of the quinquennium.

The primary aim of the building programme in the early years of the University's life was to provide the largest possible number of student places in time to meet the 'bulge' in qualified candidates expected during 1964-67, without prejudicing the longer-term interests of the University. Two decisions of major significance in the building sphere followed. Firstly, it was decided to adopt a very high rate of building, aiming to complete building for 1,500 students within five years and for 3,000 students within ten years; rates of expansion which have since been doubled. Secondly, every effort was made to build permanent buildings from the start, relying to the minimum extent on temporary buildings, with each major phase (e.g. for 3,000 students) to be as complete as possible in itself.

The difficulty of constructing permanent buildings from the start, before the academic staff who would be using them were in office, was overcome by the help, liberally given, of assessors from other universities. It would have been possible either to delay taking in students while the buildings were being planned by the ultimate users—an unacceptable solution in the historical setting—or to have used temporary buildings on a large scale. This latter solution was rejected, not only because it would have been more expensive in the long run, but because the first generation of students, whose pace-setting was considered to be of fundamental importance, would have been unduly handicapped. It is generally believed by members of the University that the decision taken was the right one. The building programme has kept pace with the expansion of student numbers, and this has been an important factor in the development of the University, since it was at one time feared that building delays would impede its progress.

## C. Residential capacity

The choice of Brighton as the location of the first of the new universities was based in part upon the assumption that there was sufficient accommodation available locally to match at least the first stages of growth. The decisions about residential accommodation on campus have been particularly important for Sussex, since the University is located about four miles from the centre of Brighton and four miles from Lewes, with a regular bus and train service to it from both towns. Although United Kingdom students tend to go away from home to university, and consequently in many towns to rely on the provision of halls of residence, statements about national policy seemed to make it clear that Sussex would for a long time, and probably indefinitely, have to rely on accommodation in neighbouring towns, primarily Brighton. In 1966/67 the number of residential places available in universities was about 64,000 i.e. 35 per cent of the total student population at that time. The ideal recommended in the Niblett report (1957), a sub-committee of the UGC on halls of residence, was that residential places should be provided in most universities for two-thirds of the increase in student numbers. In fact, the amount of residence provided from UGC building funds in recent years has been as shown in Table 6.

TABLE 6. Allocation for residence, 1964-1969/70 (in £ million)

|  | 1964 | 1965/66 | 1966/67 | 1967/68 | 1968/69 | 1969/70 |
|---|---|---|---|---|---|---|
| Total allocation | 48.5 | 46.1 | 39.3 | 35.1 | 29.0 | 29.0 |
| Allocation for residence | 12.5 | 7.9 | 5.3 | 2.7 | 2.1 | 2.3 |

Nevertheless, the University of Sussex has consistently aimed at a target figure for residence of one in three. Accordingly, it was thought important to concentrate on as efficient as possible a grouping of the academic and social facilities that would be used by all the members of the University rather than to insist on grouping academic and residential buildings together. The availability of suitable local accommodation has of course been an important factor in enabling the University to attract faculty with families. Local accommodation is available to the University in private homes (with service and meals as required), small hotels, bedsitters (without board), flats of different sizes. The University established an accommodation office in 1962/63 to advise and secure accommodation for students and for faculty.

There are, however, other sources of pressure on local accommodation, especially from neighbouring institutions such as the Brighton College of Technology and the Brighton College of Art, both of which are entirely non-residential, and the Brighton College of Education, which is part-residential. The future expansion of all these institutions will depend in fact upon the availability of suitable accommodation, and it is likely that a larger proportion of residential facilities on campus will have to be provided. Nevertheless, it has been possible so far for the Brighton area to absorb the large numbers of students from all the various institutions.

# D. Selection of undergraduates

The University, from its earliest days, has devoted a great deal of its energy to the design of its first degree courses and to the selection of its undergraduates. In view of the large excess of demand for University places over supply (see Table 7), the University felt itself under an obligation to establish an efficient selection procedure, and to be seen to be so doing by schools and candidates. In particular, it was hoped that such a procedure would reduce student wastage rates to a minimum.

It has been recognized that the quality and type of the graduates of the

TABLE 7.   Applications, acceptances and relative indices, 1961-68

|  | Applications | | Acceptances | | Relative indices | |
|---|---|---|---|---|---|---|
|  | Arts | Science | Arts | Science | Arts | Science |
| October 1968 | 8 411 | 5 221 | 449 | 509 | 18.73 | 10.02 |
| October 1967 | 7 594 | 4 675 | 453 | 564 | 16.76 | 8.29 |
| October 1966 | 6 691 | 3 433 | 434 | 467 | 15.42 | 7.34 |
| October 1965 | 7 345 | 2 987 | 395 | 397 | 18.59 | 7.52 |
| October 1964 | 4 994 | 966 | 316 | 235 | 15.81 | 3.86 |
| October 1963 | 3 876 | 889 | 224 | 201 | 17.30 | 4.42 |
| October 1962 | 2 453 | 627 | 199 | 159 | 12.033 | 4.0 |
| October 1961 | 475 | — | 52 | — | 9.13 | — |

University is due in great part to the quality and type of the applicants admitted. The nature of the courses, the quality, type and amount of teaching, the level of motivation of students during the course and the general ethos of the University are equally important, but their effectiveness depends upon the quality of the intake. The University therefore needed a systematic admissions procedure as one of the tools of its central planning. The University's control over the allocation of its resources, and its ability to adjust that allocation, has depended to a large extent upon the effectiveness of its control over its intake.

The University of Sussex is unusual, though not unique, amongst British Universities in that the admission of students to first-degree courses is organised and controlled centrally. The desirability of such a degree of centralisation also arose from the structure of the curriculum at the University, with its integration of neighbouring disciplines and its liberal transfer policy, both of which have tended to render a subject-based admissions system inappropriate and unduly rigid. The advent in 1962 of the Universities Central Council on Admissions (UCCA) as a national central clearing house for undergraduate admissions not only relieved universities of a large clerical burden (at a cost to this university of some £5,000 per year), but also made a central office necessary rather than merely desirable. It is interesting to recall that Lord Fulton, the first Vice-chancellor of the University, was the first chairman of UCCA, and this again emphasised the University's concern with admission problems.

It has been one of the admissions office's tasks, from year to year and throughout each year, to strike balances between the distribution of places to applicants by School and major subjects, and the relative quality of applicants applying for the various courses. There is no formula for achieving the right balance; statistical tools for weighting the various factors are used but the factors are not constant. However, to date the University has achieved its

TABLE 8. Applications and acceptances by major subject, 1968

| Subject | Applied | Accepted[1] | Applications/place ratio[2] | Subject | Applied | Accepted[1] | Applications/place ratio[2] |
|---|---|---|---|---|---|---|---|
| *Arts and social studies* | | | | *Science and technology* | | | |
| American st. (hist.) | 94 | 5 | 18.8 | Automatic control | 53 | 8 | 6.6 |
| American st. (lit.) | 162 | 5 | 32.4 | Applied physics | 92 | 11 | 8.4 |
| Anthropology | 291 | 17 | 17.1 | Biochemistry | 558 | 38 | 14.7 |
| Art | 306 | 12 | 25.5 | Biology | 685 | 62 | 11.0 |
| Biology | 8 | 0 | — | Chemistry | 713 | 94 | 7.4 |
| Economics | 848 | 37 | 22.9 | Chemical physics | 56 | 7 | 8.0 |
| English lit. | 1 688 | 89 | 19.0 | Electronics | 576 | 42 | 13.7 |
| French | 574 | 41 | 14.0 | Electrical engineering | 224 | 17 | 13.2 |
| Geography | 502 | 29 | 17.3 | Engineering operational research | 34 | 3 | 11.3 |
| German | 213 | 15 | 14.2 | | | | |
| History | 743 | 49 | 15.2 | | | | |
| International rels. | 300 | 15 | 20.0 | Engineering and social studies | 65 | 5 | 13.0 |
| Law | 412 | 7 | 58.9 | Experimental psychology | 218 | 14 | 15.6 |
| Mathematics | 71 | 7 | 10.1 | Geography | 113 | 5 | 22.6 |
| Philosophy | 267 | 15 | 17.8 | Materials science | 95 | 13 | 7.3 |
| Philosophy and religion | 41 | 4 | 10.2 | Mathematics | 594 | 72 | 8.3 |
| Physics | 10 | 0 | — | Philosophy and the theory of science | 58 | 4 | 14.5 |
| Politics | 225 | 20 | 11.2 | | | | |
| Psychology, developmental | 297 | 11 | 27.0 | Mathematical physics | 124 | 14 | 8.9 |
| Psychology, social | 434 | 21 | 20.7 | Mechanical engineering | 406 | 28 | 16.1 |
| Religious studies | 68 | 0 | — | Physics | 553 | 72 | 7.7 |
| Russian | 46 | 9 | 5.1 | Others | 4 | 0 | — |
| Russian studies | 28 | 6 | 4.7 | | | | |
| Sociology | 775 | 35 | 22.1 | | | | |
| Others | 8 | 0 | — | | | | |
| Total | 8 411 | 449 | 18.7 | Total | 5 221 | 509 | 10.3 |

1. The figures for accepted students should not be confused with those who actually began courses in October 1968. Some students who are accepted in August subsequently withdrew. The final intake figures were 422 in B.A. courses and 487 in B.Sc. courses.
2. Although the applications/place ratio is a test of competition, it should be regarded with caution. It ignores, for instance, the *quality* of the applications received, which varies between subjects. English and History, for example, are more competitive than Economics, despite the figures.

TABLE 9. Sussex applicants also applying to Oxbridge: percentage preference for Sussex

| | 1st | 2nd | 3rd | 4th | 5th | 6th | Total |
|---|---|---|---|---|---|---|---|
| 1966 | 1.3 | 19.3 | 27.4 | 21.4 | 16.3 | 14.3 | 100.0 |
| 1968 | 10.6 | 34.4 | 28.4 | 16.9 | 7.2 | 2.5 | 100.0 |

targets and the balance within those targets with considerable accuracy. There was a slight shortfall in science in 1964, but the annual intakes have always been 1 per cent or 2 per cent higher than the targets set.

In 1967/68 the University received 13,632 applications for the 908 places which were available in terms of the logistic development of the University. 1967/68 was characterised by large increases in the number of applications for both B.A. and B.Sc. courses (see Table 8). The B.Sc. increase of 11.9 per cent (from 4,675 in 1967 to 5,221 in 1968) should be set against a national increase of 6.9 per cent in the subject areas offered by the University. These figures confirm the trend of previous years, in all but one of which the University has increased its share of the applicant market in arts, and in all of which that share has been increased for Science courses.

The University receives many tributes each year from Schools and individuals on its attitude to admissions and upon the effort made to be fair and to treat applicants as individuals. A relative decline in the demand for places might have been expected, in view of the publicity given to the difficulty of obtaining a place at Sussex and in view of the opening of other new universities. In fact, applications as a proportion of the total national applications have continued to rise year by year (approximately 15 per cent of all UCCA applicants in 1965 named Sussex as one of their choices, and the percentage is approximately 18 per cent if applications for courses not offered by Sussex are discounted (e.g. medicine, dentistry, law, agriculture, etc.).

In percentage terms, Sussex has, over the past two years, improved its position in relation to Oxbridge. The figures for Sussex applicants also applying to Oxbridge are shown in Table 9.

Of all Sussex applicants in 1968, 14.3 per cent applied to Oxbridge, compared with 19.0 per cent in 1966, the last available figure. The figures for each group are: arts men 18 per cent, arts women 7.5 per cent, science men 15.7 per cent, science women 10.0 per cent.

TABLE 10. Preference for Sussex amongst applicants also applying to Oxford or Cambridge, 1968

| Sussex preference | B.A. courses | | B.Sc. courses | | Total applicants |
|---|---|---|---|---|---|
| | Men | Women | Men | Women | |
| 1st | 101 | 32 | 61 | 12 | 206 |
| 2nd | 392 | 71 | 181 | 26 | 670 |
| 3rd | 243 | 88 | 195 | 28 | 554 |
| 4th | 108 | 49 | 159 | 14 | 330 |
| 5th | 54 | 15 | 64 | 7 | 140 |
| 6th | 22 | 3 | 20 | 3 | 40 |
| Total | 920 | 258 | 680 | 90 | 1 948 |

# E. Academic faculty

Figure 4 illustrates the growth in staff numbers during the period 1961-68 (see also Table 11). From the outset, the University has been fortunate in both the quality and quantity of the applicants for nearly all the academic and administrative posts it has offered. In only a small number of subjects has there been a reflection of a national shortage, though it is clear that there is increasing competition for applicants from other institutions. Most members of faculty have been recruited after public advertisement, though some have been invited to take up posts at the University.

TABLE 11. Total university staff

| Session | 1962/63 | 1963/64 | 1964/65 | 1965/66 | 1966/67 | 1967/68 |
|---|---|---|---|---|---|---|
| Date of count | April 1963 | March 1964 | March 1965 | April 1966 | March 1967 | February 1968 |
| *Faculty* | | | | | | |
| Teaching and research | 61 | 111 | 176 | 253 | 321 | 344 |
| Administrative | 18 | 21 | 34 | 45 | 61 | 57 |
| Other non-academic | 5 | 9 | 11 | 16 | 26 | 30 |
| Total | 84 | 141 | 221 | 314 | 408 | 431 |
| *Non-faculty* | | | | | | |
| Clerical and secretarial | 34 | 66 | 128 | 189 | 245 | 275 |
| Technical | 19 | 38 | 60 | 102 | 140 | 164 |
| Estate wages staff | 29 | 57 | 92 | 146 | 190 | 187 |
| Catering wages staff | 34 | ( ) | 43 | 52 | 59 | 72 |
| Total | 116 | (161) | 323 | 489 | 634 | 698 |
| Grand total | 200 | (302) | 544 | 803 | 1 042 | 1 129 |

NOTE  The above figures are of full-time equivalent staff in posts payable from University funds (i.e., excluding grant-aided and visiting and associated posts).

Vacancies in establishment have been mainly due to time-lag, not lack of quality applicants—except in certain science fields, such as mathematics and physics. In 1965, for example, there were six vacancies only, which was 3 per cent of all logistic posts. In 1968, there were 11 vacancies, again 3 per cent only of all logistic posts. Figure 5 sets out the distribution of academic faculty by grade during the period 1961-68; the distribution of academic faculty by subject group is shown in Figure 6.

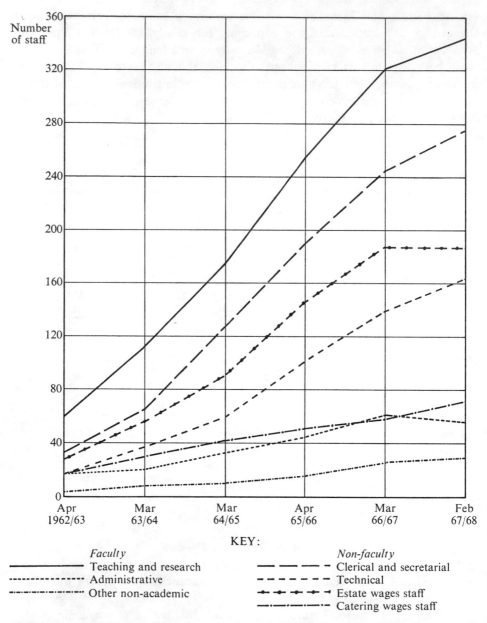

KEY:

| Faculty | Non-faculty |
|---|---|
| Teaching and research | Clerical and secretarial |
| Administrative | Technical |
| Other non-academic | Estate wages staff |
| | Catering wages staff |

Figure 4. Growth of staff numbers (total University staff), 1961—1968

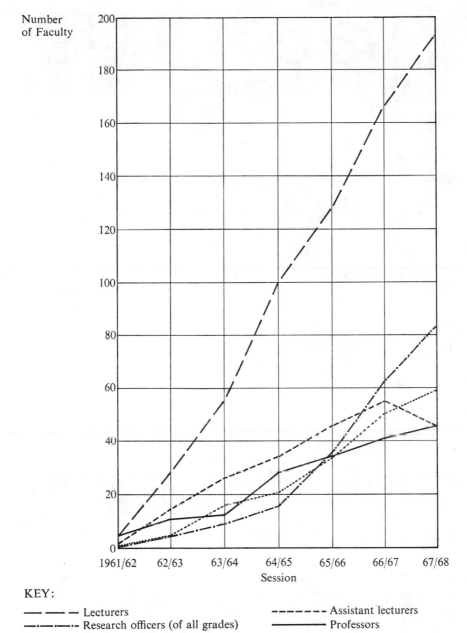

Number of Faculty

Session

KEY:

— — — Lecturers      - - - - - - Assistant lecturers
—·—·—·— Research officers (of all grades)      ——————— Professors
·················· Readers and Senior lecturers

NOTE   The figures up to and including 1964/65 are those of full-time teaching and research faculty paid directly from University funds. From 1965/66 the numbers are of all academic faculty whether financed from University funds or not, except visiting and associated faculty. The difference is due to a change in UGC definitions from 1965/66.

Figure 5.   Academic faculty by grade, 1961—1968

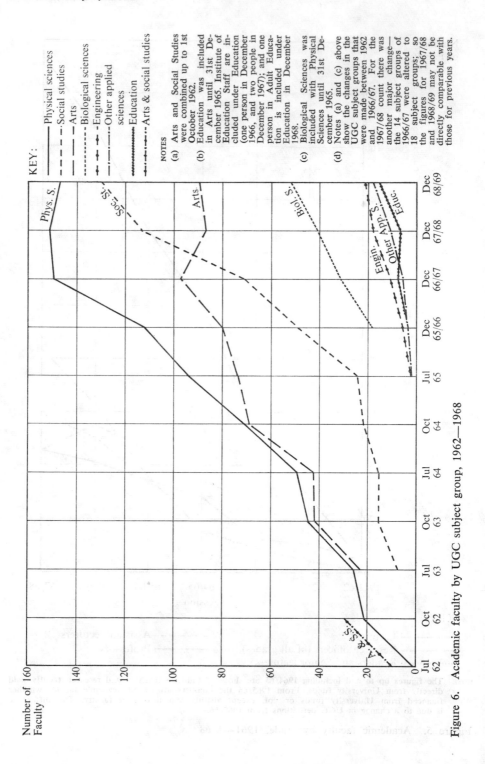

KEY:

——— Physical sciences
– – – Social studies
— — Arts
·········· Biological sciences
–·–·– Engineering
—··—··— Other applied sciences
▪▪▪▪▪ Education
–··–··– Arts & social studies

NOTES

(a) Arts and Social Studies were combined up to 1st October 1962.

(b) Education was included in Arts until 31st December 1965. Institute of Education Staff are included under Education (one person in December 1966, and two people in December 1967); and one person in Adult Education is included under Education in December 1968.

(c) Biological Sciences was included with Physical Sciences until 31st December 1965.

(d) Notes (a) and (c) above show the changes in the UGC subject groups that were made between 1962 and 1966/67. For the 1967/68 count there was another major change—the 14 subject groups of 1966/67 were altered to 18 subject groups; so the figures for 1967/68 and 1968/69 may not be directly comparable with those for previous years.

Figure 6. Academic faculty by UGC subject group, 1962—1968

Academic titles for full-time faculty fall into four categories: professors, readers, lecturers and assistant lecturers. Professors, readers and senior lecturers are normally the three senior grades, the latter two being broadly parallel in age and salary structure. In 1968, the University decided to abolish the traditional distinction made in British universities between readers and senior lecturers, and all faculty at Sussex at that grade are now called readers. Research posts have their own range of titles, such as Professorial fellow, Senior fellow and Fellow.

In December 1965 an analysis was made of the ages of academic faculty compared with some national data (see Table 12).

TABLE 12.  Ages of academic faculty

| | University of Sussex 1.10.64 | National (Robbins report) 1961/62 | National (AUT survey) 1.10.61 | National survey 1.10.64 |
|---|---|---|---|---|
| | % | % | % | % |
| *Ages* | | | | |
| Under 30 years | 45 | 19 | 22 | 28 |
| 30-39 years | 36 | 37 | 41 | 36 |
| 40-49 years | 15 | 25 | 22 | 22 |
| 50 years and over | 4 | 19 | 15 | 14 |
| *Average (median) age in years* | | | | |
| Professors | 44.5 | 51 | 50 | 49 |
| Readers/Senior lecturers | 37.5 | 47 | 43.5 | 43.5 |
| Lecturers | 30 | 37 | 34.5 | 33 |
| Assistant lecturers | 26.5 | 28 | 26 | 25.5 |
| All teaching staff | 31 | 38 | 37 | 36 |

The numbers of resignations of academic faculty in the period 1965-68 are given in Table 13.

TABLE 13.  Resignations of academic faculty, 1965/68

| | 1965/66 | 1966/67 | 1967/68 |
|---|---|---|---|
| Teaching faculty resignations | 10 | 7 | 18 |
| *Reasons for academic faculty leaving* | | | |
| To U.K. university | 6 | 3 | 5 |
| To overseas university | 1 | 2 | 7 |
| Others and not known | 3 | 2 | 6 |

NOTE  The rate of annual turnover was under 1 per cent in 1961-65, rising to 4 per cent in 1965/66, 2.5 per cent in 1966/67 and 6 per cent in 1967/68. The low rate of turnover has been one of the distinctive features of the faculty pattern.

TABLE 14.   Staff-student ratios, 1961/62-1968/69

| | 1961/62 | 1962/63 | 1963/64 | 1964/65 | 1965/66 | 1966/67 | 1967/68 | 1968/69 |
|---|---|---|---|---|---|---|---|---|
| **Number of students** (full-time only) | 52 | 434 | 883 | 1 482 | 2 090 | 2 763 | 3 233 | 3 457 |
| Undergraduates | 52 | 416 | 813 | 1 299 | 1 723 | 2 161 | 2 580 | 2 713 |
| Postgraduates (4th year) | | | | | | | | |
| Cert. ed. & Dip. soc. work | — | — | — | 37 | 40 | 83 | 72 | 86 |
| Arts (MA) | — | — | — | 19 | 92 | 120 | 185 | 205 |
| Science (MSc) | — | — | — | 12 | 28 | 140 | 162 | 195 |
| Postgraduates (research) | | | | | | | | |
| Arts | — | 4 | 15 | 34 | 64 | 132 | 109 | 78 |
| Science | — | 14 | 55 | 81 | 143 | 150 | 164 | 180 |
| **Number of teaching staff** (full-time only) | 9 | 56 | 107 | 172 | 250 | 310 | 346 | 362 |
| **Staff-student ratio:** | | | | | | | | |
| UGC formula[1] | 5.8 | 8.3 | 9.4 | 10.1 | 10.3 | 11.5 | 11.7 | 12.4 |
| Unweighted | 5.8 | 7.75 | 8.25 | 8.6 | 8.4 | 8.9 | 10.45 | 9.6 |
| Sussex formula[2] | 5.8 | 7.4 | 7.6 | 8.0 | 7.5 | 8.8 | 8.7 | 8.9 |

1. *UGC formula:* undergraduates and educational postgraduates=1; arts and social studies postgraduates=2; science postgraduates=3.
2. *Sussex formula:* same as UGC formula except that all first-year postgraduates=1.

TABLE 15.   Faculty time: average hours per student

| | Undergraduates | | | Graduate and research students | | |
|---|---|---|---|---|---|---|
| | Number of students | Total faculty teaching hours | Hours per student | Number of students | Total faculty teaching hours | Hours per student |
| Science | 998 | 24 790 | 24.9 | 325 | 22 642 | 70.0 |
| Arts | 1 128 | 67 006 | 59.4 | 280 | 16 345 | 58.8 |
| Total | 2 126 | 91 796 | 43.2 | 605 | 38 987 | 64.4 |

As already stated, the figures in Table 16 represent the activities which are easily quantifiable and obtainable from University records; they exclude research, general reading, outside and professional activities, etc. They are presented in percentages rather than actual hours since without adequate allowance for research time the table would be misleading, particularly the arts/science comparison.

TABLE 16.  Faculty time: activities as percentages of total hours (of non-research time)

|  | Science | | Arts | | Total | |
|---|---|---|---|---|---|---|
| Undergraduate teaching | 31.6 | | 57.05 | | 47.9 | |
| Graduate courses | 1.7 | | 10.3 | | 7.0 | |
| Research supervision | 28.7 | | 3.75 | | 13.35 | |
| Total teaching | | 62 | | 71.1 | | 68.25 |
| Personal tutors | 13.1 | | 10.1 | | 11.0 | |
| Undergraduate admission | 2.1 | | 1.3 | | 1.5 | |
| Graduate admission | .5 | | .25 | | 0.3 | |
| University examinations | 7.7 | | 4.7 | | 5.75 | |
| University committees | 4.0 | | 4.05 | | 4.0 | |
| Officer duties | 10.6 | | 8.5 | | 9.2 | |
| Total non-teaching | | 38 | | 28.9 | | 31.75 |
| Total | 100.0 | | 100.0 | | 100.0 | |

# F. Undergraduate programme

The Sussex undergraduate's career is based on one of the nine Schools of studies. There are close links of different kinds between all Schools; links between the Deans, among members of faculty who may teach in more than one School, and those which result from a series of common procedures for admissions, transfer and 'wastage'. There are also some common assumptions about tutorials, teaching methods and teaching loads and joint examining procedures. Policy in regard to personal tutors, the use of the health service and the careers advisory service is common to all the schools.

On coming up to the University, a new undergraduate follows a preliminary course during the first two terms. Much of this course is common to all first-year undergraduates in the arts (or science) group of schools; the undergraduates therefore share a common ground-work. This is thought to be doubly valuable; first, the undergraduate starts out by acquiring a broad basis of knowledge, principles and techniques which he can later develop in different ways; secondly, in the light of the work in several subjects, he may be able to change his intended School or major subject provided that he is suitably qualified and provided that he obtains the permission of the Deans concerned.

The opening week of each academic year is devoted to the registration of all students. A programme of activities is organised by the Registrar's office in consultation with Schools of studies and the Union, and is designed to introduce new students to the life of the University. Because of the many important inter-faculty and faculty-student discussions and consultations on academic matters which occur during the first week, either on an official or an informal basis, members of faculty are expected to be in attendance at the University throughout the whole of this week to advise students on their course, plans, etc.

Undergraduates are set written work to produce on a weekly basis, either in the form of essays or of answers to problem papers. Tutors report on this work to Deans of Schools. Each School office keeps a record of each individual undergraduate's academic progress. The record card is brought up to date regularly by the School office in the light of tutors' reports, examination results, comments by personal Tutors, notes from the University health service, etc. Each tutor is expected to complete a form (which contains a graded assessment section and a prose report section) reporting on the work of each of his pupils in a given term and to return it duly completed to the student's personal Tutor and to the School office. Tutors are asked to submit special reports to the Dean at any time if they are anxious about the attendance, performance or progress of a particular undergraduate, and the Dean will then determine what action should be taken. This is considered particularly important during an undergraduate's first term. Tutors' reports are intended to provide Deans and personal Tutors with regular and confidential information about the academic progress of an undergraduate; they also provide the basis of end-of-term discussions between Deans, personal Tutors and undergraduates.

It is considered uniquely valuable for students to meet their tutors frequently and face to face—whether in tutorials or in seminars and problem classes. Members of a small tutorial group can ask searching questions and consider the pros and cons of suggested possible answers. If an undergraduate is obliged, as he is at Sussex, to produce regular written work—anyone proposing to enter the University must come with that clear understanding— any difficulties he may have should quickly come to light. By these means the tutor hopes to guide his pupils towards understanding, discrimination and inventiveness.

Some of an undergraduate's tutors change from term to term. To ensure that someone can advise him on his work throughout his university career each undergraduate has a personal Tutor, who teaches some of his major subject courses. He can always approach his personal Tutor informally for help on personal as well as academic matters. Many members of faculty act in the capacity of personal Tutor to a limited number of undergraduates. The appointment of personal Tutor rests with the Dean of each school. As a general rule, a personal Tutor will be pre-appointed for each new undergraduate by the Dean from amongst those members of the faculty who have stated a primary affiliation to his particular School.

In the arts and social studies Schools, the chief responsibilities of the personal Tutors are to assist and advise their undergraduates in the drawing-up of their study plans for their projected courses and to supervise their progress thereafter. Discussion of course selection and study plans has particular significance, partly because an undergraduate may change his School or major subject with the permission of the relevant Deans, and partly because undergraduates have alternative major subject or contextual courses to choose from in studying for Finals—and they are expected to consult their personal Tutors before making their choices. The personal Tutor will normally be one of the undergraduate's teachers, and continues to act in an advisory capacity throughout the undergraduate's course.

In the science Schools, the role of the personal Tutor is essentially similar. In general, the personal Tutor's subject will be the undergraduate's major subject, and he will teach his personal students for at least one term and if possible much more; he will maintain personal contact with them throughout their course and will help and advise them in academic and other matters.

Through the tutorial and personal Tutor systems the University is able to keep an eye on how its undergraduates are getting on. If one of them seems to be in difficulty, for academic or other reasons, his tutor or personal Tutor is expected to discuss the matter with him; or the Dean of his School may advise him. Very serious cases may go to the students' progress committee; this committee, which consists of the Vice-chancellor, the Deans and the Director of the health service, and which meets twice a term, can enter an undergraduate's name on the Vice-chancellor's List. This means that the undergraduate is sent an official letter warning him that, unless his work improves, he may be required to leave the University. The decision to send down an undergraduate can only be taken if and when the subject tutor, the personal Tutor, the Dean, the Vice-chancellor and the students' progress committee are in agreement, after all the information on the undergraduate has been fully reviewed by all concerned. This procedure applies even though an undergraduate may have failed a University examination. Because of these measures the percentage of students leaving the University without a degree is among the smallest at any British University (see Tables 17-19).

A considerable volume of transfer is permitted, indeed encouraged, at the beginning and the end of the first two terms of the undergraduate's career (see Tables 20 and 21). Undergraduates may prefer to transfer to another School, probably because they prefer its contextual courses, or they may wish to change both School and major course. The question of transfers between courses has been exercising a wide variety of opinion within the University for some time. The University has operated this flexible transfer policy from the outset, and this is becoming increasingly important nationally in view of the changing pattern of secondary education and the consequent changes in the direction of flexibility and experience in the School curricula.

TABLE 17.  Wastage: withdrawals in each academic year

| Academic year | Intake | Student's year at university | | | | Total Students |
|---|---|---|---|---|---|---|
| | | 1 | 2 | 3 | 4/5 | |
| *Arts and social studies students* | | | | | | |
| 1961/62 | 52 | 2 | | | | 2 |
| 1962/63 | 204 | 11 | 1 | | | 12 |
| 1963/64 | 225 | 7 | 4 | — | | 11 |
| 1964/65 | 313 | 18 | 2 | 2 | — | 22 |
| 1965/66 | 365 | 5 | 4 | 3 | 2 | 14 |
| 1966/67 | 448 | 15 | 3 | 2 | 1 | 21 |
| 1967/68 | 438 | 18 | 10 | 8 | 1 | 37 |
| 1968/Feb. '69 | 433 | 3 | 9 | 1 | — | 13 |
| Totals | 2 478 | 79 | 33 | 16 | 4 | 132 |
| *Science students* | | | | | | |
| 1961/62 | — | | | | | — |
| 1962/63 | 159 | 13 | — | | | 13 |
| 1963/64 | 199 | 6 | 2 | — | | 8 |
| 1964/65 | 234 | 6 | 1 | — | — | 7 |
| 1965/66 | 383 | 12 | 3 | — | — | 15 |
| 1966/67 | 449 | 23 | 11 | 1 | — | 35 |
| 1967/68 | 531 | 31 | 10 | 5 | 1 | 47 |
| 1968/Feb. '69 | 493 | 12 | 6 | 7 | 1 | 26 |
| Totals | 2 448 | 103 | 33 | 13 | 2 | 151 |
| *All students* | | | | | | |
| 1961/62 | 52 | 2 | | | | 2 |
| 1962/63 | 363 | 24 | 1 | | | 25 |
| 1963/64 | 424 | 13 | 6 | — | | 19 |
| 1964/65 | 547 | 24 | 3 | 2 | | 29 |
| 1965/66 | 748 | 17 | 7 | 3 | 2 | 29 |
| 1966/67 | 897 | 38 | 14 | 3 | 1 | 56 |
| 1967/68 | 969 | 49 | 20 | 13 | 2 | 84 |
| 1968/Feb. '69 | 926 | 15 | 15 | 8 | 1 | 39 |
| Totals | 4 926 | 182 | 66 | 29 | 6 | 283 |

NOTES
1. *Intake*=new undergraduates, excluding visiting or exchange students, in the academic year.
2. *Academic year*=October to September inclusive, except for 1968/69.
3. Each row of the above table shows the number of students withdrawing in a given academic year, split according to the number of years each individual had been studying here. ('Year at University' is not quite the same as 'year of course', but the latter is not generally available without copious research).
4. Each column shows the numbers leaving after a given period of years here.
5. Each diagonal shows the numbers of a *particular intake* leaving at different stages. For example: in the *All students* section: in October 1963, 424 students entered the University (see row 3) and, of these, 13 left after being here up to one year, 3 left during their second year of study, etc.

TABLE 18. UGC Wastage survey 1965/66: progress of undergraduates by subject groups

| University | Number who would normally have graduated in 1965/66 (1) | Obtained first degree | | | | Re-admitted in October 1967 | | Left without having obtained a first degree | | | | Withdrew during course | |
| | | In normal period | | In more than normal period | | | | Failed degree | | Academic failure | | Other than academic failure | |
| | | Number | % of column 1 | Number | % of column 1 | Number | % of column 1 | Number | % of column 1 | Number | % of column 1 | Number | % of column 1 |
| *All subject groups* | | | | | | | | | | | | | |
| Sussex | 422 | 385 | 91.2 | 6 | 1.4 | — | — | 4 | 0.9 | 8 | 1.9 | 19 | 4.6 |
| Total England | 27479 | 22046 | 80.2 | 1850 | 6.8 | 227 | 0.8 | 357 | 1.3 | 2036 | 8.4 | 683 | 2.5 |
| Total Great Britain | 35386 | 27496 | 77.2 | 2770 | 7.8 | 432 | 1.2 | 488 | 1.4 | 3349 | 9.5 | 851 | 2.4 |
| *Arts subjects* | | | | | | | | | | | | | |
| Sussex | 151 | 130 | 86.1 | 2 | 1.3 | — | — | — | — | 3 | 2.0 | 16 | 10.6 |
| Total England | 6542 | 5669 | 86.7 | 350 | 5.3 | 26 | 0.4 | 83 | 1.3 | 186 | 2.8 | 228 | 3.5 |
| Total Great Britain | 8988 | 7441 | 82.8 | 619 | 6.9 | 80 | 0.9 | 127 | 1.4 | 435 | 4.8 | 286 | 3.2 |
| *Social studies* | | | | | | | | | | | | | |
| Sussex | 91 | 91 | 100.0 | — | — | — | — | — | — | — | — | — | — |
| Total England | 4912 | 4220 | 85.9 | 240 | 4.9 | 19 | 0.4 | 60 | 1.2 | 248 | 5.0 | 125 | 2.6 |
| Total Great Britain | 5819 | 4913 | 84.4 | 351 | 6.0 | 29 | 0.5 | 63 | 1.1 | 315 | 5.4 | 148 | 2.6 |
| *Physical sciences* | | | | | | | | | | | | | |
| Sussex | 120 | 108 | 90.0 | 3 | 2.5 | — | — | 3 | 2.5 | 4 | 3.3 | 2 | 1.7 |
| Total England | 4492 | 3638 | 81.7 | 204 | 4.5 | 20 | 0.4 | 84 | 1.9 | 431 | 9.6 | 85 | 1.9 |
| Total Great Britain | 5336 | 4237 | 79.4 | 235 | 5.5 | 25 | 0.5 | 100 | 1.9 | 582 | 10.9 | 97 | 1.8 |
| *Mathematics* | | | | | | | | | | | | | |
| Sussex | 60 | 56 | 93.2 | 1 | 1.7 | — | — | 1 | 1.7 | 1 | 1.7 | 1 | 1.7 |
| Total England | 1884 | 1553 | 82.7 | 82 | 4.3 | 7 | 0.4 | 29 | 1.5 | 171 | 9.1 | 37 | 2.0 |
| Total Great Britain | 2273 | 1819 | 80.0 | 133 | 5.9 | 12 | 0.5 | 37 | 1.6 | 225 | 9.9 | 47 | 2.1 |

NOTE The comparisons in the above table of the Sussex position by subject categories. On the basis of percentage obtaining first degree in normal period Sussex is placed 2nd out of the 29 English universities for all subjects, 12th in arts, 1st in social studies, 4th in physical sciences and 3rd in mathematics; only in arts was our 'failure' rate higher than the national average.

259

TABLE 19.  All students: reasons for withdrawal from University

| | Reasons for withdrawal | | | | | | | |
|---|---|---|---|---|---|---|---|---|
| | Failed prelims | | Other academic reasons | | Any other reasons | | Total students | |
| Academic year | M | F | M | F | M | F | M | F |
| 1961/62 | — | — | 1 | — | 1 | — | 2 | — |
| 1962/63 | 13 | 7 | — | — | 1 | 4 | 14 | 11 |
| 1963/64 | 5 | 1 | — | 1 | 2 | 10 | 7 | 12 |
| 1964/65 | 5 | — | 1 | — | 6 | 17 | 12 | 17 |
| 1965/66 | 6 | 2 | 2 | — | 11 | 8 | 19 | 10 |
| 1966/67 | 12 | 2 | 7 | 3 | 20 | 12 | 39 | 17 |
| 1967/68 | 8 | 2 | 8 | 1 | 34 | 31 | 50 | 34 |
| 1968/Feb. '69 | — | — | 7 | — | 21 | 11 | 28 | 11 |
| Totals | 49 | 14 | 26 | 5 | 96 | 93 | 171 | 112 |

NOTES
1. See note 2 to Table 17.
2. Each row of the above table shows the number of students, divided into male and female, withdrawing in a given academic year for the specified reason.
3. Each column shows the numbers of male and female students withdrawing for the specified reason.
4. *Other Academic Reasons*=failed school examinations or poor work and/or poor attendance.

Since the University ceased its initial phase of rapid expansion, during which the character of the undergraduate intake was to a significant degree determined by the demand for places in various fields of study, it has become increasingly important to maintain a student population which mirrors as far as possible the physical and teaching resources which are available within the University. The restricting factors on the number of undergraduates following a particular course are basically the physical amenities which can be provided for them (e.g. laboratory space) and the number of hours of teaching available for their use. As a result of these pressures, together with the fact that the distribution of teachers in each subject can change less rapidly if little or no expansion is taking place, some restrictions have been placed on transfer between subjects. The conditions under which transfers can take place are that the Dean of the receiving School must be satisfied that the undergraduate is properly qualified for the course he intends to follow, and that adequate teaching resources are available. In the case of undergraduates wishing to transfer from science to arts, or *vice-versa,* these conditions must be satisfied, but in addition it will normally be the case that the undergraduate will be required to attend for a selection interview with a regular admissions interview panel, which will take into account, in formulating a recommendation, whether he or she appears to measure up to the standards being imposed on new applicants. Further, an undergraduate making such a

TABLE 20. Undergraduate School and major subject changes due to transfer (1st year only): transfer by School: 1966/67

| School | Transfer within School | | Transfer to another School | | Total transfers | | Transfers into School | Net change in School population | |
|---|---|---|---|---|---|---|---|---|---|
| | Number | % | Number | % | Number | % | Number | Number | % |
| African & asian studies | 13 | 29 | 8 | 18 | 21 | 47 | 18 | 10 | +23 |
| Educational studies | 5 | 10 | 4 | 8 | 9 | 18 | 12 | 8 | +16 |
| English & american studies | 19 | 18 | 6 | 6 | 25 | 24 | 19 | 13 | +13 |
| European studies | 36 | 31 | 12 | 11 | 48 | 42 | 4 | −8 | −7 |
| Social studies | 15 | 11 | 28 | 20 | 43 | 31 | 13 | −15 | −11 |
| Arts total | 88 | 20 | 58 | 13 | 146 | 33 | 66 | +8 | |
| Applied sciences | 4 | 5 | 2 | 2 | 6 | 7 | 9 | 7 | +8 |
| Biological sciences | 13 | 15 | 3 | 4 | 16 | 19 | 10 | 7 | +8 |
| Mathematical & physical sciences | 0 | 0 | 16 | 10 | 16 | 10 | 6 | −10 | −6 |
| Molecular sciences | 19 | 16 | 14 | 11 | 33 | 27 | 2 | −12 | −10 |
| Science total | 36 | 8 | 35 | 8 | 71 | 16 | 27 | −8 | |
| Grand total | 124 | 14 | 93 | 10 | 217 | 24 | 93 | 0 | |

NOTES  1. The percentages are based on the School totals at 31 December 1966.
2. *Science to arts transfers:*
*School of biological sciences:* 3 biology majors transferred; two to science B (biology) in the School of educational studies and one to English in the School of English and American studies.
*School of mathematical and physical sciences:* 5 mathematics majors transferred; three to mathematics, one to social psychology and one to sociology, all in the School of social studies.
Both the Table and the science to arts transfers exclude transfers which took effect in October 1967.

transfer will, unless there are quite exceptional circumstances, be required to start the new course from scratch, involving an extra year at the University, and such transfers will in all cases be subject to the approval of the senior Dean.

The operation of this system preserves the liberal transfer policy operated at the University—it is, even with these restrictions, much easier to change courses at Sussex than at the great majority of universities—and at the same time allows the University to plan its teaching and other commitments on a realistic basis in order to make the best use of resources at its disposal. A by-product of the new arrangement is that, since there can be no absolute guarantee of transfer into any particular subject, and in particular into the subjects under heaviest pressure, applicants will presumably be discouraged from deliberately applying for a subject under comparatively light pressure with every intention of transferring on entry. Although there has been no

TABLE 21.   Undergraduate School and major subject changes due to transfer (1st year only): transfer by School and major subject 1966/67[1]

*African and asian studies*

| | |
|---|---|
| Economics | +2 |
| Geography | +1 |
| History | +1 |
| International relations | −1 |
| Literature (English) | 0 |
| Literature (French) | 0 |
| Philosophy & religion | 0 |
| Politics | 0 |
| Social anthropology | +12 |
| Sociology and politics | −5 |
| Total | +10 |

*Educational studies*

| | |
|---|---|
| English | +2 |
| Geography[2] | +1 |
| History | 0 |
| Philosophy | +2 |
| Psychology | −1 |
| Religious studies | 0 |
| Science (biology) | +2 |
| Sociology | +2 |
| Total | +8 |

*English and American studies*

| | |
|---|---|
| American studies | +12 |
| Art | +1 |
| English | −2 |
| History | −2 |
| Law | 0 |
| Philosophy[2] | +4 |
| Politics | −1 |
| Sociology | +1 |
| Total | +13 |

*European studies*

| | |
|---|---|
| Art | 0 |
| Economics | −3 |
| English | +5 |
| French | −16 |
| Geography | +1 |
| German | −3 |
| History | +1 |
| International relations | +4 |
| Law | 0 |
| Philosophy | +1 |
| Politics | +1 |
| Religious studies | 0 |
| Russian | 0 |
| Russian studies[2] | −1 |
| Sociology | +3 |
| Sociology and politics | −1 |
| Total | −8 |

*Social studies*

| | |
|---|---|
| Economics | −4 |
| Geography | −7 |
| History | 0 |
| International relations | 0 |
| Law | +1 |
| Mathematics | +1 |
| Philosophy | 0 |
| Politics | +2 |
| Religious studies | −1 |
| Science (physics) | 0 |
| Social anthropology | −1 |
| Social psychology[3] | 0 |
| Sociology[2] | −5 |
| Sociology and politics | −1 |
| Total | −15 |

*Applied sciences*

| | |
|---|---|
| Automatic control | +1 |
| Applied physics | +2 |
| Electrical engineering | 0 |
| Science | 0 |
| Mechanical engineering | 0 |
| Science | +2 |
| Mathematics | +2 |
| Materials science | 0 |
| Total | +7 |

*Biological sciences*

| | |
|---|---|
| Biology | −10 |
| Biochemistry | +8 |
| Experimental psychology | +3 |
| Geography | +6 |
| Total | +7 |

*Mathematical and physical sciences*

| | |
|---|---|
| Mathematics[3] | −9 |
| Physics[3] | 0 |
| Mathematics/Physics | −2 |
| Philosophy and the Theory of Science[3] | +1 |
| Total | −10 |

*Molecular sciences*

| | |
|---|---|
| Chemistry[3] | −20 |
| Theoretical chemistry | 0 |
| Chemical physics | +8 |
| Biochemistry | +6 |
| Materials science | −3 |
| Physics | −3 |
| Total | −12 |

1. The science to arts transfers are included in these figures.
2. Students also transferred into these subjects, as 1st year students, from science courses in October 1967.
3. Students also transferred from these subjects to the 1st year of arts courses in October 1967.

direct evidence of this in the past, some concern has been expressed that a system of unrestricted transfer would cause this to happen, and would cause unfairness towards applicants who made genuine statements as to their likely specialization. It should perhaps be said that this concern has not yet appeared to be well-founded in more than a very small number of cases.

# G. Graduate studies

There were many prophets (among them members of the University's academic advisory committee) who foresaw a protracted future for the University of Sussex in which postgraduate teaching (apart from professorial courses in education and social work) would have no part. The event has falsified these prophecies as the figures of growth in student numbers at the postgraduate level (Table 22 and figure 7) show.

TABLE 22. Increase in numbers of postgraduate students

| Year | MA | MSc | Research | | Dip. in social work and cert. in education | Total |
| | | | Arts | Science | | |
|---|---|---|---|---|---|---|
| 1962/63 | — | — | 4 | 14 | — | 18 |
| 1963/64 | — | 8 | 17 | 48 | — | 73 |
| 1964/65 | 16 | 12 | 37 | 81 | 37 | 183 |
| 1965/66 | 92 | 28 | 64 | 143 | 40 | 367 |
| 1966/67 | 112 | 66 | 107 | 214 | 86 | 585 |
| 1967/68 | 128 | 58 | 186 | 295 | 70 | 737 |

It is noteworthy that even in the first year in which undergraduates were admitted to read science (1962/63) over 8 per cent of those entering the Schools of studies in science were postgraduate. The explanation of such a high proportion of postgraduate students in that and subsequent years, in arts as well as in science, is probably far from simple. The general interest at home and overseas stimulated by the work and report of the Robbins committee in the foundation of the new universities; the geographical proximity to the libraries and learned societies of London; the fact that the University had succeeded in attracting a number of distinguished academics with international reputations, who in turn attracted other research workers to join them; the migration to Sussex of a number of research students from other universities when their supervisors left to take up posts here—all these had their influence in strengthening the postgraduate element of the student population.

It was also in part due to the establishment at the University of a number of research institutes, centres or units. These have been established at the University by special financial arrangements, in many cases because they depended for their success on developing inter-disciplinary (as opposed to single or even multi-disciplinary) research. Examples of such establishments are the Unit for Research in theoretical astronomy (in co-operation with the Royal Observatory at Herstmonceaux); the Nitrogen Fixation Unit (in co-operation with the Agricultural research council); the Institute of development

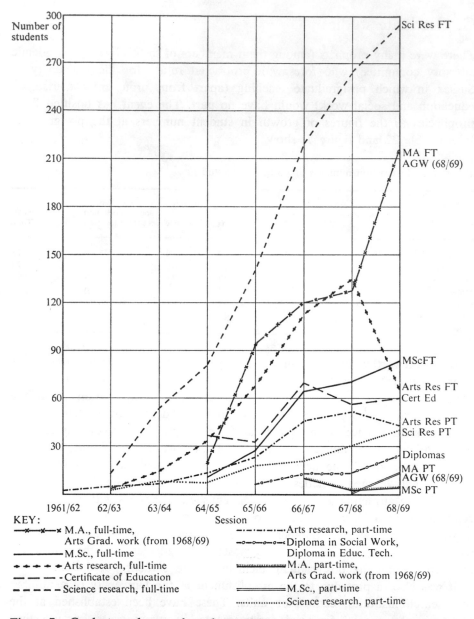

Figure 7. Graduate and research students, 1961—1968

studies (in co-operation with the Ministry of overseas development); the Centre for contemporary European studies; the Centre for multi-racial studies; and the Science policy research Unit. Their sponsors felt that at Sussex, with its emphasis on inter-disciplinary studies, there would be an output of graduates specially suited by their undergraduate training to contribute to interdisciplinary research.

Great increases in the size of the undergraduate intake had much enlarged the number of those qualified to enter on graduate study. The nature of this postgraduate study was considerably diversified during the course of the last quinquennium. Perhaps the most significant development in this context has been the growing proportion of graduate students undertaking advanced courses of instruction; this trend has been especially marked in the arts and social sciences. There was also awareness of the need to give students an understanding of the role of graduates in industry, commerce and the professions, and there has been a marked development of postgraduate courses specially geared to these needs and aimed at increasing the flow into careers in production and management. Sussex had developed a number of such M.A. or M.Sc. courses.

The Social science research council, through its applications for research studentships, obtains information on the preferences of students wishing to undertake research in the social sciences. In the 1967 applicant field, the University of Sussex was listed as the university of first preference by more applicants than any other university in the United Kingdom, with the exception of the London School of Economics. In 1968/69 Sussex received more awards than all other institutions except the London School of Economics and Oxford.

In the academic year 1967/68, Sussex received 198 studentships from the 'Science research council'; this placed Sussex in the top eight of all unversities in the United Kingdom receiving such studentships. Research Fellows supported by the Science research council in 1967/68 totalled 14; only four institutions received more awards than Sussex.

# H. Research activity

Research activity within the University has been maintained at a notably high level since the earliest days of the University, despite the pressures on the faculty to commit time and effort to a host of duties inextricably associated with the establishment of a new institution. It has not been possible to date to express this in quantifiable terms. The weekly programme of symposia and seminars on research topics reflects the range of research interests inside the University. The Schools and Centres sponsor interdisciplinary seminars as a natural extension of the structure of the University, which is geared to bring together faculty and students from various disciplines.

Allocations of recurrent grant from the UGC are not divided between teaching and research. There are two broad categories of research activity at the University, which in practice interlock at many points but are separable in financial terms. These are:

(a) Research work performed by members of the University faculty who are financed from UGC funds, and whose equipment, materials, etc. are also financed from UGC funds.

(b) Research work financed from non-UGC funds. The finances in this category would normally cover personnel and non-salary items. The predominant situation is for a member of the University's established faculty to be involved in a research project in which the equipment and materials are provided from non-UGC funds.

Postgraduate courses are treated separately from research work, though in some cases postgraduate students are members of a research team.

In its Development Report for 1962-67 (paragraph 447) the UGC states 'that it should be the autonomous responsibility of each university itself to determine, at the various decision-making levels involved, how much of its block grants should be applied to the support of research and what particular lines of research should be supported'. The UGC has reiterated the conclusion of the Trend committee in their report on the Organization of Civil Science (Cmnd 2171, 1963) that the functions of teaching and research 'are so organically interwoven that it would be disastrous to separate them for purposes of administration'. The Trend committee also emphasized:

> It is important that there should be more than one source of funds for research: centralized provision carries with it the serious risk that potentially fruitful ideas may be nipped in the cold winds of chance or academic prejudice. Moreover, fields of research are often opened up, and individual projects often come forward, which, although important, may not seem of immediate interest to the universities from the standpoint of association with teaching but may—or may not—become an integral part of university work, either in the short or the long term. Universities cannot be expected to finance these 'experimental' research developments from their general income; yet it is clearly advantageous that they should be located in the universities. In addition, the rapid advance of science gives rise to new and unpredictable developments, often calling for very expensive equipment, which are not easily accommodated within the universities' quinquennial budgeting. The system of earmarked grants, provided by Research Councils, caters for these unforeseeable contingencies.

During the period 1965-69, the University established a number of Research Units or Centres on the campus. They have been specially and deliberately located in the University in order to have the benefits of its facilities and to

266

enjoy and encourage co-operative work with academic colleagues. In turn, the staff of the Institutes, Centres or Units contribute to the University's undergraduate and postgraduate teaching programmes. The University has been anxious to attract research centres to the University when the particular research activities seem to lie close to the academic and research interests of University faculty and where co-operative work would be facilitated by proximity of location. The pattern of funding for these Centres or Units has, however, been variable and there is little doubt that in future they will have to be more or less self-financing, because the University will have increasingly less scope to commit any of its own resources to their establishment. The University finance office is consequently consulted about all new developments of this kind and, where possible and necessary, provision is made for a continuing contribution towards University overheads from the research grants or contracts. In some cases, the University agrees to take over financial responsibility for the Unit or Centre in the following quinquennium, provided adequate funds are made available by the UGC.

One of the interesting features of the University development, meriting a study in its own right, would be to trace the impact of the Research Centres on the curricular organization of the University. This interchange is expressing itself in the development of new courses of study and new schools of studies.

As in all universities, it is difficult to express the research output of faculty in quantifiable or qualitative terms. The number of publications, completed projects and inventions flowing from Sussex has been of a high order from the outset, though again it is not possible to compare these with other universities, since no such data exist. Inter-disciplinary teamwork has resulted in the emergence of new Research Units, additional funds from Research councils (e.g. brain research), and contracts for large publishing projects (e.g. the History of Contemporary European Literature). Scientific inventions and technological developments have also occurred from time to time. The confidence gained by the University in securing additional funds for research and development and attracting excellent faculty has obviated the need to use data of this kind as an indicator of the University's performance.

Tables relating to the research activities of the University will be found on pages 268-270.

TABLE 23.  Research expenditure from UGC recurrent grant

|  | 1965/66 | 1966/67 | 1967/68 |
|---|---|---|---|
| **(i) *By area*** | £ | £ | £ |
| Maths, physics and molecular sciences | 121 078 | 175 058 | 198 170 |
| Applied sciences | 9 616 | 22 412 | 42 566 |
| Biological sciences | 29 918 | 44 743 | 57 382 |
| Social sciences | 30 639 | 58 840 | 51 378 |
| Arts | 57 124 | 54 349 | 51 196 |
| Education | 3 827 | 704 | 901 |
| Total | 252 202 | 356 106 | 401 593 |
| **(ii) *By all University faculty*** | | | |
| (a) Academic salaries | 180 681 | 236 003 | 245 941 |
| Wages | 39 679 | 67 239 | 86 939 |
| Total | 220 360 | 303 242 | 332 877 |
| (b) Percentage of academic and staff | % | % | % |
| salary and wages spent on research | 30.2 | 29.7 | 28.3 |
| Percentage of academic salaries only spent on research | 30.4 | 29.3 | 26.8 |
| (c) Equivalent faculty committed to research, based on percentages in (b) above | 72.5 | 89.5 | 90.0 |
| Out of a total faculty of | 238 | 306 | 336 |
| **(iii) *By individual member of faculty*** | | | |
| (a) By individual as proportion of total faculty | 1 060 | 1 164 | 1 195 |
| (b) By individual as proportion of equivalent number of faculty committed to research | 3 478 | 3 979 | 4 462 |

SOURCE  Estimates based on a study of the University's annual returns to the UGC

TABLE 24.  Research expenditure from non-UGC sources, 1964/65-1967/68

|  | 1964/65 | 1965/66 | 1966/67 | 1967/68 |
|---|---|---|---|---|
|  | £ | £ | £ | £ |
| (i) Volume of research in terms of cost | 87 402 | 198 853 | 366 472 | 586 035 |
| *By area* | | | | |
| Mathematical and physical sciences and molecular sciences | ... | 134 315 | 211 221 | 243 852 |
| Applied sciences | ... | 11 725 | 15 022 | 48 151 |
| Biological sciences | ... | 25 125 | 56 690 | 148 611 |
| Social sciences | ... | 15 243 | 59 146 | 105 860 |
| Arts | ... | 4 408 | 6 114 | 5 985 |
| Education | ... | 1 214 | 5 547 | 5 453 |
| Other | ... | 6 825 | 12 732 | 28 123 |
| Total | | 198 853 | 366 472 | 586 035 |
| (ii) By number of 'research' faculty[1] | ... | 37 | 68 | 88 |

1.  Wholly financed from external non-UGC grants        ... Data not available

TABLE 25.  Summary of 'research' data, 1964/65-1967/68

|  | 1964/65 | 1965/66 | 1966/67 | 1967/68 |
|---|---|---|---|---|
|  |  | £ | £ | £ |
| (i) Total volume of research expenditure[1] | ... | 451 055 | 722 578 | 987 628 |
| (ii) Percentage of income expended on research | % | % | % | % |
| (a) based on total University income | 8.1 | 12.0 | 15.7 | 20.3 |
| (b) excluding income from non-UGC sources | 8.8 | 13.6 | 18.6 | 25.5 |
| (iii) Total number of 'research' faculty | | | | |
| (a) Committed primarily but not exclusively to research activity and financed by non-UGC grants | ... | 37 | 68 | 88 |
| (b) Total number of academic faculty inclusive of (a) above | ... | 275 | 374 | 424 |

1.  This represents non-UGC expenditure together with the estimated UGC commitment to research (see Table 23 [i])        ... Data not available

TABLE 26.   Scientific equipment: total purchases, 1964/65-1967/68[1]

|  | 1964/65 | 1965/66 | 1966/67 | 1967/68 |
|---|---|---|---|---|
|  | £ | £ | £ | £ |
| *(i) From UGC funds* | | | | |
| Mathematical and physical sciences | 49 987 | 43 816 | 42 373 | 74 811 |
| Molecular sciences | 29 768 | 200 737 | 84 060 | 37 773 |
|  | 109 | 43 295 | 164 207 | 92 799 |
| Biological sciences (including experimental psychology) | — | 137 950 | 99 809 | 146 168 |
| Total | 79 864 | 425 798 | 390 449 | 351 551 |
| *(ii) From non-UGC funds* | | | | |
| Mathematical and physical sciences | 11 479 | 25 137 | 43 993 | 25 335 |
| Molecular sciences | 3 383 | 765 | 11 472 | 62 365 |
| Applied sciences | 1 606 | 5 693 | 984 | 22 762 |
| Biological sciences (including experimental psychology) | — | — | 1 500 | 71 682 |
| Total | 16 468 | 31 595 | 57 949 | 182 144 |
| *(iii) Value per 'research' faculty member* | | | | |
| (a) From UGC expenditure by the notional number of 'research' faculty[2] | ... | 5 873 | 4 362 | 3 906 |
| (b) From non-UGC expenditure by non-UGC-financed 'research' faculty | ... | 854 | 852 | 2 070 |

1. This equipment is used for both teaching and research, and except in certain cases cannot be costed separately.
2. I.e., the equivalent as calculated in Table 23 (ii) (c).
... Data not available.

# 11. Conclusion

Several facts must be borne in mind about this study. It is, in the first place, a highly condensed version of a fuller study which, with its supporting materials, ran to a total length of 280 pages. It has been summarised partly in the interests of clarity and partly in order to reduce it to a manageable length by the elimination of very specialised information. Secondly, it must be remembered that it was conducted by three members of the staff of the institution concerned. There are advantages in this, since all three have been intimately connected with the University of Sussex since its earliest days and have therefore had access both to documentation and experience that could not easily be reached by an outsider. But there are also possible disadvantages for which allowances must be made. Inevitably, it is difficult to achieve objectivity or to secure adequately comparative outlook on some of the developments described. One of the reasons that we have drawn heavily upon existing documentation is to enable the reader to judge for himself the manner in which Sussex has tackled its problems and the style in which it discussed them. Thirdly, we emphasise that this case study has been seen by us as part of a continuing exercise. The earliest days of the University were described in *The Idea of a New University:*[1] the story is carried forward in this case study and it is already envisaged that other reviews of this kind will follow. Seen in this light, it may be understood that this study is not merely a special exercise undertaken for a particular research programme but is also in itself an active part of the process which it is describing.

This process is the slow but accelerating transition in the United Kingdom from a traditional and somewhat élitist university structure towards a situation in which it is beginning to be possible to speak of mass higher education. For reasons that have been described elsewhere the growth of post-secondary

1. David Daiches (ed.), op. cit.

education of all kinds is likely to continue, and variations in the rate of growth as a result of demographic factors, changes in educational policy, and economies imposed by government and other planning agencies are unlikely to do more than produce temporary fluctuations in a process of expansion that cannot now be arrested. It may be said that education is becoming a major characteristic of the social system and that both in market terms and in social implications it is likely to exercise an unprecedented influence upon society in the next two decades.

In this context the role of universities is bound to change—both in what is expected of them and in what they actually seek to do. The belief, held by some academics, that the golden age of universities is coming to an end can only be sustained on a narrow conception of what that phrase implies. The golden age of isolation from social pressures, of relative leisure and undefined goals may indeed be ending; but in a different sense a new era of growth, influence and relevance can be dawning. The question is to what extent, and how fast, universities are capable of adapting to the unavoidable crises of transition. Some of their treasured independence may go, but all the evidence suggests that they are in fact acquiring new responsibilities and a greater degree of integration with the social, economic and cultural life of their societies than has ever before been the case.

It is difficult at this moment in time to predict the precise forms which this transition will take. It is possible only to discern that change is coming to replace stability as the one constant factor, that the time-scale over which institutions must review and renovate their structures, curriculum and other activities is rapidly shortening, and that the growth of alternative means of providing post-secondary education is beginning to furnish governments with a form of leverage which did not exist in the days when universities were the main and extremely restricted centres for higher education.

How then should universities approach this critical period? The most general and useful advice that can be offered is that they should adopt a responsible rather than a negative attitude to change: that is to accept its inevitability and to establish procedures whereby the processes of change can be observed, evaluated and to some extent controlled. This means a new and radical approach to the problem of 'management' within universities, because procedures are becoming a much more decisive element in a university structure than has ever previously been the case. The old method of government where a delicate balance between administrators and faculty was maintained largely unchanged for long periods of time, within institutions which seldom faced the need for major adjustments in their organisation, structure, use of plant, their curriculum and teaching methods, or their student population, is no longer viable; it is simply an obsolete model which is inappropriate to contemporary conditions. In this case study we have been endeavouring to describe the ways in which the University of Sussex has begun to recognise this fact and to make preliminary attempts to create the new machinery that is required.

This explains why, in this study, we have dwelt upon theories of management. The first model that we have used rests on the mechanistic theory of management which was described in the editorial to Volume 46 of *Public Administration:*

> Ultimately this managerial model rests upon the belief that administration is something like a production process. You define what you want to produce and you devise means for efficient production. The production process is broken down into a series of measurable operations and these are fitted together in a manner which ensures that the end product emerges (and is disposed of) at the minimum cost in resources expended. Management techniques are those which are conducive to understanding and controlling these production processes. Much of classical organisation theory, as well as some contemporary management theory, amounts to an attempt to transfer the concepts applicable to the manipulation of physical resources for production or analogous processes to any form of human organisation.

We believe that much progress can be made in University management by making use of this kind of model.

We must stress, however, that our view of University planning and management is mainly a behavioral one; in the words of the *Public Administration* editorial, we see the process as 'essentially one of regulative action, a process of balancing and optimising, in which by definition, goals can never be exactly fixed, tasks cannot be exhaustively specified and the methods chosen must themselves take account of value judgements on the part of the administrator and in the society at large which affect both priorities and modes of procedure.' We need the quantitative and comparative information supplied by the process to set parameters to the area in which the art of judgement has to be used.

The development of manpower planning at the national level will gradually force universities in the United Kingdom to review their own manpower inputs, costs and outputs. It will have particular implications for the organisation and planning of universities, selection policies, careers advice within universities, the design of curricula and the balance between 'academic' and 'professional' courses, the University's relationships with schools and prospective employees both locally and nationally. Manpower planning is, however, only one of a range of techniques which will provide more accurate predictions about the role and purpose of higher education; it will help remind institutions of higher education that they exist in a dynamic and changing environment. The degree of responsiveness of the individual institution will depend upon a range of internal and external factors. The Sussex case study has been prepared in its present form because the authors believe that the forms of organisational structures and the mechanics of processes play a significant role in either inhibiting or encouraging innovation.

Universities are by their nature best suited to evolution through small, continuous adjustments, yet their internal structures and processes are infrequently designed with this in mind. The central necessity is that the university has to obtain information about the external requirements and about its internal activities. Most of the impetus for change is external in origin and information on it reaches the university through multiple channels. It needs to be co-ordinated, assessed, and considered in relation to the university's internal activities. The achievement of those objectives can be helped by the assignment of primary responsibility for them to a particular officer, unit or range of units.

Decision-making processes in a university have to consist of checks and balances and the final decisions need to be collective, but it remains the case that the lesser mechanics of those processes can either encourage or discourage change. High numbers of large committees arranged in multi-tier structures tend to discourage and slow down change, whereas shorter chains in the processes, the devolution of clear responsibilities to sectors of the institution, the assignment of assessment work to individuals or very small groups rather than to tiered committees, tend to encourage and speed change without reducing the university's ability to choose between the 'good' and the 'bad'.

Change and the attitude towards self-renewal can also be supported or suppressed by the role of planning in the decision-making processes. A university which institutionalises planning as a continuous process, requiring all of its parts to produce development plans, combining them into a university plan, and then requiring each of its parts and itself to each year re-evaluate those plans and objectives, is optimising, through constructive participation in an annual process, its ability to adapt to changing circumstances in comparison with institutions where planning does not exist or is too rigid. The values of decisions are dependent upon the ability to implement them. The degree of flexibility in the structures and processes concerned with implementation is the decisive factor in a university's ability to change in time for the change to be effective. The academic structure can either inhibit or encourage change; a structure highly specialised along disciplinary lines with a large number of departments tends to be less flexible than a structure which is less divisive and contains larger units.

The structures of the Administration can have similar effects; if it is divided into specialist permanent departments with little inter-change of personnel it tends to rigidify and retard the diffusion of ideas, whereas if the boundaries and existence of its sub-divisions are kept under review and if there is re-assignment of individuals across those boundaries then it can be a more flexible instrument. Building programmes and individual buildings can be designed with or without change in mind; space in buildings can be allocated to units in perpetuity or space allocation can be made subject to periodic review. Budgetary and other internal resource allocation processes can be designed to facilitate institutional flexibility; if most of the resources of internal units (faculty numbers, support staff numbers, running costs, overhead costs) are allocated to it on various formulae each related to a factor within the control of the institution (e.g. student numbers in the unit) the ability to adjust or change quickly is increased and the institution is making explicit its attitude towards flexibility and improvement. The relatively small mechanics of those resource allocation processes can have significant effects; for example, a procedure whereby on the resignation of a member of faculty the post reverts to a pool common to several units which then have to collectively consider the comparative strength of their needs is more flexible than if the post automatically remained within the unit to which it had hitherto been allocated. The processes for the review of teaching and curricula are also relevant; the clear assignment of responsibility for that review, whether that be done by the creation of units concerned with instructional resources and of educational development programmes designed to assist teaching units, or by releasing specific members of faculty from other duties for periods of time, or any other similar method, should increase the university's ability to adjust its teaching and learning processes.

The design of structures and processes concerned with information-gathering and assessment, decision-taking, and decision-implementing can thus either increase or decrease a university's ability to adjust to changing requirements. In the designing of structures there are factors other than adaptability to be taken into account and the factors may conflict; but, to a greater or lesser extent, in each structure or process there is usually some room for choice between elements of rigidity and flexibility. This case study has provided a few examples of some of those areas of choice. If a university does wish to be able to adjust itself to the shorter-term requirements of its environment, as well as to help shape the longer-term requirements of that environment, it can do so by giving greater weight to the dynamic than to the static in ways which best suit its special circumstances.

# Appendixes

*General note*

All the appendixes are working documents which were produced for internal University purposes. They should be read as such. It was decided to include a selection of these internal papers to give the interested reader more detailed information of the planning machinery developed at Sussex. Sometimes these papers contain references to other subsidiary University documents which have not been included. Those who are interested in obtaining any further documentation should apply to the University planning officer.

The planning process: outline

The planning process is an abbreviated title for the complex of systems which contain the strategic and operational plans, the budgetary system, control mechanisms, and parts of both the information and institutional research programmes of the University.

The process was introduced at the end of the major review of the government and organisation of the University in the Spring term 1968, and it became operational at the beginning of the 1968/69 session. It is an experimental process, which will be reviewed annually as part of the organisation of the University documents.

## A. Planning in a university

The purpose of planning is to illuminate the future ramifications of action. In order to do so, past actions and trends have to be analysed, the present state has to be assessed, the environment has to be taken into account and the possible future changes in it have to be assessed. Planning is not the implementation of a series of fixed future actions; it can be used to construct rigid development plans, but it can also be used as a continuous and flexible method of creating and adapting to change. The University has never taken the former approach; it has always regarded planning as a flexible process. The social, economic, scientific and technological requirements and processes which affect the University are changing at an increasing rate and are becoming more complex both in themselves and in their inter-actions. The environment is clearly dynamic and the University needs to be able to adapt, frequently and rapidly, to the changing circumstances the ways in which it fulfils its less-changing fundamental purposes (i.e. teaching and research).

It should be noted that planning as such is of little use if the University does not have the ability to change or if the University is not given the opportunity to change. They are the two pre-requisites for successful planning. In regard to the ability to change, the design of the structures and processes concerned with

279

information, decision-taking, decision-implementation and budgeting can either increase or inhibit that ability; one of the central aims of the structures which emerged in the University after the major review of government and administration was to increase the ability to change. In regard to the opportunity to change, that depends largely upon the decisions of the University Grants Committee and other major sources of finance or incentives; but the University can influence those decisions (e.g. by keeping unit costs low, plant utilisation high, student wastage low, etc.; by submitting proposals for change in areas which coincide with national needs or expectations). The fact that the above elements are pre-requisites for planning illustrates why the University's planning processes are regarded as an integral part of the organisational structure and why budgeting is seen as part of the planning process.

The fact that the University is a small constituent of a national higher educational system places restraints upon its planning. The following are the two major examples of the technical restraints of belonging to a national system; there is little point in forward planning more than seven years ahead so long as the total system operates on a quinquennial planning cycle; it is extremely difficult for the University to combine capital and recurrent finance in its planning since these two sources are planned separately in the total system and on different time-scales. However, the existence of a national system, which is itself making significantly more use of planning, underlines the need for the University to plan ahead.

Not that the need requires underlining. Apart from the need to change as the environment changes, apart from the necessity of being required to plan by the demands of the national system, and apart from the benefits of planning one step ahead of the national system, the University is a large complex organisation which could not function without planning.

## B. Method of planning

Planning is essential; every time an appointment is made to the faculty, student intakes are fixed, or a building project is approved, someone is involved in planning. There is no alternative to planning, but there are alternative ways of planning.

The University has made more use of planning since its foundation than have most of its older sister institutions. In 1968 it was decided that planning should be made more systematic, its co-ordination should be improved, its timetabling should be made more explicit, and it should be made more effective by increasing the information flows necessary for planning and by improving the subsequent control reports. The University attempted to achieve those aims by the creation of a continuous planning process which requires each unit in the University to prepare plans which flow through areas to the major committees of the University and which are re-evaluated and revised each year. The University could have attempted to achieve those aims by other methods (e.g. the creation of a highly-centralised planning team which would work under the planning committee's authority). The planning process method was chosen for two main reasons:

1. The organisation of the University is based upon the devolution of responsibilities and initiatives to its areas and units within a co-ordinated system which makes them aware of their interdependence; forward planning cannot be separated from those responsibilities; when responsibility for the academic, financial and physical management was develved to areas it was logical that initiative in forward planning should similarly be devolved; equally, planning decisions have to be taken continously in the areas and planning would be inefficient and ineffective if it was highly centralised.

2. It was felt that planning should be a participative process; all members of faculty cannot participate equally and very few will be able to be involved in the total process, but the aim is that there should be no mystique surrounding planning and everyone should have an opportunity to contribute to some aspect of planning; the planning process is concerned with the future ranges and standards of teaching, research, social, and cultural provision in all areas of the University; participation is essential in such a process.

The methods contained in the planning process are experimental and will be reviewed each year. Clearly the comprehensive and participative nature of the process means that as a method of planning it has to be structured more elaborately, timed more precisely and controlled more closely than more limited and less-participative methods. It also requires an exercise of self-restraint by units and areas if the process is to function efficiently and in accordance with its timetable.

## C. Contents of the process

The main elements of the planning process are shown in Table A.1, and are as follows:

(a) *Strategic plans.* Strategic planning is the setting of objectives and selecting strategies to meet those objectives over a four- to seven-year period; its primary focus being long-term, to identify major issues and point to major decisions which will change the fundamental character and direction of the enterprise. In the context of the University it involves such issues as the long-term rate of growth, the balance between arts and science, the balance between undergraduate teaching, postgraduate training and research.

(b) *Operational plans.* Operational planning is the translation of agreed objectives and strategic plans into specific action programmes over the short term (i.e. one to four years). In the University context this involves such issues as the logistics of faculty and students, curriculum changes, and the re-allocation of space, etc.

(c) *Budgets.* The process is budgetary as well as planning; provisional budgetary allocations for the following year will also flow through the annual cycle outlined in Figure B.1 in Appendix B. The budget can be seen as the financial/numerical expression of the operational plan for one year ahead (e.g. financial budget, manpower budget). The budget consists of a grid

Table A.1. The planning process: outline of the contents

| Type of plan | STRATEGIC (5-year plan) | OPERATIONAL (2-year plan) | BUDGET (1-year plan) |
|---|---|---|---|
| Contents | e.g. major academic developments, long term rate of growth, phased building programme. | e.g. student numbers by courses and subjects, curriculum changes, space allocation. | i.e. allocation of monies for agreed programmes, and consequential matters (e.g. manpower budget, student number targets). |
| Aids to preparation | Statement of financial situation. Planning Guide for Units. Strategic Assumptions (e.g. size of University). Statistics and research findings, national and internal (e.g. Arts/Science swing). | Statement of monies available in each year. Planning Guide for Units. Operational Guidelines (e.g. projections of faculty numbers). Statistics on current state of the University (e.g. student numbers, admissions pressure, faculty distribution etc.). | Guidebook of Regulations. Budgetary System Description. Current Year's Accounts. Budgetary Assumptions (i.e. monies available in the year and provisional internal allocations). |
| Progress controls | Operational Plans and Budget preparation, progress reports and controls. | Regular reports and statistics (e.g. admissions, current students, space, manpower). Records and Statistics Description. Various progress and control mechanisms to be set up by relevant committees (e.g. Arts and Science Committees for curriculum, teaching methods etc.). | Control Statements to the Planning Committee every term. Finance Office monthly statements to the Vice-chancellor. Finance Office monthly reports to each main spending unit. Establishments Office progress reports. Admissions Office progress reports. |

linking spending programmes and spending units. The first step is the construction of a programme budget, i.e. to provisionally allocate on the basis of previously agreed operational plans sums of money for each function (e.g. academic salaries, library books). The second step is to apportion the allocation for each spending programme amongst the spending units involved in the programme (the academic salaries programme budget would be divided at least between arts and science on a student numbers basis) and thus arrive at provisional budgets for each spending unit.

*(d) University Planning Assumptions.* These are produced annually and will contain information needed by the units in reviewing and developing plans. They will contain the existing plans and essential statistical information for use by the units in their work e.g. the statement of the known grant situation, costs of students, wastage and transfer rates of students, and ratios used in the calculations.

*(e) Control reports.* The finance office will produce control reports and statements of expenditure for each unit showing performance against budget, and for the major committees at stated frequencies throughout the year. Other offices will produce similar reports (e.g. establishments office in regard to manpower, the admissions office in regard to student numbers).

*(f) Information.* Firstly, it is essential that the process is understood by members of the University, and thus reference works on detailed aspects of the process will be made available (e.g. a guidebook of regulations, a description of the budgetary system, a description of the University's records and statistics systems, etc.). Secondly, University and unit plans cannot be efficiently constructed unless information about internal and external factors and trends is made available; thus a network will be created along which information can flow to and through the planning officer from and to the persons concerned with teaching, research, admissions, examinations, appointments, health, accommodation, finance, space, educational technology, social policy, etc. Thirdly, it is intended to develop an institutional research programme designed to evaluate past actions and their results in order to provide knowledge of use in future decision-taking and planning.

# D. The units in the process

The four main planning areas of arts, science, social policy and general are shown in Figure A.1, together with their subsidiary planning units. Planning units are not identical with spending units. There are three categories of spending units; main spending units (the units to which the planning committee and the Senate allocate monies, e.g. arts, science, library, computing centre, arts centre), secondary spending units (the units to which main spending units allocate monies, e.g. Schools) and subsidiary spending units (the units to which secondary units allocate monies, e.g. Subjects). A detailed list of spending units is contained in Appendix B.

284

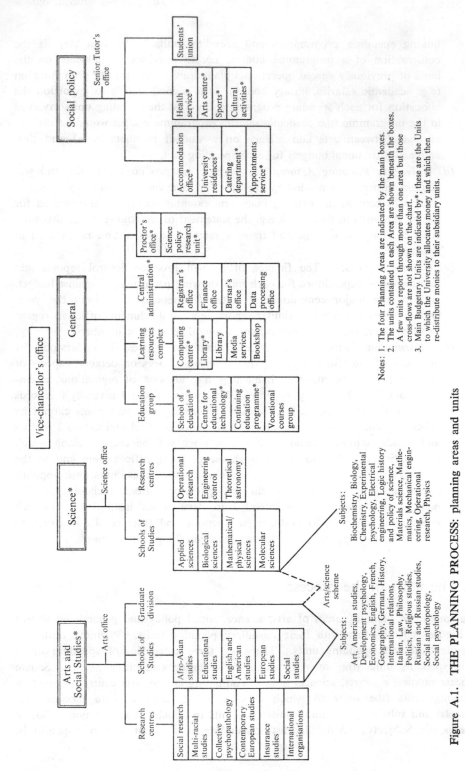

**Figure A.1. THE PLANNING PROCESS: planning areas and units**

Notes: 1. The four Planning Areas are indicated by the main boxes.
2. The units contained in each Area are shown beneath the boxes. A few units report through more than one area but those cross-flows are not shown on the chart.
3. Main Budgetary Units are indicated by*; these are the Units to which the University allocates money and which then re-distribute monies to their subsidiary units.

# E. The planning cycle

There are two cycles, the annual and the quinquennial. Figure A.2 overleaf shows the annual cycle, illustrating the flow of the planning assumptions through the whole structure for comment and amendment as unit plans are up-dated at each stage. Thus each year each unit will be provided with the strategic plans (e.g. rate of growth, etc.), the operational plans (e.g. staff and student logistics for two to four years ahead) which have already been made, and the next year's budgetary assumptions of the University. The unit will then review and propose any changes in their own plans; these will then be discussed in the appropriate bodies before the University plans are revised and detailed budgets agreed. It needs to be stressed that the system involves at each stage considerable amounts of informal discussion amongst academic and administrative officers, mainly arranged by the chairman of arts and science, the senior Tutor and the deputy Vice-chancellor, if the flow is not to be disrupted and in order that committees can concentrate on the major issues.

The quinquennial cycle is derived from the annual cycle. In essence, the University's strategic plans have to be formally converted into a quinquennial plan every five years because of the national system of finance. The fixed points are that the University must submit its quinquennial 'existing commitment' estimates in the April of two years prior to the new quinquennium, and its full quinquennial submission in November of the year prior to the new quinquennium. It follows from the timetable that the annual cycle two years prior to the beginning of the next quinquennium is the critical one, since the quinquennial estimates will be based upon its outcome. Thus although units can suggest alterations to their strategic plans in any year, the quinquennial cycle means that they must conduct their major review in the third year of each quinquennium and that they will then probably need to revise the plans in the first year of each quinquennium in the light of the monies received.

# F. Conclusion

The complex of systems in the planning process is intricate; it will take time to adjust them to actual operations and it will take time for members of the University to become fully acquainted with them. The process is an attempt at a systematic approach to the development of the University by placing an orderly exposition of assumptions and information into a flow of creative discussion; the hope being that such an approach involving all members will produce greater possibilities for acceptable progress and improvement than those which would result from the dictates of *ad hoc* decisions and undisciplined experience.

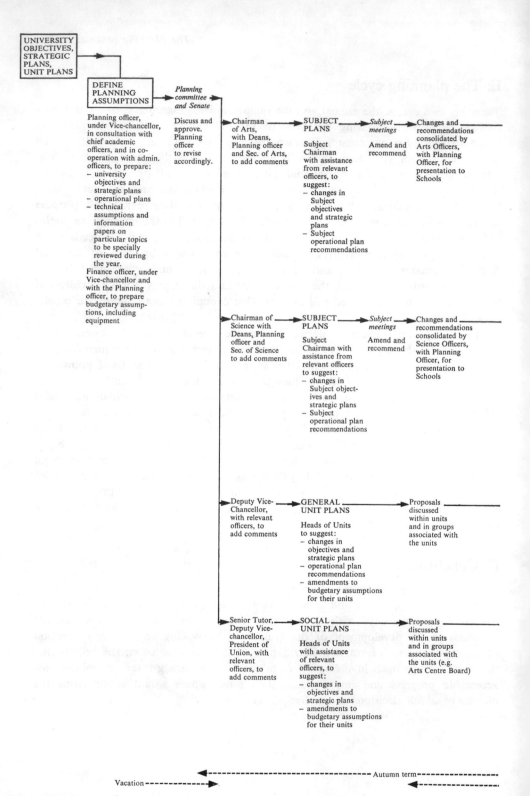

| UNIVERSITY OBJECTIVES, STRATEGIC PLANS, UNIT PLANS | DEFINE PLANNING ASSUMPTIONS | *Planning committee and Senate* | | | |
|---|---|---|---|---|---|
| | Planning officer, under Vice-chancellor, in consultation with chief academic officers, and in co-operation with admin. officers, to prepare: <br>– university objectives and strategic plans <br>– operational plans <br>– technical assumptions and information papers on particular topics to be specially reviewed during the year. <br>Finance officer, under Vice-chancellor and with the Planning officer, to prepare budgetary assumptions, including equipment | Discuss and approve. Planning officer to revise accordingly. | Chairman of Arts, with Deans, Planning officer and Sec. of Arts, to add comments | SUBJECT PLANS <br><br>Subject Chairman with assistance from relevant officers, to suggest: <br>– changes in Subject objectives and strategic plans <br>– Subject operational plan recommendations | *Subject meetings* <br><br>Amend and recommend | Changes and recommendations consolidated by Arts Officers, with Planning Officer, for presentation to Schools |
| | | | Chairman of Science with Deans, Planning officer and Sec. of Science to add comments | SUBJECT PLANS <br><br>Subject Chairman with assistance from relevant officers to suggest: <br>– changes in Subject object-ives and strategic plans <br>– Subject operational plan recommendations | *Subject meetings* <br><br>Amend and recommend | Changes and recommendations consolidated by Science Officers, with Planning Officer, for presentation to Schools |
| | | | Deputy Vice-Chancellor, with relevant officers, to add comments | GENERAL UNIT PLANS <br><br>Heads of Units to suggest: <br>– changes in objectives and strategic plans <br>– operational plan recommendations <br>– amendments to budgetary assumptions for their units | | Proposals discussed within units and in groups associated with the units |
| | | | Senior Tutor, Deputy Vice-chancellor, President of Union, with relevant officers, to add comments | SOCIAL UNIT PLANS <br><br>Heads of Units with assistance of relevant officers, to suggest: <br>– changes in objectives and strategic plans <br>– amendments to budgetary assumptions for their units | | Proposals discussed within units and in groups associated with the units (e.g. Arts Centre Board) |

Vacation ------------▶   ◀------------------------------------ Autumn term------------------▶
                                                                  ◀------------------

Figure A.2.  THE PLANNING PROCESS: an outline of the annual flow

286

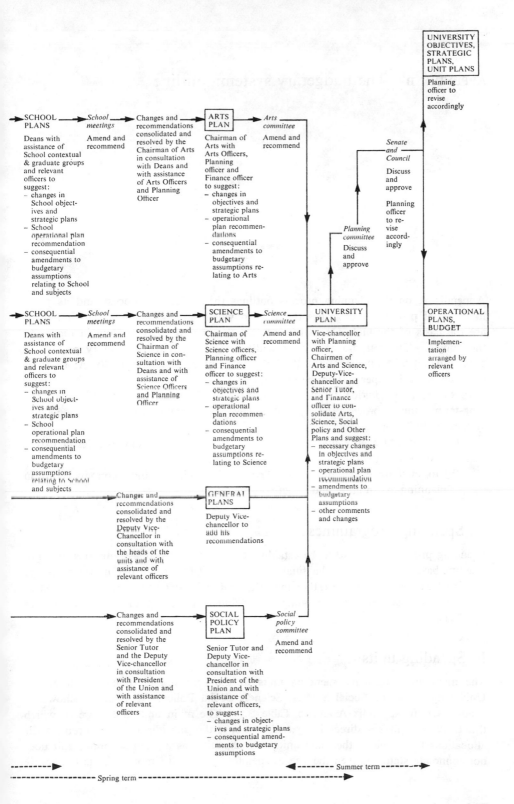

SCHOOL PLANS

Deans with assistance of School contextual & graduate groups and relevant officers to suggest:
– changes in School objectives and strategic plans
– School operational plan recommendation
– consequential amendments to budgetary assumptions relating to School and subjects

*School meetings*

Amend and recommend

Changes and recommendations consolidated and resolved by the Chairman of Arts in consultation with Deans and with assistance of Arts Officers and Planning Officer

ARTS PLAN

Chairman of Arts with Arts Officers, Planning officer and Finance officer to suggest:
– changes in objectives and strategic plans
– operational plan recommendations
– consequential amendments to budgetary assumptions relating to Arts

*Arts committee*

Amend and recommend

SCHOOL PLANS

Deans with assistance of School contextual & graduate groups and relevant officers to suggest:
– changes in School objectives and strategic plans
– School operational plan recommendation
– consequential amendments to budgetary assumptions relating to School and subjects

*School meetings*

Amend and recommend

Changes and recommendations consolidated and resolved by the Chairman of Science in consultation with Deans and with assistance of Science Officers and Planning Officer

SCIENCE PLAN

Chairman of Science with Science officers, Planning officer and Finance officer to suggest:
– changes in objectives and strategic plans
– operational plan recommendations
– consequential amendments to budgetary assumptions relating to Science

*Science committee*

Amend and recommend

UNIVERSITY PLAN

Vice-chancellor with Planning officer, Chairmen of Arts and Science, Deputy-Vice-chancellor and Senior Tutor, and Finance officer to consolidate Arts, Science, Social policy and Other Plans and suggest:
– necessary changes in objectives and strategic plans
– operational plan recommendation
– amendments to budgetary assumptions
– other comments and changes

Changes and recommendations consolidated and resolved by the Deputy Vice-Chancellor in consultation with the heads of the units and with assistance of relevant officers

GENERAL PLANS

Deputy Vice-chancellor to add his recommendations

Changes and recommendations consolidated and resolved by the Senior Tutor and the Deputy Vice-chancellor in consultation with President of the Union and with assistance of relevant officers

SOCIAL POLICY PLAN

Senior Tutor and Deputy Vice-chancellor in consultation with President of the Union and with assistance of relevant officers, to suggest:
– changes in objectives and strategic plans
– consequential amendments to budgetary assumptions

*Social policy committee*

Amend and recommend

*Planning committee*

Discuss and approve

*Senate and Council*

Discuss and approve

Planning officer to revise accordingly

UNIVERSITY OBJECTIVES, STRATEGIC PLANS, UNIT PLANS

Planning officer to revise accordingly

OPERATIONAL PLANS, BUDGET

Implementation arranged by relevant officers

--------- → Summer term ------- → 

--------- → 

----------------- Spring term -------------------------------- →

287

The budgetary system: outline

Appendix A on the planning process outlines the budgetary process and its place in the total process; it describes the way in which strategic and operational plans are the basis of the budget construction and the annual decision flow in regard to the budget. The purpose of this appendix is to explain the budgetary process in greater detail without repeating all of the relevant parts of Appendix A; i.e. it is assumed that this paper will not be read in isolation.

In essence, in addition to integrating the annual budgeting procedure into the long-term planning process, the main objectives of the changes made to the budgetary system in 1968 are:

    (a) to introduce an element of flexibility into budgeting and to a lesser extent into spending within approved 'global' budgets;

    (b) to encourage the maximum degree of efficiency and economy both in planning expenditure and in actually spending.

## A. Spending programmes

Spending programmes have to be established since the budget assumptions are programme-based even though the final budget is unit-based. Programmes represent the functions of expenditure rather than the units of expenditure and are divided as precisely as possible. The spending programmes are listed in Table B.1 (pages 290-291).

## B. Spending units

The main and subsidiary spending units in the four organisational areas of the University (Arts and Social Studies, Science, Social Policy, General) are shown in Figure A.1 in Appendix A and in Table B.1. The main units are those to which the University makes direct budget allocations; the subsidiary units receive their allocations from one of the main units. Designation as a main spending unit does not connotate status or even the size of spending power; it simply reflects the ability of the University to make a direct allocation to a unit. For example, Schools are not main spending units, since decisions on the allocation of funds to them have to be made at the arts and science level because their activities overlap to a considerable degree.

Special arrangements have been made for 'business units' (e.g. catering, bookshop). This is that given the policy on services and the general level of charges laid down by the University the business manager will prepare at the normal budget time estimates for the succeeding year. These estimates will be scrutinised by the finance officer and both officers will report to the University. On the basis of these estimates and reports a lump sum subsidy or a profit target for the year will be agreed. It will then be the responsibility of the business manager to operate the services within this subsidy. Small surpluses or deficits will be carried forward. Termly statements showing operating results during the year will be prepared by the business manager and the finance officer. Although the original estimates will be based on an estimated establishment the business manager will have discretion to vary this establishment according to the demands on the service so long as this can be done within the approved subsidy.

In addition, certain spending programmes continue, at least for the time being, to receive separate allocations and be subject to special administrative arrangements as they have been in the past e.g. scholarships and bursaries, University hospitality, Ceremonials and publicity, expenses of University meetings, post entry training, rent, rates and insurance, and Revenue contributions to capital outlay.

## C. Budgetary assumptions

Budgetary assumptions form part of the annual planning assumptions. They are drafted by the finance officer, in consultation with the planning officer, the chairman of arts and science and the senior Tutor, and under the guidance of the Vice-chancellor. At the time of preparation the next year's income and the requests from the units are largely known from their operational plans; adjustments will take place during the budgetary process, but the supply and demand for income is known with sufficient accuracy for the budgetary assumptions to be a firm basis for discussion.

(a) The first step is the allocation of the expected income to the spending programmes in the light of requests and all other relevant information. The calculations will be largely done in terms of ratios, with most ratios having average cost assumptions attached to them, e.g. the academic salaries programme allocation will be calculated from a manpower budget of one faculty member per 8+ students, assuming average salaries for each of those two groups. Ratios have been used extensively in the past and their use in calculating the budgetary assumptions will increase. Ratios are used in preference to *ad hoc* annual decisions because they provide a continuing framework of reference, because they allow for the projection of existing commitment (even if they were not used at this stage, the planning officer

Table B.1.  Budgetary process: main spending units and spending programmes

| Spending programmes | Primary base of ratios governing provisional allocation of funds | Main spending units | | | | | | | |
|---|---|---|---|---|---|---|---|---|---|
| | | Arts & social studies | Science | School of. educn. | Continuing educn. | Library | CET | Computer centre | A s |
| Academic faculty salaries | Student numbers | *ac* | *ac* | | | | | | |
| Technical staff salaries | Student and faculty numbers | *ab* | *ab* | | | | *a* | | |
| Central teaching support progms. | Student and faculty numbers | *a* | *a* | | | | *a* | | |
| Central research support progms. | Student and faculty numbers | *a* | *a* | | | | | | |
| Secretarial assist. (academic) | Faculty numbers | *ab* | *ab* | | | | | | |
| Teaching research & development | Ad hoc | *a* | *a* | *a* | | | *a* | | |
| Office expenses (academic) | Faculty numbers | *a* | *a* | | | | | | |
| Equipment | Student numbers | *ac* | *ac* | *ac* | *. ac* | *ac* | *ac* | *ac* | |
| Examinations | Student numbers | *ab* | *ab* | *ab* | | | | | |
| Records and statistics | Student numbers | *ab* | *ab* | *ab* | | | | | |
| Exchange programmes | Ad hoc | *ab* | *ab* | | | | | | |
| Travel & conference grants | Faculty numbers | *a* | *a* | *a* | *a* | *a* | *a* | *a* | |
| Grants to learned societies | Faculty numbers | *a* | *a* | | | | | | |
| Merit and hardship grants | Student numbers | *a* | *a* | | | | | | |
| Recruitment & personnel | Staff numbers | *ab* | *ab* | *ab* | *ab* | *ab* | *ab* | *ab* | |
| Hospitality | Faculty numbers | *a* | *a* | *a* | *a* | *a* | *a* | *a* | |
| Library running costs | Student numbers | | | *ab* | | *a* | | | |
| Library books, binding etc. | Student numbers | | | *ab* | | *a* | | | |
| Computer fixed costs | Faculty numbers | | | | | | | *a* | |
| Computer marginal costs | Faculty numbers | *a* | *a* | | | | | *a* | |
| Data processing programme | Ad hoc | *ab* | *ab* | | *ab* | | | | |
| Learned publications | Faculty numbers | *a* | *a* | | | | | | |
| Internal publications | Student and faculty numbers | | | | | | | | |
| External official publications | Ad hoc | *ab* | *ab* | *ab* | *ab* | | | | |
| Health services | Student numbers | | | | | | | | |
| Careers services | Student numbers | | | | | | | | |
| Accommodation services | Student numbers | | | | | | | | |
| Sports services | Student numbers | | | | | | | | |
| Catering services | Self-financ. or fixed subsidy | | | | | | | | |
| Admissions service | Student numbers | *ab* | *ab* | | | | | | |
| Social research unit | Faculty numbers | *a* | | | | | | | |
| Ceremonials | Ad hoc | *ab* | *ab* | | | | | | |
| Telephones | Staff numbers | *ab* | *ab* | *ab* | *ab* | *ab* | *ab* | *ab* | |
| Cleaning | Size of plant | *ab* | *ab* | *ab* | *ab* | *ab* | *ab* | *ab* | |
| Portering | Size of plant | *ab* | *ab* | *ab* | *ab* | *ab* | *ab* | *ab* | |
| Transport | Ad hoc | *ab* | *ab* | *ab* | *ab* | *ab* | | | |
| Fuel, light, water & power | Size of plant | *ab* | *ab* | *ab* | *ab* | *ab* | *ab* | *ab* | |
| Internal mail service | Size of plant | *ab* | *ab* | | | *ab* | | | |
| Sub post office | Ad hoc | | | | | | | | |
| Post-entry training | Staff numbers | *ab* | *ab* | | | *ab* | | | |
| Univ. contribs to off. bodies | Ad hoc | | | | | | | | |
| Public lectures | Ad hoc | *a* | *a* | | | | | | |
| Socio-educ. research programme | Ad hoc | | | | | | | | |
| Cultural activities | Student numbers | | | | | | | | |
| In-service training of teachers | Ad hoc | | | *a* | | | | | |
| Colleges of education support | Ad hoc | | | *a* | | | | | |
| Adult education | Ad hoc | | | | *a* | | | | |
| General grounds maintenance | Size of plant | | | | | | | | |
| General buildings maintenance | Size of plant | | | | | | | | |
| Buildings minor alterations | Size of plant | *ab* | *ab* | | | *ab* | | | |
| Buildings major alterations | Size of plant | *ab* | *ab* | | | *ab* | | | |
| Buildings re-decoration | Size of plant | | | | | | | | |
| Furniture | Size of plant | *ac* | *ac* | | | *ac* | | | |
| Rents | Ad hoc | | | | | | | | |
| Insurances | Ad hoc | | | | | | | | |
| Legal & audit expenses | Ad hoc | | | | | | | | |
| General administrative salaries | Student numbers | | | | | | | | |
| Discipline | Student numbers | | | | | | | | |
| Reserve fund | Ad hoc | | | | | | | | |

*a* indicates that the Budgetary assumptions for that main spending unit will include an amount for that programme.

*b* indicates that for that programme the unit exercises its main control at the budget construction stage and has less or no control at the spending stage.

| | Main spending units | | | | | | | |
|---|---|---|---|---|---|---|---|---|
| n. | Catering | Univ. res. | Arts centre | Health serv. | Sports | Accom. office | Senior tutor's office | Proctor's office |
| c | | | ac | ac | ac | | | |
| c | | | | | | | | |
| c | | ab | ab | ab | ab | ab | | |
| | | a | a | a | a | a | a | a |
| b | | | | | | | | |
| c | | | | | | | | |
| c | | | | a | | | | |
| | | a | | | | | a | |
| | | | | | a | | | |
| c | a | | | | | | | |
| c | | ab | ab | ab | ab | ab | ab | ab |
| c | | ab | ab | ab | ab | ab | ab | ab |
| c | | ab | ab | ab | ab | ab | | |
| c | | | ab | | ab | | | |
| c | | ab | ab | ab | ab | ab | ab | ab |
| | | | a | | | | a | |
| c | | | | | a | | | |
| c | | ab | ab | | ab | | | |
| c | | ab | ab | | ab | | | |
| c | | | | | | | | |
| c | | | | | | | ac | |
| | | | | | | | | ac |

NOTES:

1. This grid has been produced for *illustrative purposes;* its contents have not yet been fully implemented in the existing Budgetary Process.
2. The spending programmes differ from the existing budget heads. *The Guidebook of Regulations will contain a detailed statement on each programme* e.g. Teaching Support Programme includes teaching materials and other aids, running costs of the Language Laboratory; Research Support Programme includes grants to individuals for research projects etc.; Office Expenses include stationery, postages, copying costs etc.; Academic Salaries Programme includes all payments for the teaching of internal students (e.g. Arts/Science posts, Tutorial Fund, demonstrating payments, payments to College of Education for Cert. Ed. students etc.); Merit and Hardship Grants include the Vice-Chancellor's Fund, Overseas Student Bursaries etc.; Recruitment and Personnel includes all advertising, interview expenses, removal expenses, etc.. Hospitality includes catering expenditure on the Bulletin, the Diary of Events etc.
3. Self-financing (e.g. Conferences, Printing) are not included.

*c* indicates that savings arising during the year on that programme revert partly or wholly to the University Reserve Fund and are therefore not fully available for use on other programmes within that Unit.

would have to construct them in order to produce the planning assumptions), because they reflect the links which exist between items of expenditure, and because they simplify the issues and therefore concentrate discussion on matters of policy.  However, it is important to realise that it is not the intention to mechanically apply fixed ratios each year in a rigid structure; ratios will need to be altered from year to year, since the activities and the priorities they represent will be altering and since the resources available will change.  It is also important to appreciate that although ratios will be used in the construction of the budget and will represent guidelines on expenditure, the spending units have considerable freedom to depart from these guide-lines so long as they are prepared to finance additional expenditure by making offsetting savings.

Details of the ratios used will be set out in each year's planning and budgetary assumptions.  The majority of the ratios will be related to student numbers, since that has become the unit of measure for almost all purposes at the national level and since the majority of the expenditure of the University can be related to student numbers (e.g. academic salaries, technical staff salaries, library books, equipment, etc.).  It is mainly for that reason that the number of students in all categories is under the direct control of the planning committee.  A significant number of ratios will be based upon square-footage or other space measures (e.g. cleaning, portering, grounds, maintenance programmes, etc.).

(b) The second step in the drafting of the budgetary assumptions is the dispersal of spending programmes amongst the main spending units.  In many cases a spending programme belongs exclusively to one spending unit (e.g. health services and the University health service) but in other cases the programme has to be divided amongst units (e.g. the academic salaries programme has to be divided into arts and science). Table B.1 illustrates the grid formed by the relationships between spending units and spending programmes.

In most cases the allocation of a spending programme's monies to the relevant units will be determined by the ratios referred to in (a) above.  The result is a single sum for each main spending unit but with clear indications as to how it is made up.  Thus for arts and social studies $£x$ would be provisionally allocated on the assumption of $y$ students of $z$ 'mix' (combining $£a$ for faculty, $£b$ for secretarial services, $£c$ for administration staff, $£d$ for materials, $£e$ for office expenses, $£f$ for equipment, $£g$ for technical staff, $£h$ for examinations, $£i$ for telephones, $£j$ for portering, $£k$ for cleaning, etc.).

# D. Annual cycle

The annual cycle has been outlined in Appendix A and is illustrated in Figure B.1 (on pages 294-295).  The budgetary assumptions are first submitted to the planning committee and the Senate for general comment.  The four main areas of them (arts, science, social policy, and general) are then considered by the senior officers responsible for those areas, and it is at that stage that their assumptions or comments concerning the allocations to sub-units are added. For example, the basic budgetary assumptions will contain an allocation to the science unit, but before they are passed to the science sub-units (Schools, Subjects) it is necessary to indicate the provisional allocation to those sub-units; thus the chairman of science and the science office will analyse the science funds and provisionally allocate them, indicating the basis on which they have made the allocations.

Each main unit may decide for itself:

(a) The extent to which the various spending programmes under its control are divided between sub-units—e.g. science may decide to 'charge-out' technicians and electricity to Schools but arts may only charge-out the traditional school fund items.

(b) The method by which particular spending programmes are allocated between sub-units, e.g. although the University allocates technicians on the basis of 1.25 to each logistic member of faculty in science laboratory subjects, science is not bound to use this basis in allocating the resultant number of technicians between Schools.

The budgetary assumptions and the main unit comments are then scrutinised and commented upon. Clearly it is open to units to suggest that they should be given more monies than they have been provisionally allocated, but main units will also be specifically asked to decide, on the assumption that they will eventually receive only the provisional sums contained in the budgetary assumptions, whether they intend to significantly alter the balance of spending programmes. It is at this stage that the units have a major opportunity to exercise control over the distribution of expenditure. This opportunity has to be taken at the budget preparation time rather than at the actual spending time for many programmes, since the officers responsible for those programmes need to know the funds at their disposal with some degree of accuracy.

At the end of the decision flow the planning committee, the Senate and the Council will make the final allocations to the main units. Those allocations will be block sums, and the main units will then allocate funds to their sub-units to fulfil the agreed range of programmes; in making those allocations the main units have a further opportunity to exercise initiative since, with the following restrictions, they do not necessarily have to follow the guide-lines set by the planning committee:—

(a) they cannot deliberately under-achieve the agreed programmes (e.g. accept fewer students than the targets upon which the allocations have been based);

(b) they cannot significantly increase future commitments by their re-allocations (e.g. appoint more permanent staff than is allowed for in the agreed manpower budget);

(c) they cannot cut their expenditure on a programme but expect additional services from outside their budget (e.g. cut their administrative expenditure and ask for administrative services from other units);

(d) they cannot alter the allocation to certain stated spending programmes.

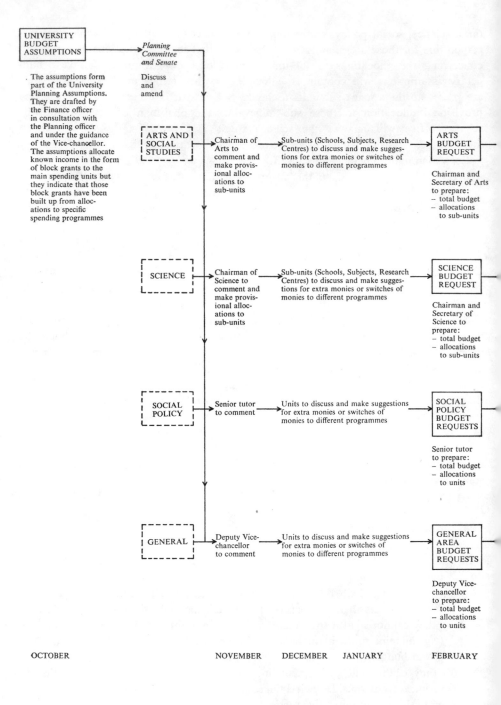

Figure B.1.    BUDGETARY SYSTEM: an outline of the annual flow

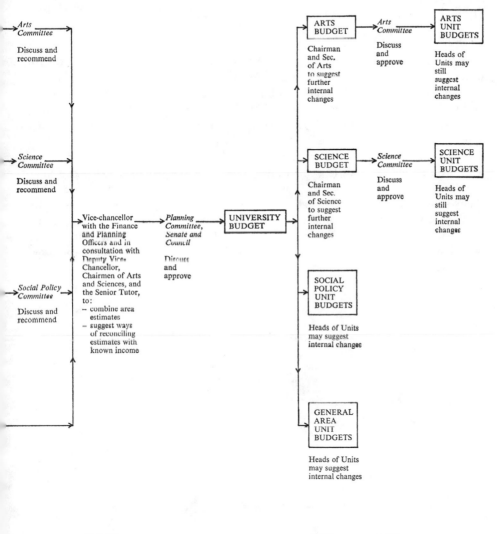

Proposals for varying the detailed make-up of the budgets of units and sub-units will be discussed with the finance officer and the planning officer so that those officers can confirm to the planning committee that the above restrictions have been observed. The finance officer will then draw up a document detailing the budgets of all units and sub-units which will be the basic budgetary control document for the year.

## E. Use of budgets

Once the allocations have been agreed, the control over expenditure rests primarily with the main spending units. The units must work within the Guidebook of regulations and they will be supplied with control statements from the finance office, but at this stage too they have some discretion to alter the pattern of expenditure over a range of programmes. The restrictions mentioned in D above continue to apply at this stage. The allocations to certain programmes will be fixed, and any savings which accrue in those programmes will revert to the University or be shared with it on an agreed basis (e.g. the academic salaries programme). One reason for this further restriction is that the University budget will not contain a large contingency item, since experience has shown that sufficient savings accrue to meet normal contingencies. Apart from those stated programmes, units will be able, subject to conditions and procedures set out in the Guidebook, to switch savings between programmes according to need. The ability to carry forward balances for use in future years will also be governed by the regulations contained in the Guidebook.

Planning guide for units, 1968-72

## Introduction

The papers on the planning process describe the role of the plans of units. Units will be asked each quinquennium to define their educational objectives and to prepare strategic plans to meet them. They will also be asked annually to revise these objectives and strategic plans for shorter term action (e.g., curriculum changes).

The initial task of preparing the unit plan involves considerable discussion and work but it is hoped that thereafter the existence of the plan will reduce annual discussion and preparation as well as making it more effective. It is recognised that the first attempts at plans, which the units are now being asked to undertake, may not be able to cover the whole range of contents listed below. The sections on objectives and strategic plans should be fully covered, but it may require experience of at least one annual process before operational plans can be put forward in the detail listed below.

Units should be as concise as possible in their plans. The lengths of the plans may need to vary according to the nature of the unit, but all units should aim to keep them as short as is compatible with their purpose. The chairman of Arts, the chairman of Science, the Senior tutor and the Deputy vice-chancellor will give guidance on this point to the units in their spheres of responsibility.

The papers on the planning process also state that units will be provided with as much as possible of the information which they require for their plans and that the relevant officers (e.g. planning officer, secretaries of Arts and Science, finance officer) will assist the units when requested. In particular, the units require information on lead times (i.e. the lead time to introduce a new major subject is approximately twenty-two months). A standard list of lead times for the main items of School and Subject plans prepared by the Arts and Science officers and the planning officer is attached.

Unit Plans

1. *Contents*

The following is an outline structure of a unit plan. The structure is applicable to all types of units; for purposes of illustration the examples used relate to a School Plan.

(a) *Objectives:* A brief statement of the academic philosophy of the School and its objectives.

(b) *Strategic Plan:*

   (i) A statement of the long-term aims in regard to teaching methods, range of subjects or areas, curriculum structure, particular areas of research interest, links with other Schools and outside institutions, etc.

   (ii) An analysis of the present state in relation to those aims, e.g., areas of strength and weakness.

   (iii) A statement of the specific four or five major problems and opportunities facing the School in the next five years.

*Note:* It is expected that (a) and (b) would normally require only up-dating on an annual basis but would be subjected to major review at one point in the quinquennial cycle.

(c) *Operational Plans,* which mainly consist of specific recommendations normally falling into one of the following headings:—

   (i)    Curriculum changes (including the Arts/Science Scheme)
   (ii)   Teaching methods
   (iii)  Undergraduate numbers and distribution
   (iv)   Graduate numbers and distribution
   (v)    Academic faculty and distribution
   (vi)   Research staff and distribution
   (vii)  Technical staff and distribution
   (viii) Secretarial staff and distribution
   (ix)   Equipment and teaching aids
   (x)    Admissions policy and procedure changes
   (xi)   Students' Progress policy and procedure changes
   (xii)  Examinations policy and procedure changes
   (xiii) Exchange Programme and other external relations proposals
   (xiv)  Other

Each proposal should be specific (i.e. naming the branch of a discipline in which a new appointment is needed rather than just the title of the discipline); each proposal should have a recommended date of implementation (e.g. course $x$ to be withdrawn for 1st year students with effect from October 1970, and course $z$ to be introduced for 2nd year students from October 1971, etc.) and should state what action which bodies have to take for its approval and implementation; the resource implications of each proposal must be stated either in terms of a transfer of stated resources from another area or in terms of the additional monies, accommodation, etc. required.

The plan should end with a summary statement of the recommendations and of the cost effects in each of the following three years if the proposals are approved.

*Summary of recommendations*

| Recommendation | Timing | Cost | Other resource implications |
|---|---|---|---|
| 1. Appoint an Asst. Lecturer/Lecturer in History with interests in 19th Century British Social History | October 1969 | Cost £2000 per annum | One tutorial |
| 2. Change teaching method of the School Prelim. course to tutorials of 3 instead of tutorials of 2 without increasing the frequency or length | October 1970 | Reduces demand for faculty time by $x$ hours | Room |
| 3. Etc. | | | — |

*Summary of resource implications*

| Additions | Deletions | Additions | Deletions |
|---|---|---|---|
| 69/70 70/71 71/72 | 69/70 70/71 71/72 | 69/70 70/71 71/72 | 69/70 70/71 71/72 |

(d) *Comments on other Unit Plans:* Schools will receive plans from subjects and possibly from other units; the School's recommendations concerning those plans will largely be included in the School's own plan. However, if Schools do not accept particular recommendations of other units, then they should explain their reasons in this section.

2. *Annual Process*

Thus the steps each year in regard to a unit plan will be as follows:

    (i) *Receive and review planning assumptions*

    (ii) *Approve or change existing statement of unit objectives*

    (iii) *Approve or change existing strategic plan statement.* This should particularly concentrate on re-defining the 4 or 5 major problems or opportunities facing the unit.

    (iv) *Develop a list of recommendations for change*

    (v) *Prepare summary statement* of selected changes to be recommended in standard form, together with their resource implications.

    (vi) *Prepare short statement of comment* on other unit plans.

    (vii) *Send unit plans to next stage in planning process* for further discussion.

    (viii) *Receive results of discussions* and make any further comments as appropriate.

(ix) *Receive budgets.*

(x) *Receive control reports* showing progress against budget periodically and take appropriate action where necessary.

*Conclusions*

There are many differences between units and the outlines of their plans will need to be considered individually by the 'heads' of the units with their own staff and with the Planning and Finance Officers. In general, however, they should be able to conform to the above pattern.

## Attachment to Planning Guide for Units: Lead times for the plans of Academic Units

Units require advice about the timings involved in the devising and implementing of plans. The following is a list of the main topics of relevance to academic units, and of the minimum periods required between decision-taking and operational implementation for each topic. Column B indicates the time by which the *Arts or Science Committee* needs to take a decision if it is intended to implement changes by the date in Column C; Schools, Subjects etc. need to reach decisions before the time in Column B, which means they need to start discussing the topics two or three months ahead of those times.

| A | B | C |
| --- | --- | --- |
| | Arts or Science Committee final | Operational |
| *Topics* | decision | start time |
| Addition or deletion of a *major subject* in the B.A. or B.Sc. curriculum; addition or deletion of a Masters Degree or Diploma Course | 22 months | October |
| *Major changes of course options* for first or higher degrees i.e. changes which significantly affect the balance of the course | 22 months | October * |
| *Minor changes of course options* | 8 months | October * |
| *Prelim. examination* changes of timing, procedures and policies | 10 months | March |
| *School examination changes* | 5 months | October |
| *Final examinations* changes of procedures, examiners, marking, etc. | 10 months | May |
| *Final examinations* changes in method of examining etc. | 28 months | May |
| *Graduate examinations* changes in procedure, method of examining etc. | 15 months | May |

| A | B | C |
|---|---|---|
| | *Arts or Science Committee final* | *Operational* |
| *Topics* | *decision* | *start time* |
| *Entrance requirements* for all degree courses | 22 months | October (of entry) |
| *Undergraduate admissions* changes in published procedures | 10 months | October (of appl.) |
| *Undergraduate admissions* changes in unpublished procedures | 5 months | October (of appl.) |
| *Graduate admissions* changes in procedures | 5 months | October (of appl.) |
| *Teaching Methods* changes for particular courses or options which do not affect over-all pattern | 3 months | Termly |
| *Teaching Methods* changes which affect over-all pattern of a degree course | 22 months | October |
| *Intakes of Students* to all courses — changes to projections | 15 months | October |
| *Students' Progress* — changes in procedures | 3 months | Various |
| *Student Records and Statistics* changes in main system (including Registration procedures) | 10 months | October |
| *Exchange Programmes* — institution and changes | 11 months | October |
| Allocation of *existing space* | 3 months | Various |
| Main requests for *additional space* | 10 months | October |
| Major requests for *new buildings* | 46 months | October |
| Requests for *alterations to buildings* | 8 months | Various |
| Acceptance of a *research grant* | 3 months | Various |
| Changes in *faculty* numbers and distribution | 8 months | Various |
| Changes in *research appointment* numbers and distribution | 6 months | Various |
| Changes in *technical staff* numbers and distribution | 6 months | Various |
| Changes in *clerical staff* numbers and distribution | 6 months | Various |

\* These are minimum periods; in most other universities curricula are changed only on a cohort basis; thus the lead time for a change in a third-year course is over four years and it is over three years for a second-year course etc.; the above times are based on the assumption that courses can be changed provided students are given eight months notice of minor changes and twenty months notice of major changes.

The above is not a comprehensive list but it sufficiently indicates the fact that Schools and Subjects need to allow for an almost two-year gap between discussion and implementation of significant changes; in many cases that gap is due to external requirements.

The above list will be revised after the secretary of Arts, the secretary of Science and the planning officer have held the first series of discussions with Schools and Subjects.

Student numbers

# Introduction

Projections of student numbers, both in total and by categories, have been used as one of the bases of planning by the University since the 1964/65 session. At that time it was decided to produce tables of projections in order that the distribution of students in each of the next five years could be ascertained assuming that there were no basic changes in the University's plans; they allowed members of the University to see the long-term results of current assumptions and plans; they also allowed the effects of proposed changes in those assumptions or of proposals (e.g. for new major subjects) to be seen before final decisions had to be taken. The projections also allowed the shape of the curve of development to be seen, and they were used for some resource allocation purposes.

The introduction of the Planning Process in 1967/68 gives a more systematic role to the projections of student numbers. The projections of student numbers for five main groups (B.A. including Arts visiting students, B.Sc. including Science visiting students, the Professional courses, Arts and Social studies graduates, and Science graduates) are approved on a rolling five-year basis by the planning committee and the Senate; they are compiled, using the Assumptions listed below, in the light of the monies allocated and guidance given to the University by the University Grants Committee and in the knowledge of the developments requested for those five groups in the plans of the relevant units of the University. The projections and the assumptions are checked and reviewed annually.

# 1. Content

The series of projections contain various elements, several of which have different status. The main points which require explanation are:—

1. *Definitions of student numbers* for resource allocation purposes. The numbers contained in the projection of total numbers approved by the planning committee are termed the *logistic student numbers:* they are the numbers upon which all

resource allocation decisions other than academic faculty numbers are based (e.g. School funds, allocation of space); they represent minimum rather than fixed targets since, within certain limitations, the Arts and Science committees can accept higher numbers of students provided that extra resources are not thereby requested from the University. In the determination of academic faculty numbers not all categories of logistic students are included in the calculations; the student numbers used for this purpose are termed the *ratio student numbers,* and they consist of the logistic B.A. and Arts visiting students (in which, from 1969/70, Year Abroad students count as one-sixth of a full-time student), the logistic B.Sc. and Science visiting student numbers, the logistic Professional course student numbers (excluding courses where the teaching inputs are not financed from the UGC recurrent grant) and the logistic numbers of first-year Arts and Science graduate students; the methods of calculating academic faculty numbers are explained in detail in paper P/95/5.[1]

The difference between logistic and actual student numbers is accounted for by the *extra-logistic student numbers,* of which there are two categories. Firstly, those numbers which arise from the Arts or Science committee's decision to exceed the logistic targets; in regard to this category the planning committee does offer guidance as to maximum numbers and reviews the numbers each year. Secondly, those numbers which arise from externally-financed courses or from externally-financed units associated with the University (e.g. Institute of Development Studies); in regard to this category it is the responsibility of the Arts or Science committee to negotiate the student number targets with the units concerned.

Finally, it should be noted that there is a category of *'external' student numbers* which is not included in the projections, e.g. students of the School of education (including B.Ed. students), of the Continuing Education programme, etc.

2. *The use of the projections for resource allocation purposes:*
   (a) Firstly, this varies according to the distance ahead of the projections. The projections for the full five years do not represent fixed plans; they are reviewed each year and they are simply the best estimates available of future logistic numbers and their distribution. As such they are used as the main base of the projections of resource allocation (e.g. budgets, faculty logistics, etc.) embodied in the University's operational and strategic plans.

   However, once the annual process of review has been completed in March of each year, then elements of the projections become fixed plans until the next annual review and other elements become alterable only at the margin. Thus when the attached projections are approved in March 1969:—
   (i) the 1969/70 ratio and logistic numbers contained in them will be used for the final resource allocation decisions for that year, i.e. the budgetary, academic faculty, space etc. allocations will be based upon them and will not be altered thereafter (even if the logistic numbers are under-achieved);

---

1. Not reproduced

(ii) the 1970/71 ratio and logistic numbers contained in them will be used as the basis of the budgetary assumptions for that year (which will then be discussed during the 1969/70 cycle of the planning process), as the basis for the calculation of provisional faculty numbers for that year, and by the Admissions office as the provisional intake targets for October 1970. Thus although the 1970/71 numbers do not represent fixed plans they are capable of only marginal alteration during 1969/70, since some actions will have had to be taken using them as a base (e.g. the majority of faculty appointments for 1970/71; since the admissions selection for October 1970 will be largely completed before March 1970 the Admissions office will have used the provisional 1970/71 numbers for that purpose).

(b) Secondly, the question as to how and when the actual number of students affects the projections and resource allocation needs explaining. It has already been stated above that the overshooting of ration and logistic student numbers by units has no effect upon the use of the projections as the base for resource allocations. Such gaps between actual and logistic numbers are only taken into account in the framing of the Quinquennial Submission and in the resulting Quinquennial Development Plan at the beginning of each quinquennium. However, the under-achievement of logistic numbers is a different matter; it is taken into account through a procedure which allows marginal under-achievement without any corrective action, which spreads any necessary alterations over a period of time sufficiently long for the unit to make the necessary resource adjustment, but which prevents major disparities amongst units. The details of the procedure are:—

(i) under-achievement is calculated separately for each of the five main groups of students (e.g., over-achievement of the Arts graduate logistic numbers would not compensate for under-achievement of the B.A. logistic numbers);

(ii) under-achievement is calculated in relation to total numbers within a group and not solely in relation to the annual intake of a group; the count to be taken at the end of October of each year (i.e. immediately before the budgetary assumptions for the following year are finalised); this procedure allows for a backlog of extra-logistic numbers from previous years' intakes to compensate for under-achievement in one year's intake up to the agreed total number of logistic students (it does not allow promises of over-achievement in the following year to be taken into account);

(iii) if the B.A. and B.Sc. (both including visiting students) total student numbers in a year fall below 98 per cent of the logistic targets or if the relevant categories of the Professional course, Arts graduate or Science graduate total student numbers fall below 95 per cent of the ratio or logistic targets, then the difference between the actual and the 100 per cent logistic numbers will be taken into account in the operational plans and budgetary assumptions for the following year (but not the current year's budget).

3. *Responsibility for projections* and their implementation: As explained above, the planning committee is responsible for the student number projections for the

five main groups. The Arts committee is then responsible for the allocation to courses or Schools and subjects of the B.A., Arts visiting, Professional course and Arts graduate numbers; the Science committee is similarly responsible in regard to B.Sc. Science visiting and Science graduate numbers. All of the projections are subject to the approval of the Senate as part of the planning process. The compilation of the projections and the procedures for resource allocation require that all of the projections be part of an integrated series and that detailed records be maintained of achievement against the targets; the Planning officer is responsible for the integrated series and for the records in consultation with the Arts, Science and Statistics offices.

Responsibility for attempting to achieve the agreed targets is divided as follows:—

(a) for B.A., B.Sc. and Visiting students, the Admissions office working under the planning committee's authority and in consultation with the Chairman of Arts and Science;

(b) for Professional courses and Arts graduates, the Arts office under the authority of the Chairman of Arts;

(c) for Science graduates, the Science office under the authority of the Chairman of Science.

## 2. Assumptions

The following are the main assumptions upon which the tables have been calculated:—

1. The projections do not include any calculations of the effects of closer ties with the *Colleges of Education or the College of Technology* (the expected 70 to 90 B.Ed. students are excluded).

2. *The number of B.A. and B.Sc. course students should be approximately equal.* Nationally, in 1965/66, Arts and Social Studies accounted for 43 per cent of undergraduates, Science 43 per cent (23 per cent Pure Science and 20 per cent Applied Science) and the remaining 14 per cent were accounted for by Medicine, Dentistry, Agriculture etc. Judging by GCE and UCCA statistics, the demand pressure for Arts (or more accurately for Social Studies) continues to increase more rapidly than for Science; on the other hand, the Robbins Report stated that, in the national interest, the aim for 1980 should be 38 per cent Arts, 24 per cent Pure Science, 23 per cent Applied Science and 15 per cent others. The attached projections, in accordance with decisions of the Planning Committee and the Senate, assume a slight excess of B.Sc. over B.A. students in 1972, mainly due to the development of the new Science Schools.

3. *The B.Sc. degree student numbers* are shown by Schools of studies. A subsidiary paper[1] will give details of the breakdown into major subjects and Schools (P/61/1/1/a revised — 2). The allocation to Schools and major subjects is determined by considering several factors (e.g. the relative demand for places

in each subject and the trends of that demand, the numbers of faculty appointed in each subject, the rate of transfer during the course, the optimum sizes of groups of faculty for teaching and research efficiency, the amount of physical facilities available, etc.) and achieving a balance amongst them. The demand pattern, the degree of transfer of students during the course, the University's needs and the national pattern may change from year to year and thus table P/61/1/1/a will be revised each year within limits imposed by the existing distribution of faculty posts.

4. *The B.A. degree student numbers* are shown by Schools of studies. A subsidiary table[1] will give details of the breakdown into major subjects by School (P/61/1/1/b revised — 3) and the School figures in P/61/1/1 will be the figures adjusted after transfers have been taken into account. The allocation to Schools and major subjects is determined by considering several factors (e.g. the relative demand for places in each subject and the trends of that demand, the numbers of faculty appointed in each subject, the rate of transfer during the course, the optimum sizes of groups of faculty for teaching and research efficiency, etc.) and achieving a balance amongst them. The demand pattern, the degree of transfer of students during the course, the University's needs and the national pattern may change from year to year and thus table P/61/1/1/b will be revised each year within limits imposed by the existing distribution of faculty posts. The figures, and particularly those by Schools, need to be treated with caution due to the high rate of transfers, the distribution of which cannot be accurately predicted.

In previous projections the B.A. student numbers have been divided into separate three- and four-year course numbers, whereas in the attached projections all are shown as three-year courses and the additional numbers of undergraduates abroad are indicated in a footnote. This procedure does mean that care has to be taken in deriving the actual number of students requiring teaching in any one year, and is only feasible in a period when the size of the intake is fairly constant over a number of years. This change has been made for two reasons. Firstly, the increasing requirements of a year abroad makes the numbers more difficult to calculate; the numbers and the Schools of language majors were easy to calculate and identify, but with all students in the School of European Studies being required to spend a year abroad from 1968 and with other existing and probable developments in this field (e.g. American Studies majors) the calculations would be very inaccurate, bearing in mind the high rates of transfer within the B.A. degree course. Secondly, undergraduates spending a year abroad make a reduced call upon the resources of the University, and since these projections are used mainly for planning and resources purposes it is less distorting to exclude than to include them. Estimates of their numbers are included in the footnote because they do count for UGC purposes and because they do have some marginal resource needs (e.g. for staff/student ratio purposes each student

1. Not reproduced

spending a year abroad as part of his course is deemed equivalent to one-sixth of a resident undergraduate). Finally, there are some students undertaking four-year courses who require teaching in all four years (e.g. some Science majors) but their number is so small as to come within the degree of error in the estimates of total numbers.

5. *The University will aim to undertake its share of the national programme of teacher-training and vocational training for graduates but will not be able to fully achieve that aim by 1972* (this assumption does not take into account the possibility of a Certificate in Education becoming compulsory for graduate teachers). In 1965/66, approximately 16 per cent of new graduates nationally went on to take a Certificate in Education. In the projections it is assumed that *approximately 20 per cent of Arts graduates and 10 per cent of Science graduates will take the Professional courses (excluding the M.A. in Education) in the School of Educational Studies.* A subsidiary table[1] gives details of the breakdown of the total numbers by course (P/61/1/1/c).

In drafting the tables, the numbers for these courses are calculated on the basis of Sussex graduates. The assumption being that *we shall take graduates from other universities in proportion to the graduates of this University who go elsewhere for their course.* This is not to imply that Sussex graduates be given preference in the selection process, it is simply a method of calculating the available places.

6. The University should increase its numbers of *graduate students* and that it is in this field that we should make our main contribution to the teaching of overseas students. The Robbins aim was that the present percentage of home graduates who go on to advanced study other than education (20 per cent) should be increased by 1980 to 30 per cent. The attached tables assume Sussex will achieve an average of approximately 40 per cent in both Arts and Science before 1972 but that percentage does include overseas students who constituted approximately 30 per cent of all graduate students in the United Kingdom in 1965/66. Numbers of undergraduates proceeding to graduate work are not readily available across all subjects for years later than 1961/62. The latest UGC published figures are for 1965/66 and they show that 12.5 per cent of all Arts students (11.5 per cent for Arts and 14.5 per cent for Social Studies) were at the graduate level (excluding Cert.Ed. etc.) and that 18 per cent is the equivalent figure for Science (19 per cent for Physical Sciences, 23 per cent for Biological Sciences, and 15 per cent for Applied Sciences). The equivalent percentages for Sussex in the attached projections are 16 per cent and 21 per cent for Arts and Science respectively in 1969/70.

The projections of graduate student numbers exclude those 'extra-logistic' students who are taught entirely by bodies attached to the University which have their own independent resources (e.g. the Institute of Development Studies). Those students are registered students of the University but are excluded from

1. Not reproduced

the projections since their demand for University resources is much less significant.

7. *Arts Advanced Courses and Research.* *The assumption at Sussex is that the equivalent of 35—40 per cent of its own B.A. graduates will enter advanced courses or research (other than professional courses in education).* A subsidiary table[1] gives details of the breakdown of the numbers amongst Graduate Sub-Divisions (P/61/1/1/d). It is assumed that all first-year graduate students will undertake course work terminating in either an M.A. examination or a qualifying examination for a research degree. The distinction between M.A. and first-year research is retained in the projections solely to illustrate the likely division. It is further assumed that 65 per cent of Arts graduate students will complete their courses at the end of their first year and that the remaining 35 per cent will continue for two further years. It is assumed that after three years all students will be registered as 'continuation fee' students (i.e. will be finishing their theses but not making significant use of University resources and therefore not included in the projections). Clearly if more than 35 per cent of the graduate students continue beyond their first year then the first-year graduate intake ought to be cut in the following year (or increased if less than 35 per cent continue).

The assumption is that *we shall take graduates from other United Kingdom universities, particularly overseas students, in proportion to the graduates of this University who choose to go elsewhere for their courses or research* (i.e. it is not implied that Sussex graduates be given preference in the selection process, it is simply a way of calculating the available places).

8. *Science Advanced Courses and Research.* *The assumption at Sussex is that the equivalent of 40 per cent of its own B.Sc. graduates will enter advanced courses or reserach (other than in education).* A subsidiary table[1] gives details of the breakdown of the numbers amongst the Subjects approved by the Planning Committee (P/61/1/1/e). It is also assumed that the first-year courses will be similar for graduates whether they be doing the M.Sc. course, a Diploma course, or research (i.e. that students doing their first year for the M.Phil. or D.Phil. will cover much of the same course and seminar work as the M.Sc. student). In that sense, it is best to divide these students into first-year research, second-year and third-year, rather than into M.Sc., Diploma, M.Phil. or D.Phil. etc. It is therefore assumed that 40 per cent will enter the first year, that 65 per cent of those will go on for two further years and that a small number will continue as full-time research students for a fourth year. Clearly if more than 65 per cent of the graduate students continue beyond the first year then the first year intake ought to be cut in the following year (or increased if less than 65 per cent continue etc.). It is assumed that after three years the vast majority of research students will be registered as 'continuation fee' students (i.e. will be finishing their theses but not making significant use of University resources and therefore not included in the projections).

1. Not reproduced

The assumption is that *we shall take graduates from other universities, particularly overseas students, in proportion to the graduates of this University who choose to go elsewhere for their course or research* (it is not implied that Sussex graduates be given preference in the selection process, it is simply a way of calculating the available places).

9. *Wastage Rates.* The recent UGC Report states that of the 1962/63 intake 10 per cent in Arts, 11.5 per cent in Social Studies, 15 per cent in Physical Sciences, 13.5 per cent in Biological Sciences and 23 per cent in Applied Sciences 'failed' (82 per cent for academic reasons). The Sussex rate so far has been between 5 per cent and 7 per cent. *A 6 per cent wastage rate for the B.A. and a 7 per cent rate for the B.Sc. course have been assumed and for simplicity it has been deducted at the end of each first year.* Wastage rates have not been calculated at the postgraduate level. This University has not had sufficient experience upon which to calculate the graduate rates and there is a conspicuous lack of information on this topic at the national level. It is therefore assumed that the intakes stated in the projections will be increased each year by the same amount as the number of withdrawals in the previous year. It is also assumed that if a significant number of full-time graduate students are given permission to study or research abroad for a year then the intakes can be increased correspondingly.

10. *Transfers.* The rate of transfer between major subjects on the B.A. and B.Sc. degree courses is sufficiently significant for it to be taken into account. Thus actual intakes for the October of each year have been calculated, the net losses or gains by subjects have been calculated, it has been assumed for simplicity that those gains and losses take place in the first year of the course, and thus adjusted intakes have been derived. The intakes shown on the two main tables are the adjusted intakes and the subsidiary tables show both the actual and the adjusted intakes.

The net losses and gains amongst the B.A. major subjects have been calculated on the basis of loss and gain trends since 1962. The gains and losses amongst the B.Sc. major subjects are less firmly based due to the full effects of the two new Schools not yet being known. *No net loss or gain between the B.A. and B.Sc. degree courses has been assumed.*

11. *Visiting students.* The definition of a Visiting student is a full-time student accepted for one year to undertake a series of undergraduate courses. Visiting graduate students, even though they may take undergraduate courses for a year before undertaking the M.A. for example, are included in the graduate number projections.

12. *Occasional students.* These have not been taken into account, since they are not full-time students.

13. *Part-time students.* Part-time students not undertaking courses of instruction are excluded from the projections but a part-time student undertaking a course of instruction is counted as the equivalent of one-third of a full-time student (i.e. 3 part-time M.A. students are counted as equivalent to one full-time M.A.

student but three part-time research students who have completed the course work part of their requirement are not counted in the projections). *Continuation fee* research students are not included in the projections.

## 3. UGC Guidelines

The UGC in announcing the level of recurrent grant given to the University for the quinquennium 1967/72 indicated the student numbers for 1971/72 upon which that grant had been based. The UGC explicitly stated that those numbers were in no sense targets, still less 'ceilings'. The following table compares the UGC's numbers for 1971/72 with those arrived at in the attached projections.

| Category | UGC | | University projections | |
|---|---|---|---|---|
| | Total | % | Total | % |
| Arts-based | 1325 | 39.9 | 1346 | 37.7 |
| Science-based | 1290 | 38.9 | 1461 | 40.9 |
| Total undergraduate | *2615* | *78.8* | *2807* | *76.6* |
| Arts-based | 360 | 10.8 | 375 | 10.4 |
| Science-based | 345 | 10.4 | 395 | 11.0 |
| Total graduate | *705* | *21.2* | *770* | *21.4* |
| Total | 3320 | 100 | 3577 | 100 |

It is extremely difficult to compare the UGC sub-divisions with those contained in the attached projections, since there is no evidence of the basis of the UGC's divisions into Science and Arts; thus with one exception the Arts and Science figures in the attached projections have been used without any attempt to adjust them (e.g., it could be claimed that B.A. Science majors should be switched into the 'Science-based' category and the B.Sc. Psychology majors switched into the 'Arts-based' category); the one exception is that the Science-based Cert.Ed. students have been placed in the Arts category since the UGC has never differentiated between types of Cert.Ed. student.

## 4. Attachments

Table P/61/1/1 (revised 6)[1] contains the total numbers approved by the Senate and the Planning committee in the summer term 1968. Subsidiary tables on the B.Sc., B.A., Professional course, Arts graduate and Science graduate numbers are attached to that main table and their status is indicated in the notes in the main table.

1. Not reproduced

## Conclusion

In considering the actual size of the University (i.e. the number of registered students) it is important to bear in mind the extra-logistic numbers. In 1971/72 the attached projections total approximately 3,600 students plus 100 B.A. Year Abroad students; given that there are approximately 200 extra-logistic students in 1968/69 it seems likely that there will be at least an equivalent number in 1971/72, thus the total of full-time students in 1971/72 is likely to be approximated 3,900; to which a further approximately 100 continuation fee students and 100 B.Ed. students could be added. Thus the number of registered students in 1971/72 is likely to be nearer 4,100 than the 3,600 total in the table above.

Academic faculty establishment notes

These notes describe the method by which logistic academic faculty members are calculated. They are explanatory notes to the attached *Academic Faculty Establishment Chart*[1] which replaces the Manpower Budget which used to be attached to the University Financial Estimates each year. The Chart gives details of the calculations and results in each of the following steps.

The Planning Process results in a University plan which includes projections of faculty and student numbers; that plan is reviewed annually and these notes describe the annual process of adjustment.

# 1. Student numbers

The five-year projections of student numbers prepared on the basis of the financial allocation to the University are reviewed each year by the Planning committee. The committee agrees student number targets for the following year for groups of courses, i.e. B.A., B.Sc., (both including Visiting students), professional courses, Arts and Social Studies graduates, Science graduates; those are termed the logistic student numbers since they are the basis of the allocation of a range of resources (e.g. space, School funds); they represent minimum rather than fixed targets since the Arts and Science committees can, with certain limitations, accept a higher number of students (extra-logistic students) provided extra resources are not asked for.

However, not all categories of logistic students count for staff/student ratio purposes. The *ratio students* consist of B.A. students (in which from 1969/70 Year Abroad students count as 1/6th of a full-time student), B.Sc. students, Professional course students (excluding those courses where the teaching inputs are not financed from the UGC recurrent grant), and first-year Arts and Science graduate students.

1. Not reproduced

## 2. Student/staff ratio

The second step is that the Planning committee then applies a staff/student ratio to the groups of ratio students agreed in 1 above. The ratio is fixed in accordance with the financial situation of the University. From 1969/70 the Planning committee will apply the same staff/student ratio to all three groups of students, but in the years 1965/67 the ratios got out of alignment and it was not possible to apply a common ratio for 1968/69.

Thus by applying a ratio to those groups of students, faculty numbers are derived for the Arts, Science and Professional course groups; these are termed the *area-based faculty logistics.*

## 3. Arts and Science committees

The third step is the calculations carried out by the Arts and Science committee to translate the area-based logistics into faculty *group-based internal logistics.* This list of faculty groups presently recognised for this purpose by the Arts and Science committees is listed on the Establishment Chart. *A Classification Table of Academic Faculty Groups* has also been produced to help members of faculty understand the nature of the groups, their inter-relationships and their links with the classifications used by national bodies.

The stages in this step are:

(a) to remove a number of posts from the total for Arts or Science general needs (e.g. Tutorial funds, research posts, 'administrative' posts) as determined by the Arts and Science committees;

(b) logistical guides have been produced for the Arts, Science and Professional courses which indicate the proportions of teaching input into each course by each faculty group. The Arts and Science committees can thus either decide upon the course allocation of the student numbers indicated by the Planning committee (i.e. divide them into Schools, majors, optional courses) and use the logistical guide to derive faculty group numbers, or they can decide upon the faculty group allocation of the area-based logistics and use the logistical guide to determine the allocation of the student numbers. Whichever way round the exercise is done, it will result in the allocation of student numbers to courses and the allocation of faculty members to faculty groups. To date, common staff/student ratios have been used within each of Arts and Science in the above calculations, but whereas the Planning committee does not include non-UGC financed posts in its calculations the Arts and Science Committees may do so (e.g., the teaching input of an externally financed research post in Economics does not affect the Planning committee's allocation of area-based logistics but it may affect the Arts committee's allocation of posts to faculty groups);

(c) faculty groups belong to either Arts or Science, whereas the B.A., B.Sc., and Professional courses each contain elements of both Arts and Science. This had led to some confusion in the past when a system of net trade-off had been used. For example, if the balance of the curriculum resulted in the Arts committee allocating 3 posts to Mathematics and 1 post to Biology, 3 posts to Sociology and 1 post to Geography, then 3 posts would have been switched from Arts to Science at the end of step 2 above, thereby resulting in inequalities amongst faculty groups when the calculations in (b) above were undertaken. Given an overlapping curriculum, any description of faculty logistics must relate area-based logistics to faculty-group based logistics more clearly and accurately than has been the case previously. Area-based logistics are those which come within the planning control of the Arts and Science committees (i.e., they derive from the Arts and Science curricula, e.g., the Arts committee by altering the B.A. curriculum can effect the distribution of posts to a Science faculty group). Faculty-group based logistics are the logistics within the control of the Arts and Science committees for annual operational purposes (e.g. recruitment and manpower control, teaching allocations).

The main purpose of the *Academic Faculty Establishment Chart is to relate these two sets of logistics,* e.g., to demonstrate that of the posts allocated to the sociology faculty group, $x$ posts are derived from Arts, $y$ posts are derived from Science and $z$ of a post is derived from the Professional courses. The Chart can be made more sophisticated within Arts and Science if that is desired (e.g., the $a$ posts allocated to Economics on account of Arts teaching can be further divided into $.m$ for Economics majors, $.n$ for other specific majors, $.e$ for Arts/Science Scheme, $.p$ for School of Social Studies contextuals, etc.);

(d) at present the *Arts/Science Scheme* logistics are not adequately built into the above calculations. The procedure is that 5 posts are extracted at the end of Step 2 (2.5 each from Arts and Science) for the Arts/Science Scheme and the requirements of the Scheme are not built into the B.A. and B.Sc. logistical guides. Discussions are now proceeding with a view to including the Arts/Science Scheme in the B.A. and B.Sc. logistical guides so that it can be taken into account in the determination of faculty-group logistics in the same way as all other elements in the B.A. and B.Sc. curricula.

# 4. Adjustments

The fourth step is that having derived faculty-group based logistics there might then be agreements between groups about the transfer of posts (e.g. 3 posts could be transferred from the Mathematics group to the Physics group on condition that the latter group provides an agreed amount of teaching in Mathematics); or posts could be transferred from the Education group to the Centre for Educational Technology on condition that the Centre provides an agreed amount of teaching). Again, it is important to record such agreements on the Faculty Establishment Chart, since the lack of clear records on such transfers has in the past led to confusion. A considerable amount of cross-teaching does take place, but the only adjustments which affect the Chart are those where a post or a specified part of a post is actually transferred between groups or units. The resulting figures are termed the *adjusted faculty group-based internal logistics.*

## 5. Other courses

As explained in Step 1 above, the calculations are related to a set of courses. However, the University is responsible for courses which do not appear in that list (e.g. courses in the School of Education, the Continuing Education programme). The Planning committee makes separate budgetary allocations to the units responsible for those courses, but it may then be the case that those units and the faculty groups reach agreements under which the latter undertake teaching on the courses organised by the units. In cases where that involves the transfer of a post (or a significant part of a post) from such a unit to a faculty group then the transfer should be shown on the Faculty Establishment Chart. A considerable amount of cross-teaching does take place but the only adjustments which affect the Chart are those where a post or a specified part of a post is actually transferred between groups or units. The resulting figures are termed the *composite faculty group-based logistics*.

## Conclusion

The above description is complicated because it reflects the patterns of the curriculum of the University and the structure of the academic organisation of the University. In those circumstances, clarity is different from simplicity. The previous simple statements of faculty logistics have led to misunderstandings. The recent devolution of new responsibilities to Arts and Science have made it all the more important for statements about faculty logistics to be complete and comprehensive.

Responsibility for the production of the Academic Faculty Establishment Chart rests jointly with the Arts, Science and Establishment Offices in consultation with the Planning Officer.

# List of participants and observers[1]

| | |
|---|---|
| M.-Y. Bernard | Director of Higher Education, Ministry of National Education, Paris |
| L. Cerych | Centre for Educational Research and Innovation, OECD, Paris |
| S.C. van Dorsser | University of Amsterdam |
| P.J. Gilbert | Assistant to Secretary, London School of Economics and Political Science |
| S. Graubard | Editor, *Daedalos,* Harvard University, Cambridge, Mass. |
| S. Ichimura | Director, Center for South-east Asian Studies of Kyoto University |
| J. Jadot | Catholic University of Louvain |
| II. Jones | Deputy Director, Centre for Educational Technology, The University of Sussex |
| Makonnen Kebret | Associate Academic Vice-President, Haile Selassie I University, Addis Ababa |
| T. Kobayashi | Director, Unesco Institute for Education, Hamburg |
| J. Kershaw | Programme Officer, Division of Education and Research, The Ford Foundation, New York City |
| H.M.R. Keyes | Secretary-General, International Association of Universities, Paris |
| A. Khan | Centre for Educational Research and Innovation, OECD, Paris |
| R.G. King | Lecturer on Education, Harvard University, Cambridge, Mass. |
| G. Lockwood | Planning Officer, The University of Sussex |

1. This list gives the positions held by the participants at the time of the symposium.

| | |
|---|---|
| V. Massakovsky | Rector, Dnepropetrovsk State University |
| M.V. Mathur | Director, Asian Institute of Educational Planning and Administration, New Delhi |
| N. MacKenzie | Director, Centre for Educational Technology, The University of Sussex |
| M. Meyerson | President, State University of New York at Buffalo, New York |
| C. Nelson | Principal, Peat, Marwick, Mitchell & Co., New York City |
| N.T. Nujin | Rector, Kazan State University |
| S. Petracek | Chair of Educational Planning, University of 17th November, Prague |
| G.S. Papadopoulos | Head, Educational Investment and Development Division, Directorate for Scientific Affairs, OECD, Paris |
| H.M. Phillips | Consultant in education, Paris |
| K. Podoski | Pro-rector, Pedagogical High School, Gdansk |
| K. Rybnikov | Director, Division of Higher Education, Unesco, Paris |
| V. Shorin | Head, University Department, Ministry of Higher and Specialized Secondary Education of the RSFSR, Moscow |
| M. Soliman | Director, Provisional Bureau, Association of Arab Universities, Cairo University. |
| O. Vera | Director, Planning Office, University of Chile, Santiago |
| P. Walckiers | Catholic University of Louvain |
| J. Walter | Systems Research Group, University of Toronto |
| J. Westenberg | University of Amsterdam |
| R. Whaley | Cresap, McCormick & Paget Inc., New York |
| W. Wolter | Director, Institute for Higher Education, Humboldt University, Berlin |
| V. Yarushin | Ministry of Higher and Specialized Secondary Education of the USSR, Moscow |
| IIEP Staff Members | R. Poignant, *Director*<br>V.G. Onushkin, *Head of research project*<br>P.H. Coombs<br>R.F. Lyons<br>G. Bartagnon ⎫<br>B. Sanyal ⎭ *Consultants to IIEP* |

# IIEP book list

The following books, published by Unesco/IIEP, are obtainable from the Institute or from Unesco and its national distributors throughout the world:

*Educational development in Africa* (1969. Three volumes, containing eleven African research monographs)

*Educational planning: a bibliography* (1964)

*Educational planning: a directory of training and research institutions* (1968)

*Educational planning in the USSR* (1968)

*Fundamentals of educational planning* (series of monographs: full list available on request)

*Manpower aspects of educational planning* (1968)

*Methodologies of educational planning for developing countries* by J.D. Chesswas (1968)

*Monographies africaines* (five titles, in French only: list available on request)

*New educational media in action: case studies for planners* (1967. Three volumes)

*The new media: memo to educational planners* by W. Schramm, P.H. Coombs, F. Kahnert, J. Lyle (1967. A report including analytical conclusions based on the above three volumes of case studies)

*Problems and strategies of educational planning: lessons from Latin America* (1965)

*Qualitative aspects of educational planning* (1969)

*Research for educational planning: notes on emergent needs* by William J. Platt (1970)


The following books, produced in but not published by the Institute, are obtainable through normal bookselling channels:

*Quantitative methods of educational planning* by Héctor Correa
Published by International Textbook Co., Scranton, Pa., 1969

*The world educational crisis: a systems analysis* by Philip H. Coombs
Published by Oxford University Press, New York, London and Toronto, 1968